CU00403394

BUCKS AND BRUISERS

A drawing of Pierce Egan by George Sharples

❧ J. C. Reid ❧

BUCKS AND BRUISERS

Pierce Egan and Regency England

Routledge & Kegan Paul

LONDON

First published 1971
by Routledge and Kegan Paul Ltd
Broadway House,
68–74 Carter Lane,
London, EC4V 5EL
Printed in Great Britain by
Cox & Wyman Ltd, London, Reading and Fakenham
Set in Monotype Plantin
© J. C. Reid 1971

ISBN 0 7100 6967 7

✿ Contents ✿

❧ Illustrations ❧

Illustrations 1, 3, 6, 7, 8 and 10 are reproduced by kind permission
of the British Museum.

✿ Foreword ✿

I first became interested in Pierce Egan through a concern with Dickens. In various accounts of Dickens's life and works, Egan's name kept cropping up as one of the popular writers of the preceding age whom the young Dickens had set out to rival. But when I was drawn to investigate the nature of Egan's accomplishment, I found two major obstacles in the way. The first was the extreme rarity of Egan's books and the bibliographical problems connected with his output; the second was the almost complete lack of accurate information in print on the man himself, his life and his activities.

To obtain and read what Egan wrote has been a task, albeit an interesting one, that has occupied several years. Even important works, such as *Life in London* and *Finish to Life in London*, which ran through several editions numbering many thousands, are today both scarce and expensive. At the time of writing, a London bookseller is offering a first edition of *Life in London* for £145, while another is prepared to exchange one of that book's many imitations, *Real Life in London*, for £125. Number parts of Egan's books are very much harder to come by than those of Dickens's—so much harder, in fact that, despite assiduous searching, I have been unable to view any at all and I tremble to think what they would fetch on the modern collectors' market. Other books by him survive only in single copies in libraries in Great Britain or the United States or in private collections.

Although I have done my best to locate everything he published in book or pamphlet form, there are still, I have no doubt, fugitive publications of his which remain to be identified. The bibliographical tangle which surrounds several of his works and which is discussed in the Bibliography to this book is a complicated one. The situation is not made any easier by the ascription to Egan in certain major library catalogues—that of the British Museum, for instance—of works which are demonstrably not his. None of his books is in print today, although extracts from *Boxiana* regularly turn up in anthologies of boxing and sporting literature. The last edition of *Life in London* appeared in 1909.

The second problem is the biographical one, and it, too, is of a formidable nature. Largely because of the mainly sub-literary character of his writings and the fact that he did not mix in literary circles, partly because of the disdainful attitude the Victorians took towards 'coarse and vulgar journalism from a low-caste Irishman', partly, too, because of the reaction against Regency mores and the brutality of bare-knuckle fighting which Egan was, mistakenly, regarded as uncritically supporting, few of his letters have been thought worth preserving, and contemporary memorials of him are few and hard to find. The Press obituaries were brief, if kindly, and none of his acquaintances thought it worth while to pay him the tribute of a memoir or biography. While adequate biographical material survives of fourth-rate nineteenth-century poets and abysmal novelists, many of whom possessed not a tittle of Egan's vitality or originality, the life and character of 'Fancy's Child', as he was known in his day, must be constructed laboriously from such scanty records and papers as are still extant and from the evidence, fortunately often highly suggestive, in his published writings. Unhappily, the entry on Egan by J. W. E(bsworth) in the *Dictionary of National Biography* is riddled with gross inaccuracies and misinformation which have misled almost every literary historian who has noticed the writer. John Camden Hotten's Preface to his 1869 edition of *Life in London* is helpful concerning the reception of the original work, but he has hardly anything to say about Egan's life (as he remarks, 'The biographical dictionaries are silent upon the subject of Mr Egan's literary and social career'), and what he records is second-hand and sometimes apocryphal.

It is then perhaps not surprising that, in the course of my investigations, I have found that at least three projected studies of Egan have been abandoned—one by an American professor and two by British men of letters. It may seem presumptuous of me to shape up to the problem where others have thrown in the sponge or not come up to the scratch, as Egan himself would have said. My only excuse is that I believe that a study of this writer is long overdue, first and foremost, because he is in himself an interesting man, with unquestioned talent and skills not to be despised and because a great deal that he wrote can still give pleasure; secondly, because his writings constitute, in my opinion, one of the most valuable, if most neglected, sources for important aspects of the social history of the Regency period; thirdly, because of the rich mine he offers of the cant, slang, colloquial language and sporting jargon of his time; fourthly, because, in the many fields of writing in which he engaged, he epitomizes the variety of popular publishing activity in the first three decades of the nineteenth century; fifthly, because in his personality as much as in his books, he is a fascinating transition figure, reflecting a good deal of the eighteenth century and yet anticipating so much in Victorian popular writing, showing, in short, how many attitudes and forms we tend to designate as 'Victorian' were already shaped before the young Queen came to the throne; and, finally, because, as I hope I have demonstrated herein, Egan was a not insignificant predecessor of, and influence upon, more than one Victorian novelist, most notably Dickens. One further reason for this book—and, to be honest, the major one—is that, in reading his works and tracing his life, I have come to have a genuine admiration and affection for this energetic, eccentric, raffish, indomitable, cocky character.

Areas of Egan's life and activities still remain obscure. I have been as thorough in this chronicle as the discoverable records allow, and I have seldom allowed myself the luxury of guesses, save where sound evidence seemed to justify the leap. I should not be surprised to learn from later investigators that some of my speculations have been false, but at least I have tried to make plain what is fact and what is reasonable conjecture. I hope this book will not be the last, as it is the first, to be devoted to him; it is a beginning and certainly not offered as a final word.

Because almost all his books are inaccessible to the general reader—indeed, to many students of literature—I have thought it necessary to give fairly complete accounts of the more important of them, as much for the social history they contain as for the light they throw upon Egan's own concerns and for their value as popular literature. I make no high claims for Egan as a writer, except in the field of sport, but I believe that as a recorder of particular, widespread interests of his time he is without peer. The understanding of great writers is enhanced by a knowledge of those they began by imitating and came to surpass, and the history of literature is enriched by a study of such writers as Egan, who reflected much of the spirit of their age and were in their day phenomenally popular. Literary history, in constant and justifiable pursuit of the major names, cannot afford to neglect the phenomenon of contemporary popularity, if only because our own age has its Egans too.

His early books were produced while the great Romantic poets, as well as Jane Austen and Walter Scott, dominated literature; he was still active and widely read during the interregnum, after the death or exhaustion of the Romantics and before the rise of the major Victorians; he wrote his last books after Dickens and Tennyson were fairly launched. He is essentially a writer of the Regency and the interregnum periods. The latter age, the time of Thomas Hood, Beddoes, Darley, Clare, Leigh Hunt, Samuel Rogers and Felicia Hemans, was an important one, as much for its pleasant, if minor, accomplishments as for its seminal character. Far from being a waste-land diversified only by a few oases, it was a nursery where several modest blooms flourished and seedlings for a future age were carefully cultivated. From the literature of the quarter of a century immediately before the Queen's accession we can still learn many of the reasons why Victorian writing took the directions it did and why certain subjects and genres flourished well into the century. I have already, in my study of Thomas Hood, tried to show how much of the popular poetry of Egan's age leads into both popular and serious poetry of the succeeding generations. To some extent, this book aims to establish similar links in a quite different area of popular writing. But, above all, it is Pierce Egan himself and his unusual accomplishment that concern me.

❧ Acknowledgments ❧

I am happy to acknowledge the generous assistance of the following individuals and institutions in the making of this book:

The Chief Herald, Genealogical Office, Dublin Castle, who carried out a search for me into Pierce Egan's antecedents.

The Rev. R. N. Talbot, Rector of Ballyhay Parish, Charleville, County Cork, Eire, who searched his parish registers for details of the Egan family.

Mr Stanley J. Osborne, Beadle and Assistant to the Clerk, Stationers' Hall, London, who supplied me with information concerning apprenticeships to the printing trade.

Mr Ernest Crowsley, Secretary of the Charles Lamb Society, London, who lent me some useful newspaper cuttings relevant to Pierce Egan.

The Chief Librarian and Curator, Islington Public Libraries, who gave me information about Egan's interment.

Miss Olive Johnson, Acquisitions Officer, University of Auckland Library, who was of particular help in enabling me to obtain some rare Egan items.

The Librarians of the Bodleian Library, Oxford, the Birmingham University Library, the Huntington Library, California and the Carl H. Pforzheimer Library, New York, who drew my attention to Egan material. The section of Egan's letter to Mrs Hill quoted in Chapter IX is reproduced by special permission of the Carl H. Pforzheimer Library,

The staffs of the British Museum Manuscript Room and Print Room. of the British Museum Newspaper Library, Colindale, and of the

Acknowledgments

London Public Record Office, who gave me courteous and willing help with my inquiries.

The various people with the surname Egan in the London area who cordially replied to my circular letter.

And, in particular, Mr John Ford of Reading University, who kindly shared with me some of his encyclopaedic knowledge of Regency boxing. My conversations with him have been among the chief pleasures arising from my quest for Pierce Egan.

J. C. REID

Antibes

❧ I ❧

A Printer by Trade

In July 1819 *Blackwood's Edinburgh Magazine* ended a glowing review of *Boxiana or Sketches of Pugilism* by 'One of the Fancy' with the only half-jesting words: 'We see no reason why the author of this celebrated work should remain anonymous any more than the author of *Waverley*. He seems to us to be, on many accounts, far better deserving than the latter personage, of the title of the GREAT UNKNOWN.' The enterprising editor of the London *Weekly Dispatch* promptly reprinted the *Blackwood's* article with a proud note to the effect that the gentleman alluded to 'is the person who furnishes the Sporting Intelligence exclusively for this Paper—Mr Pierce Egan'. The first volume of *Boxiana*, the *Dispatch* went on to say, 'had been published anonymously for nearly seven years; but, previous to the appearance of a second volume . . . in April 1818, the author, at the request of several distinguished persons in the sporting world, was induced to add his name'.

In thus drawing the laggard *Blackwood's* attention to something that the entire sporting world of London already knew, the editor of the *Weekly Dispatch* was merely confirming the reputation of Pierce Egan as the most popular and successful of all the sporting journalists in an age when noblemen and dustmen alike shared a passion for sport—above all for pugilism—and eagerly scanned the columns of the various competing newspapers for blow-by-blow accounts of the most recent bare-knuckle bouts between giants of the ring. More than any others, it was Egan's graphic first-hand descriptions in the *Dispatch* that they sought, trusting in his accuracy and relishing his vivacity. When

1

subsequently these reports were reprinted in the successive numbers and volumes of *Boxiana*, the same readers bought the books in their thousands, making them among the most considerable best-sellers of their day. *Boxiana* was an indispensable part of a sporting gentleman's library, the provoker of innumerable discussions and the unique authority in the settling of arguments relating to 'the gentle science'.

England had never had a sporting journalist to match Pierce Egan— a connoisseur of 'milling', and expert in almost every sport, a racy, colourful, wholly individual writer, a just and fair judge of a contest, an intimate of pugilists and their backers, trusted by them and having access to inside information no other journalist could pretend to, and one so familiar with the slang of the Fancy and the private languages of sportsmen that he used the lingos as if he had created them, as, indeed, in part he had. In the highly competitive world of sports reporting, with its fierce rivalries and jealousies, Egan's name was, for over twenty years, the only one that was known to every sportsman, literate and illiterate. For was he not something more than a reporter—the very Thucydides of the Ring, the historian of boxing, the permanent chronicler of events that, in the eyes of his Regency contemporaries, equalled, if they did not outclass, the feats of arms of the heroes of classical mythology themselves? 'Fancy's Child', 'Glorious Pierce', 'Immortal Pierce', 'The Great Lexicographer of the Fancy', 'The Veteran Historian of the Ring' were a few of the names bestowed upon him by his legions of admiring readers. And *Blackwood's* itself, doing penance for its ignorance of the identity of the author of *Boxiana*, went on to print eight lengthy articles in praise of both pugilism and of its historian. The series concluded in March 1821 with 'A Letter to Pierce Egan, Esq.' from the pen of 'Christopher North' himself, taking some credit for enlarging Egan's reputation and for making

> The name of Egan, like an evergreen,
> To blow and blossom in the northern sky;

and ending with a somewhat superfluous exhortation to him to 'keep writing books that will stir up the old English spirit'.

Who was Pierce Egan and what qualities equipped him to become the exactly appropriate popular writer of his age? He was of Irish ancestry, a member of that branch of the ancient and numerous Egan family whose roots are in County Tipperary.[1] His grandfather, Carbery Egan, a member of that minority group, the Protestant Irish, was born in County Cork in 1720. In 1740 he entered Trinity College, Dublin, and graduated A.B. in 1743 and A.M. in 1747. He was ordained deacon in the Established Church in 1748 and priest in 1749, both at Cloyne. He was licensed to the curacy of Rathgogan or Charleville in 1748, in which humble position he remained until 1770. He was also for many years Master of the Endowed School at Charleville. From 1770 until his death in 1771, Carbery Egan was Vicar of Templebodane.

He had several sons. The most distinguished of these, John Egan, was born in 1754, studied at Trinity College, Dublin, and was admitted to the Irish Bar in 1778. In 1789 he entered the Irish Parliament, and from 1790 to 1800 he represented Tullagh and was 'Chairman' of Kilmainham—that is, County Court Judge. John Egan, or 'Bully' Egan, as he was called, was a large, corpulent man and a noted duellist. He appears to have been celebrated less for his own wit than for being, like Falstaff, the occasion of wit in others. It is recorded that he once challenged his intimate friend, Curran, but when the time for the duel came round, Egan complained of the advantage his bulk gave to his adversary. 'I'll tell you what, Mr Egan,' said Curran. 'I wish to take no advantage of you whatsoever. Let my size be chalked out on your side and I am quite content that every shot which hits outside that mark shall go for nothing.' 'Bully' Egan's retort, if any, has not come down to us, but the duel was fought without injury on either side.

When Pierce Egan, on a visit to Ireland many years afterwards, went to view the grave of 'Sir' Dan Donnelly, the Irish Champion, he found the remains of Donnelly to be interred in Bully's Acre, near Kilmainham and some three miles from Dublin. 'Bully's Acre', says Pierce in *Every Gentleman's Manual* (1845), gave its name to John Egan, to whom it had once belonged, and he goes on to tell that John on one occasion 'in a law contest with that great wit and eloquent pleader, the Master of the Rolls, Mr Grattan, observed "if the latter did not leave off his abuse he would put him in his pocket", an allusion to his being a small man. "If you do so," replied Grattan, "you will have more law in your pocket than you ever had in your head."'

John Egan's finest hour came during the final debate in the Irish Parliament on Union between Great Britain and Ireland. He delivered a vehement and stirring speech opposing the motion and sat down exclaiming, 'Ireland—Ireland for ever! and damn Kilmainham!' His instinct was sound. As a result of his voting against Union, he was deprived of his 'chairmanship' and died in poverty in Scotland in 1810.

One of 'Bully' Egan's sons, James, a cousin of Pierce's, went to Germany at the beginning of the nineteenth century and became a page at the Court of Zweibrücken, later taking up residence in Austria. He had four sons, three of whom achieved various kinds of eminence.

James, his first-born, became a professor at the University of Budapest, Alfred became Chief Engineer to the Hungarian State Railways, while Alfred, who acquired large land-holdings in Hungary, produced one son, Edward, who was Inspector-General of Dairy Farming for the Hungarian Government, and another, Lewis, who was Chief Engineer to the Maritime Government of Fiume.

Pierce Egan's father, also called James, was not to distinguish himself as his brothers and nephews did. He was the eldest of Carbery Egan's sons, born presumably before 1748, when his father became assistant curate at Charleville, since the parish register, which records most of the Egan children, is silent on him. At some stage James left home, first, perhaps, for Dublin, certainly later for London. It still remains uncertain where and when his son, Pierce, was born. More than one Irish biographical dictionary claims him as born in Ireland.[2] The English *Dictionary of National Biography* says only that he 'is believed to have been born in London in 1772', presumably thus picking up and perpetuating the 'Aged 77 years' in the *Gentleman's Magazine* obituary of November 1849 and the note in the one from *Bell's Life in London* of 12 August 1849 that he had reached 'the good old age of eleven times seven'.

On the other hand, Egan's death certificate, recording his demise on 3 August 1849, shows his age as seventy-four, and in a letter to Robert Peel dated 5 December 1842 Egan describes himself as 'upwards of 65 years of age', which would be a very curious way of saying he was seventy, as a 1772 birth-date would make him. These two pieces of evidence indicate that he was, in fact, born late in 1774 or early in 1775, more probably the former.

As for his place of birth, it is perhaps relevant that, while the high chauvinism of Egan's continual praises of English valour, English mores and the British monarchy is typical of his time, the frequency and enthusiasm of such adulation suggest a convert or adoptee rather than one native-born. At the same time, he is exceptionally partial to Irish boxers and, as such of his hostile critics as H. D. Miles, the author of *Pugilistica*, were quick to point out, he has a habit of claiming wholly English-born pugilists as Hibernian, even to the extent of putting an 'O' before their names. Miles, too, it is who describes Egan as having been, in his childhood, 'a Dublin gossoon'.[3] Unhappily, the destruction of the Dublin Record Office by fire in 1926 and the incompleteness of subsequent valiant attempts to fill the consequent gaps prevent for the present any certainty on this point. London parish registers of the time give no record of the christening of an infant Pierce Egan.

The most likely conclusion, then, in my view, is that 'Fancy's Child' was born in Ireland towards the end of 1774 and came with his parents and his two brothers, John (born in 1779) and Laurence, to London while a small boy. Nothing is known of his mother, although it is more than likely that he inherited his unusual first name, Pierce, from her maiden name.

The first certain record we have of his youth is an entry in the Record of Apprentices at Stationers' Hall, London, which shows that, on 5 September 1786 Pierce Egan, the son of James Egan, paviour, of Cross Lane, Holborn, was apprenticed to Lockington Johnson of Broad Street, Bloomsbury, printer, for seven years. No money was paid to the printer. The form of indenture signed was that still in use, which, among other things, binds the apprentice to faithfully serve

> his said Master . . . his Secrets keep, his lawful Commands
> everywhere gladly do. He shall do no damage to his said Master,
> nor see to be done of others, but that he to his Power shall lett,
> or forthwith give warning to his said Master of the same. He shall
> not waste the Goods of his said Master, nor lend them unlawfully
> to any. He shall not commit Fornication during the said term.
> He shall not play at Cards, Dice, Tables, or any other unlawful
> Games, whereby his said Master may have any loss. With his
> own Goods or others, during the said Term, without Licence
> of his said Master, he shall neither Buy nor Sell. He shall not
> haunt Taverns, nor Play-houses, nor absent himself from the said
> Master's Service without his Consent unlawfully; But in all
> Things as a faithful Apprentice he shall behave himself towards
> his said Master and all His, during the said Term.[4]

Egan's father's humble occupation, that of a road-making labourer, who helped lay pavements with the rammers or paviours of the day, indicates that James was one of those countless Irishmen who left their native land for the imagined opportunities of London and were forced to take whatever work they could find in the golden city. Except for the producing of his talented son, James Egan has left no record of achievement behind. Nor is much known of Egan's 'Master'. Lockington Johnson appears to have been a printer in a quite small way, since the Stationers' records show him as having this unique apprentice, while other printers of the time numbered theirs by the dozen.

There is no entry showing Pierce Egan's admission as a Freeman of the Stationers' Company at the expiration of his seven years' apprenticeship, but this does not necessarily mean that he did not complete his term, as not all former apprentices exercised this right. Indeed, his exceptional knowledge of the printing trade in its various branches suggests that he did, in fact, serve out his seven years.

This early employment certainly determined the bulk of his mature interests. In Johnson's printing-house he picked up the disease of book-making as well as becoming an expert compositor, typesetter, bookbinder, printer, proof-reader, and editor, and equipping himself for a life which was to be spent in great part among books, newspapers, printers' shops and booksellers.

His formal education was scanty; he was largely self-educated. Some years later, in his characteristically verbose way, he wrote,

> After all, it is not my fault that I am not *classical*—it would seem
> that it never entered the head of my daddy, poor man, to send
> me to college to become a *Graduate*, to pore over the Elements
> of Euclid and to wade through the Books of Ovid. The mode
> (though not exactly in unison with Dr O'Toole's system of
> *learning*) under which I obtained what little knowledge I possess
> —for to tell the truth it is but little—a nutshell would contain
> it—was of a more *gradual* nature; yet like the above celebrated
> Tutor, I am more indebted for what are termed 'new lights'
> in these enlightened days, to the GAS than to any other great
> body of *illuminati*![5]

This lack of formal training shows up in occasional solecisms and grammatical uncertainties in that part of his writing done under the pressure of journalistic deadlines; from time to time he is apt to lose himself in rank jungles of syntax.

In the early part of his *Life of an Actor*, Egan was to depict a young man, Peregrine Proteus, not unlike himself, who is apprenticed to a printer and who develops his education and enlarges his mind by reading the books in Mr Quarto's office and by conversations with the older printers. There can be little doubt that this reflects his own youthful experience. As a youngster and as an adult, he read avidly in the literature of his day and, like the young Dickens, he soaked himself in the major novelists and playwrights of the past. His acquaintance with Shakespeare was more than a nodding one; he has by heart many passages from the plays (or partly by heart, since, in quoting from memory, he is not always accurate) and can find an apt quotation from *Hamlet, Othello, Macbeth, Richard II, Richard III* and other plays for almost every occasion. Goldsmith, Cowper, Fielding, Pope, Sheridan, Swift, Scott, Cervantes are all laid under tribute, but the most admired of all his models was Sterne. Sterne's name pops up in his writings like King Charles's head in Mr Dick's. Sterne's sensibility, his humanity and his insight are all dear to Egan, and his style is the one he tries most strenuously at times to imitate. The breadth of reading he displays is wider than that of almost every other popular journalist of his time, but it is almost all pre-Romantic and predominantly eighteenth-century. Except for Byron, whose roots are Augustan, anyhow, there is no major Romantic poet mentioned in the whole range of his writing, despite the fact that the great members of this movement were producing their finest work when Egan was a young man. But what he lacked in knowledge and appreciation of Romantic poetry he more than made up for, as we shall see, in his encyclopaedic knowledge of popular writing and sub-literature, of street-songs, ballads, broadsides, thieves' chronicles, romances, guides and 'warnings'.

Schooled, then, in his own way, the young Pierce Egan immersed himself in the highly competitive, cut-throat world of printing and bookselling. The days of his young manhood were a curious time for literature, which, like English society as a whole, was passing through an age of transition. This expatriate Irishman was to become one of the most successful and popular writers of the Regency period and to sum up, in the various genres he attempted, in his point of view, in his level of appeal and in his style, many of the characteristics of the age. His peak of popularity was to be reached during the time of the Prince Regent and his ten years' reign as George IV and during the time of his successor, William IV. By the mid-1820s he was already beginning to be left behind by the change that had come over society as a whole and by the new literary modes that were to inaugurate the age of Victorian literature. But the world of print which he entered as a young man was a world of pulp—not that of the powerful reviews, nor of the remarkable novelists of manners, Jane Austen and Walter Scott, nor of the lesser Scott, John Galt, nor even that of Mrs Radcliffe and Letitia Landon. It was the world of the newspaper journalist, the hack-writer, the catchpenny broadside-monger, the warmer-up of other people's rejected trifles, the compiler of guides, encyclopaedias, histories on the pattern of the young Goldsmith and Borrow—all those who, in other words, set out to provide, by fair means or foul, reading matter for the newly literate and partly literate who were swelling the population of London in the decades that straddle the eighteenth and nineteenth centuries.

It was a world of 'devil take the hindmost', of impudent plagiarisms, of fly-by-night bookseller-publishers, of chapbooks, of children's books at a farthing and a halfpenny, of newspapers that failed and bankrupted their owners and of those that succeeded, like Harmer's *Weekly Dispatch*, and made their proprietor's fortune. It was the world of Jemmy Catnach of Seven Dials, King of the Broadsides, 'plodding, dirty, ignorant and successful',[6] who sold over 500,000 copies of his account of Thurtell's murder of Weare and made £500 from it, and who, in 1828, sold over 1,000,000 copies of the alleged dying speech of William Corder, who murdered Maria Marten in the Red Barn.

It was a time of golden opportunities for shrewd operators like George Virtue, who built up a successful business on the purchasing of remainders and canvassing for the books of other publishers before establishing himself as a wealthy and respected publisher of poetry and religious and art books. It was the age of Thomas Kelly and Thomas Tegg and other far from scrupulous suppliers of print for the masses, and also of poor Thomas Hood, who fought all his life for a meagre crust in the arena of popular writing, as much as it was the age of Charles Lamb, William Hazlitt and Christopher North. It is doubtful if any time before the twentieth century produced such a prodigious quantity of printed junk as did the Regency. But, as in our own day, it was avidly received junk and highly profitable to the purveyors. Also, as in our own day, there were practitioners in this sub-literary world who had in themselves a dash of something better, something more original and lasting, and who thus added to the barren pumice-land that trace of cobalt which allowed later, better writers to take root there and flourish.

In this *milieu* of popular print Egan early became at home. During his adolescent years and those of his twenties, he was not only a compositor and proof-reader in various printing establishments, but also, it seems likely, a hack-writer and compiler of chapbooks and of the biographical compendia popular at the time. Early in the new century he became associated with Joseph and George Smeeton, for whom he worked as a compositor. Joseph Smeeton, of St Martin's Lane, a typical printer-stationer of his age, established himself in the 1780s as publisher and seller of a wide variety of ephemera. In 1794 George Smeeton, Joseph's nephew, was apprenticed to his uncle for seven years and in 1802 completed his apprenticeship and was admitted into the Freedom of the Corporation.[7]

When, in May 1809, Joseph's printing-works were burnt down and both the printer and his wife perished in the flames,[8] George Smeeton carried on the business in St Martin's Lane under his own name. He was to become one of the most imaginative and successful of the popular

8

publishers of the second and third decades of the century. In association with James Caulfield of Wills Street, he published in 1814 *The Eccentric Magazine*, a forerunner of the Ripley *Believe It or Not* series, consisting of the lives of giants, dwarfs, abnormally fat men and women and human oddities of various kinds. Of a more reputable nature were the *Biographia Curiosa or Memoirs of Remarkable Characters of the Reign of George III* (1822) and the four volumes of *The Unique* (1825), with memoirs and engravings of other eminent persons, Shakespeare, Byron, Newton, Handel, Sterne and Voltaire among them. But his most original and noteworthy enterprise was his reprinting, from 1817 onwards, of several early sixteenth- and seventeenth-century pamphlets, admirably executed and with fine reproductions of contemporary portraits. These were collected into two volumes in 1820 under the title of *Reprints of Rare and Curious Tracts Relating to English History*. They included King James's *Book of Sports*, and lives of Captain James Hind, the robber, hanged in 1652, the 'Famed Mr Blood', and Captain James Simpson, the highwayman.

The production of such books from the works in which Egan was employed undoubtedly influenced his own tastes and interests. Biography, crime and sport were among the areas in which he was later profitably to employ his pen. In view of his manifest facility and his gifts as a reporter and compiler, it is reasonable to suppose that he combined his work for Smeeton as a compositor with that of 'editing' various gatherings of material for the same printer in the days before copyright law placed obstacles in the way of pirating booksellers. It is significant, too, in considering the origins of Egan's *Life in London*, with its pictures of low life and its large doses of slang and cant, to note that among George Smeeton's early publications were *The Stranger's Guide or Frauds of London Detected*, by George Andrewes (1808), one of the many contemporary books warning the uninitiated about the perils of low life in the big city, and *A Dictionary of Slang and Cant Language: Ancient and Modern*, also by Andrewes (1809).

Except for one special pursuit which Egan developed during his early manhood, he may well have remained one of the host of unknown and unsung printers' assistants and hacks of his age. This was his deep interest in sport of all kinds, but especially in boxing. Possibly his Irish ancestry provided the initial impetus, but his own personal qualities gave him unique advantages over those other members of his race who involved themselves in the chronicling of sport. He was by nature an intensely gregarious person, never happier than when he was at a booze-up or a sing-song, the normal relaxations of the sporting fraternity and their hangers-on. He had a gift for composing topical songs, impromptus, parodies and doggerel, which he would sing or recite at the drop of a hat. This talent, his good humour, his love of puns, quips and facetiae and his ability as a raconteur made him a welcome guest or chairman on numerous convivial occasions and a valued member of a considerable number of sporting and drinking clubs, the two being virtually synonymous. Even before the publication of *Boxiana* established him as the acknowledged authority on pugilism, past and present, his immense knowledge of all varieties of sport had given him a reputation among those who made such things their business or their primary recreation.

By the time he had reached his early thirties he had published nothing over his own name, but had begun to contribute small items and articles on sporting activities to various newspapers, more and more of which were beginning to devote space to this material, such as *Bell's Weekly Messenger*, founded in 1796, and the *Weekly Dispatch*, founded in 1801. By 1806, he had sufficient confidence in his ability to earn a living by his trade and by his pen to embark on marriage. On 7 July 1806 he married Catherine Povey, spinster, at the Church of St Mary le Bone, in the County of Middlesex, 'according to the rites and ceremonies of the Established Church'.[9] Little is known of Catherine, except that she bore Egan several children and apparently shared his flair for light verse. There is a brief sentimental poem, 'Lines on the Chain Pier, Brighton', in the *Weekly Dispatch* of 12 October 1823 from her hand, and some verses in the Adelphi version of *Life in London* were attributed to her by the *Weekly Dispatch* reviewer. Although this was corrected by the editor in a footnote which named Moncrieff as the author, the mistake suggests that Catherine Egan was known to be a writer of poems and songs. In 1810 a daughter, Catherine, was born to the Egans, and in 1814 Pierce Egan the younger, himself to become a very popular writer of fiction in the Victorian age.

Early in his career Egan had taught himself shorthand, which was to stand him in good stead when he came to report the blow-by-blow details of a boxing match lasting for some fifty or sixty rounds. He was proud of his speed and accuracy. This ability seems to have led him to supplement his income by serving as a Parliamentary reporter, again like the young Dickens. He certainly goes out of his way, in Chapter VI of *Life in London*, to write a lengthy footnote in praise of Luke Hansard in terms which indicate a personal acquaintance. Again, he tells us in *Epsom Races* that Richard Brinsley Sheridan once said to him that 'nothing so astonished and delighted him as the admirable *rapid* mode, as well as the great accuracy, of reporting the debates in Parliament: "It is a luxury to me that I want words to express my admiration of the system; to have found what I have said late at night in the House of Commons, correctly reported, waiting for me, the next morning, on my breakfast table."[10]

Be this as it may, Pierce Egan was almost forty years old before fame came to him. The years of his ascendancy in sporting journalism and of his reputation in wider fields were to be those when many writers are written out. Few writers have begun so late and so unpromisingly, with so many apparent disadvantages. Yet, like a good number of his contemporaries, he possessed boundless energy, an indomitable spirit, a love of life and people and a determination which lifted him out of the pulp ruck to a place of his own. From the meagre information we have of him during his first thirty-seven years or so we can, however, form some impression of the man who burst on the sporting world in 1812 with *Boxiana*—a Protestant Irishman who had exchanged ancestral loyalty to the old sod for a passionate devotion to the British monarchy and British mores, an experienced printer, book-maker and hack, a convivial spirit who loved to mix with not only sportsmen and their noble patrons, but also the humble folk of London's back streets, a militant Cockney for whom London was the centre of the universe, a self-educated man whose tastes had been formed on Shakespeare and eighteenth-century literature, but who knew equally well the ephemera of his day, an expert in sport and especially in pugilism, a 'character' of incurable facetiousness, a man of the underworld of literature and journalism, with no connections with, or interest in, the literary circles of his day, the kind of person, in fact, both ignored and despised by polite society and polite letters, for whom he and his kind were 'low'. And yet it was this same man who, to a vast number of contemporary Englishmen, became more loved, respected and read than any of his fellow writers except Sir Walter Scott. It was *Boxiana* that began it all.

The Xenophon of the Ring

Writing in 1851 in *Lavengro*, George Borrow recalled the days of his youth, the age of Egan, when pugilism was at its height:

> I have known the time when a pugilistic encounter between two
> noted champions was almost considered as a national affair;
> when tens of thousands of individuals, high and low, meditated
> and brooded upon it, the first thing in the morning and the last
> at night, until the great event was decided. . . . In the days of
> pugilism it was no vain boast to say, that one Englishman was a
> match for two of t'other race. . . . What a bold and vigorous
> aspect pugilism wore at that time! . . . Let no one sneer at the
> bruisers of England—what were the gladiators of Rome, or the
> bull-fighters of Spain, in its palmiest days, compared to England's
> bruisers!

The comic insularity, while as typical of Borrow as his Paisleyite anti-Catholicism, was not peculiar to him. In his younger days the ordinary Englishman also romanticized the pugilists and saw them as archetypal representatives of the English superiority over other nations.

Boxing was not only an English sport; it was *the* English sport, a stern, stark, fierce, clean contest between two brawny specimens of English Protestant manhood, armed only with their bare fists and 'bottom' or courage, worlds away from the dirty, dark, sly, sinister ways of wop and dago, with knives beneath the cloak, their un-English cowardice, their lack of stamina and their habit of lurking in dark alleys to strike in the back. 'The noble art' was both popular and fashionable. The Hon. Grantley Berkeley, lamenting in the 1860s that he had had to acquire 'a certain degree of proficiency' in boxing, wrote:

> In point of fact, though nothing then was said of 'muscular Christianity', the art of self-defence was considered to be as necessary to the education of a gentleman as dancing a minuet or speaking French. It was a rough time, when, if a dispute arose, a word and a blow became a matter of course—the last not infrequently coming first—and men of rank who could rely on their 'science', as it was termed, did not shrink from displaying it at the expense of their inferiors, when the latter were insolently aggressive. . . . Woe to the pugnacious snob who sought the honour of a turn-up with 'a swell'.[1]

There were many reasons for the vogue of pugilism in the years between 1800 and 1824, but among the most important of them was a national assertiveness and a sense of solidarity inspired by the long and bitter Napoleonic Wars and the confidence of a people in their superiority at arms and their possession of the virtues of doggedness and robustness. The England which survived the wars was one whose wealth was increasing by the transformations wrought in the textile and heavy industries through new techniques of manufacture and improved systems of transport. Divided and apprehensive in many ways Britain may have been; there was starvation among the poor and repression on the part of short-sighted governments; rapid industrial change had created problems which few who recognized them for what they were could face with complacency. Yet, after Napoleon's defeat Britain was the most powerful and richest nation in the world, and took pride in this fact. There was not as yet much evidence of that social conscience and reforming dynamic which were to mark the succeeding age.

In the Regency period Englishmen were very conscious of being Englishmen, and the national pride which still, to a degree, attaches to the performances of a touring football team or cricket eleven was focused passionately on the feats of boxers. When Tom Cribb fought the American negro ex-slave, Tom Molyneaux, on 10 December 1810 in the historic battle before 20,000 spectators at Copthorn, near East Grinstead, what was at stake was more than Cribb's Championship; it was the honour of England, and Cribb's victory after thirty-four tremendous rounds was hailed as not only a personal, but also a national, triumph.

The major bouts, with their huge audiences, were a social phenomenon of considerable significance. They brought together the King and the Commons, the wealthy and the poor, the nobles and the plebs, and excluded only the emergent middle classes, for whom pugilism was merely vulgar brawling (as, indeed, it sometimes was). Proscribed by law since 1750 and hounded by the magistrates, the contests persisted, partly because they objectified what Englishmen saw as their prime virtues and partly because of the patronage of the highest in the land. The Prince of Wales, who became Prince Regent and later King George IV, his brothers, the Duke of York and the Duke of Clarence, later King William IV, were supporters, patrons, bettors; the presence of one or other of these at an 'illegal' contest at Moulsey Hurst or Crawley Downs was sufficient to deter even the most zealous of magistrates from issuing a warrant. Not only did the Prince of Wales attend fights, at least until 1788, and visit the training-rooms in London, but he cultivated the society of boxers and received them at Court. On 24 July 1821, when he was crowned King, eighteen of the leading pugilists of England, including Cribb, Spring, Belcher, Richmond, Owen, Hudson and Oliver, under the direction of 'Gentleman' John Jackson, were chosen by the King to act as ushers at Westminster Hall, which action at the same time flattered his friends of the Fancy and ensured the absence of outbreaks of rowdyism. Without such patronage and wealthy backers, it is doubtful if pugilism could have survived the constant charges from the respectable as to its brutality and the vigilant persecution from officers of the law; the presence, too, of the nobility and the aristocracy at a bout acted as something of a check on the large, heterogeneous and often pugnacious crowds. During the Regency boxing came to surpass horse-racing in popularity as a diversion and an interest; as one historian has it, 'the most eagerly awaited news of the day for most people was the results of the horse races and the prize fights'.[2]

Another force in maintaining the standard and the standing of pugilism was the personal influence of 'Gentleman' John Jackson. In the eighteenth century pugilism had been in great part unscientific fisticuffs mixed with wrestling and kicking, contests of strength and endurance between untutored Goliaths. Jack Broughton, who opened his Amphitheatre in the Haymarket in 1743 and was one of the earliest of scientific boxers, formulated the rules which stood under his name and which controlled boxing for almost a century, until the London Prize Ring Rules of 1838 superseded Broughton's code. Broughton's good character helped to raise the status of pugilism and his reliance more upon his fists than on the wrestling-holds which had for generations formed an accepted part of bare-knuckle fighting led to more sophisticated boxing. It is ironical that Broughton himself, after some sixteen years as Champion, lost in 1750 to Jack Slack, a burly, untrained, not too scrupulous butcher, whose reign coincided with a general decline in standards and in the honesty with which the sport was conducted.

Tom Johnson, who became Champion in the 1780s, noteworthy for his courage, his doggedness and his refusal to entertain 'crosses', as fixed fights were called, did something to restore the good name of pugilism and to encourage participation by more reputable fighters and backers. 'That wholly British art' began slowly to rival bear-baiting, dog-fighting, cock-fighting and horse-racing in public favour, although the latter still predominated. The prestige of the sport was enhanced still further by the genius of Daniel Mendoza (1763–1836), who succeeded the next Champions, Ben Brain of Bristol, home of many of the doughtiest boxers, and 'Gentleman' Richard Humphries. Humphries, a teacher of the art of self-defence, trained Mendoza, but came to be jealous of his former pupil. In three fights between the two men, which were the best-attended bouts in Britain up to that date, Mendoza lost the first and triumphantly won the next two. This brilliant little Jew, who weighed merely 160 pounds and thus was, by modern standards, only a middle-weight, fought and defeated boxers very much his superior in weight and size. But his exceptional footwork, his speed and his lightning straight left gave him victory after victory over his slower-witted and sluggishly moving opponents. He was, as Egan points out, a dazzling fighter, moving with a swiftness rarely seen before that time in the ring. More than any other pugilist to that day, Mendoza helped to turn bare-knuckle contests from being controlled brawls into something resembling encounters of skill, agility and intelligence.

In 1795, Mendoza, after several profitable years of teaching, lost the title to 'Gentleman' John Jackson. Although Jackson was a clever boxer, he won and held the title rather cheaply. He had fought only two major bouts before meeting Mendoza, and his victory over the Jew was gained by his grabbing Mendoza's long hair and clubbing him in the face as he struggled to get free. Jackson fought no more, but set up rooms in London at 13 Bond Street with the express aim of coaching noblemen. In fact, Jackson quite frankly used his position as Champion and his knowledge of boxing as a stepping-stone into society, cultivating the nobility and assuming the airs and dress of an aristocrat himself. For all that, he was a good teacher, as one of his most notable pupils, Lord Byron, testified.

With the advent of Jackson, pugilism came wholly out of the shadows; the great era of the ring began, which lasted until his retirement in 1824. Jackson gave the sport a certain respectability. Englishmen were more than ready to embrace a sport that summed up their image of themselves at war—honest, muscular, hard-hitting, clean-fighting, not very bright perhaps, but loyal, trustworthy and never knowing when they were beaten. Jackson, as 'Commander-in-Chief', spread his influence over pugilism for about a quarter of a century. He not only gained adherents from the nobility, but he organized bouts, he acted as referee, he drew up articles of agreement, he presided over inquiries into the conduct of contests, he denounced 'crosses'. His presence was a guarantee of a decent bout. In his rooms at Bond Street the Pugilistic Club was formed in 1814. This body of aristocrats and wealthy supporters set out to fashion regular and systematic procedures for contests as well as to raise money for prize-fights and matches. Under the command of Jackson and with the supervision of the Pugilistic Club, pugilism entered its first Golden Age, perhaps its only Golden Age.

During the next fifteen years or so, whatever the political or the military situation, whatever the miseries of the poor and the sins of the rich, whatever the threat of invasion from outside or revolution from inside, whatever the ineptitude or repressiveness of governments, Englishmen found themselves able to forget their problems for a time in watching two men stripped to the waist confronting each other in an open field and pummelling each other until one of them fell exhausted or unconscious or was dragged from the ring, broken and bleeding, by solicitous seconds. And they went to such bouts in their thousands. Because of the law, matches were seldom advertised in advance; the news would go around by word of mouth or leaflet that a certain place had been chosen (often it was Moulsey Hurst) and a certain date. From London and many provincial centres crowds would set out on horseback, in coaches, gigs, carts, or on foot ('toddlers'), converging on the denominated spot. More often than not, on arrival there they would be told that an officer of the law, or an alderman, by magistrate's order, had forbidden the contest on that location. So another place would be chosen, often several miles away, and the whole caravanserai would stream to this spot, at times in the pouring rain which is so predictably a feature of the English climate on sporting occasions. Not since the religious festivals of the Middle Ages, part religious act, part carnival, part communal ritual, had England seen outdoor gatherings to match the prize-fighting crowds of the early part of the nineteenth century. When Tom Spring fought Bill Neat on 20 May 1823 at Hinckley Down,

Hampshire, the roads from Gloucester, Newbury, Winchester, Bristol, Southampton, London and other centres were, as Egan puts it, 'covered with vehicles of every description filled with amateurs' and on the hill at the back of the Down, which formed a natural amphitheatre, upwards of 30,000 spectators witnessed the fight, 'amongst them numerous well-dressed females'.

The composition of such an audience Egan describes when Tom Spring met John Langan, the Irish Champion, at Worcester on 7 January 1824:

> It was a union of all ranks, from the *brilliant* of the highest class in the circle of Corinthians, down to the *Dusty Bob* gradation in society; and even a *shade* or two below that. Lots of the Upper House, the Lower House and the *flash* house. Proprietors of splendid parks and demesnes; inmates from proud and lofty mansions; thousands from the peaceable cot—and myriads of *coves* from no houses at all; in a word, it was a conglomeration of the Fancy.

Just as a cross-section of the British people found an outlet in pugilism in a time of war and its aftermath and just as the boxers found a leader in Jackson and patrons in the Pugilistic Club, so the sport found, at the right time, its fitting chronicler in Pierce Egan. He had, unconsciously, been preparing for the role for much of his early life. His opportunity came when, in 1812, George Smeeton, always on the lookout for a topical subject, decided to issue a history of pugilism in monthly parts, illustrated with plates of the boxers. Egan was chosen for the task, or, rather, chose himself, and the result, issued first in parts and then in a volume in 1813 by Smeeton at 139 St Martin's Lane, was to be the beginning of a series of five volumes which has no parallel down to the present day.

Boxiana was not the first book to deal with pugilism. Captain Godfrey's little monograph of 1740, *A Treatise on the Useful Art of Self-Defence*, is the earliest known systematic treatment of the subject, and other volumes, such as *Recollections of Pugilism and Sketches of the Ring*, by 'An Amateur' (1801), and *Recollections of an Octogenarian*, by J. C. (1805), followed. In 1811 *Lives of the Boxers* was issued by 'Jon Bee'[3] (Jonathan Badcock), a sporting journalist and writer on veterinary subjects, who, in part because Egan's book quite overshadowed his, was to become one of the latter's most vituperative and jealous rivals, and in the same year there appeared the more elaborate *Pancratia: A History of Pugilism*, by Bill Oxberry, the comic actor, journalist and pub-keeper, with an historical Introduction, also most probably by Badcock.

In scope, detail, vivacity and expertise, none of these could hold a candle to *Boxiana*. Badcock, who was no mean sporting writer himself, lost no opportunity to disparage Egan's skill and originality. In his *Slang: A Dictionary of the Turf, The Ring, The Chase, etc.* (1823) he claims that Smeeton and not Egan was the 'compiler' of the first volume of *Boxiana*, that the book was based upon *Pancratia*, that it was, in fact, merely 'a copy essentially, but a vulgarized one, of the comedian's book', and says that anyone wanting a true history of boxing should buy 'the *Fancy Chronology*, a history of 700 battles, by John Bee, Esq, the fancy writer and present quill-man'.[4] This cannot be taken seriously; Badcock, especially when dealing with Egan, his *bête noire*, was prone to errors, exaggerations and downright falsehoods. Besides, the Fancy, by virtually ignoring Badcock's books and taking *Boxiana* as their bible and Egan as their oracle, cast their vote decisively.

What seems to have happened is that Smeeton, aware of the growing market for works on pugilism, suggested to Egan, or Egan, similarly aware, suggested to him, that something could be compiled on the lines of Bee's *Lives* and Oxberry's *Pancratia*. Possibly Egan had already tried his hand at such gatherings. *Sporting Anecdotes, Original and Select*, published in London in 1807 by J. Cundee and J. Harris and attributed to 'An Amateur Sportsman', appears to show traces of Egan's taste and preoccupations; certainly in his later acknowledged compilations he did not hesitate to draw upon this book.

The first volume of *Boxiana* undoubtedly was indebted to earlier books, Godfrey's, Oxberry's and Badcock's among them, as it had to be for a history of boxing, in the absence of more than a handful of sources. But it soon leaves them behind as it approaches 'the present milling era' and gives eye-witness accounts of major bouts and details the fighters' origins, characters and background, information which could come only from direct personal knowledge. As already mentioned, the book was published anonymously as by 'One of the Fancy'. Egan was as yet unknown to the general public as a writer; he was a familiar figure as 'an amateur', but still, it seems, thought of himself as mainly a printer and journalist, one of the many unnamed workers in the field of ephemera. The sub-title of *Boxiana* is 'Sketches of Antient and Modern Pugilism, From the Days of Broughton and Slack to the Heroes of the Present Milling Era', and it was dedicated to 'that distinguished patron of Old English Sports, Captain Barclay'. This was the same Captain Barclay, an outstanding backer of boxers, who trained Tom

Cribb for his classic bout against Molyneaux on 28 September 1811, and who is said to have won £10,000 through Cribb's victory. Egan was never modest in selecting dedicatees, and with each successive book progressed higher and higher until he arrived at the very top.

It is not difficult to understand, at this distance of time, why *Boxiana* had such an impact upon its age. For one thing, in most respects it was a good deal more comprehensive, as well as more accurate, than its predecessors and contemporaries. John Hamilton Reynolds, poet, essayist, friend of Keats and brother-in-law of Thomas Hood, writing under his pseudonym of 'Peter Corcoran', called Egan 'a Lord Eldon in the skill and caution of his judgments'. For another, it disclosed more 'inside' knowledge of the ring and its followers than any other sports writer could claim. And the manner and tone of the book made it unique. Egan's style, at times orotund and rhetorical, especially when he is stirred by national considerations or transfixed with ecstatic admiration before that 'most noble institution', the British monarchy, personified in a dissolute Regent, is also capable of an eighteenth-century raciness and energy. He uses sporting slang, cant and the jargon of the Fancy with unself-conscious ease, although by no means as consistently or as generously as he was to do in succeeding volumes of *Boxiana*. He speaks to sportsmen in their own tongue, linking amateurs together in the intimacy of a shared jargon and yet not laying it on so thickly as to exclude the interested outsider.

Stylistically, it seems to me that each of the five volumes of *Boxiana* improves upon the previous one. The peak is reached in the *New Series* of 1828 and 1829. But this first book contains much that is typical of Egan as a boxing reporter and that makes him, as A. J. Liebling calls him in *The Sweet Science*, 'the greatest writer about the ring who ever lived'.

On the very first page Egan defines 'the Fancy': 'It simply means any person who is fond of a particular amusement, or closely attached to some subject; a lively instance fortunately presents itself in illustrating the phrase beyond all doubt—as the old lady observed, when she kissed her cat, that it was "*her fancy*".' Then follows a lengthy historical introduction and defence of pugilism against the attacks of the middle class and the religious. 'Boxing', Egan declares, 'came from *Nature*! wounded feelings brought manly *resentment* to its aid—and *coolness*, checking fiery passion and rage, reduced it to a perfect science'.

No writer has been more generous in capitalized and italicized words than Pierce Egan—not even Queen Victoria—nor as prolific in exclamation marks. It would be to attribute to him greater subtlety than he possesses to suggest that these serve the same purpose as an actor's emphases, yet it is true that once the reader becomes accustomed to this idiosyncrasy, he finds that the typographical oddities impart a colloquial tone and colour to much of the writing; one can, it seems, hear the speaking voice of an agreeable, lively, enthusiastic raconteur behind the printed page. At other times, the italicizing has a comic effect, not so much from Egan's execrable puns (by comparison with his contemporary, Thomas Hood, he is a lumbering amateur) as in the quaint turn he can give to a statement by his emphases. Compare this: 'Bill Love, a *Butcher* challenged Johnson for fifty guineas, which was decided at Barnet; but the *Knight of the Cleaver* was, in a few minutes, so completely *cut up*, as to leave Johnson in possession of the ground' with this: 'No pugilist [Cribb] ever retired from the *ring* with such favours heaped upon him as the present CHAMPION, and the sporting amateurs have vied with each other in paying respect to his *milling* acquirements, that have been so often seen, *felt*, and justly acknowledged; and, doubtless, will be *long* remembered by those persons who entered the lists against his conquering arm.'

Not only is boxing natural, continues Egan; it is especially natural to Englishmen. Britain is 'a country where the stiletto is not known— where trifling quarrels do not produce assassination, and where revenge is not finished by murder. Boxing removes these dreadful calamities; a contest is soon decided, and scarcely ever the frame sustains any material injury.' Those who attack prize-fighting do not realize how much it both manifests and contributes to the soundness of the national character. If they had their way, 'the English character may get too *refined* and the *thoroughbred* bull-dog degenerate into the *whining* puppy'. He attributes the decline in duelling to the rise in the art of self-defence during the past seventy years or so. 'Where, *then*, is the relative, however high in pride and pomp, in viewing the father, husband, or brother, killed in a duel, but what would rather that they should have had recourse to the manly defence of *Boxing*, than the deadly weapons of sword and ball?'

Men are always liable to quarrel. Why should they then not settle their differences in the clean, decent way of fisticuffs, avoiding the sneaky methods of lesser breeds without the law?

In Holland the long knife decides too frequently; scarcely any person in Italy is without the stiletto; and France and Germany are not particular in using sticks, stones, etc. to gratify revenge; but in England, the FIST only is used. . . . The fight done, the

hand is given in token of peace; resentment vanishes, and the
cause generally bound in oblivion. This generous mode of conduct
is not owing to any particular rule laid down by education—it
is an inherent principle—the impulse of the moment—acted upon
by the most ignorant and inferior ranks of the people. . . . As a
national trait, we feel no hesitation in declaring, that it is
wholly—*British!*

That pugilism had become respectable Egan maintains by citing the
number of noblemen and eminent people who patronized the sport.
In 1786 the Prince of Wales, the Duke of York, the Duke of Orléans
and most of the French nobility at that time in England were among
those who witnessed the set-to between Humphries and Marton, the
Bate Butcher, at Newmarket. The 1811 battle between Cribb and Molyneaux had among its spectators the Marquis of Queensberry, Sir
Henry Smyth, Lord Yarmouth, the Hon. Berkeley Craven, Lord
Pomfret, Sir Francis Baynton and many other aristocrats. Even Dr
Samuel Johnson is called in as an example; his mastery of 'the manly
display of the pugilist, as much as his appreciation of the life of the
people, helped to form the *stamina* of his literary works and he himself
afforded a striking proof of pugilism being a national trait by thrashing
an insolent athletic brewer's servant who insulted him in Fleet Street!'

Egan goes on with some sensible remarks on the basic principles of
boxing, elementary perhaps nowadays, when the sport has become so
much more sophisticated, and unconscious of the importance of
rigorous training, but clearly aware of the need for a good deal more
than muscle and brute strength ('It is particularly recommended to
those who box, never to charge their stomachs with too much food on
the day of combat.'). The prime ingredient for success, in his estimation,
is 'bottom', or courage, 'which requires *wind* and *spirit* or *heart*'. ('You
gotta have heart,' in the words of the baseball coach in *Damn Yankees*.)

In his historical survey of boxing from its beginnings, Egan laments
the absence of detailed accounts of earlier battles in a characteristic
way (one vice he did not possess was false modesty): 'Alas! for the want
of a *Boxiana*, to record their valorous deeds. Heroes and Tyros of the
fist have, unfortunately, been suffered to "steal ingloriously to the
grave" and their qualifications buried with them, leaving the pugilistic
fraternity to mourn in silence the loss of their achievements.' But he
does all he can to recapture the mood and style of the giants of the past,
treating each boxer separately, since the various paper-covered parts of
Boxiana dealt each with a different pugilist. From the days of James Fig,

who first caught the public imagination in 1719 and held the Championship, a loosely bestowed title in those days, and of Jack Broughton, who was the next Champion of real note ('at once a Lycurgus, a Caesar and an Alfred', said *Blackwood's*), he gives a lively and lucid account of the development of the science, aware of its finer points and of all the things that went to enhance its prestige and refine its practice—among them Broughton's invention of the 'mufflers', or primitive gloves, which were not worn in the actual fights, but enabled boxers to practise without injury, Broughton's rules, which included 'that no person is to hit his adversary when he is down' and 'that no champion be deemed beaten unless he fails coming up to the line[5] in the limited time [i.e. half a minute, the time allowed after a fall], or his own second declares him beaten'; the grace and skill of Richard Humphries, the popularity of Henry Pearce or 'Hen' Pearce (hence 'The Game Chicken'), the 'science and thorough *bottom*' of John Gully, the only pugilist to become a Member of Parliament, the 'rapid dexterity and irresistible gaiety' of Jem Belcher, the native vigour of 'Sir' Daniel Donnelly, the Irish Champion, and, above all, the elegance and intelligence of Daniel Mendoza, 'a complete artist', as Egan says. *Blackwood's* found Mendoza 'a showy or *flowery* boxer', but most contemporaries agreed with *Boxiana* that the Jew 'rose up like a phenomenon in the pugilistic hemisphere and was a star of the first brilliancy'.

Throughout the whole of this giant record of almost 500 pages Egan's enthusiasm rarely slackens. Even in writing of bouts which took place before he was born, his vivacious style makes them appear to be the reports of an eye-witness. His heroes, so many of them unlettered men who had been navvies, butchers, bakers, soldiers, paviours, he surrounds with the ambiance of classical or literary allusions, raising them to the level of demi-gods. The Game Chicken, when at the height of his fame he received a challenge from his old friend, patron and tutor, Jem Belcher, is 'not altogether unlike Julius Caesar in receiving the unkind stab from his beloved Brutus'. When, in the thick of the battle, Pearce had a chance of ending it, Egan makes him cry, 'I'll take no advantage of thee, Jem; I'll not hit thee, no, lest I hurt thine other eye!' 'My *Uncle Toby*,' Egan adds, 'never uttered a finer sentiment, or performed a nobler act more worthy of registering.' When Pearce gallantly rescued a servant from a burning house in Bristol in 1807 at great peril to his own life, he proved himself, asserts Egan, 'almost more than mortal'.

Indeed, if one were to take them literally, the pronouncements Egan quotes as uttered by the bruisers of his time would indicate that they were indeed Homeric heroes or sometimes Biblical ones, as in the David versus Goliath encounter when Tom Johnson fought Isaac Perrins of Birmingham. Perrins was 6 feet 2 inches high and weighed 17 stone, 3 stone more than Johnson. At one point in the bout, according to *Boxiana,* Johnson's evasive footwork provoked the contempt of Perrins. 'Why,' Egan reports him as saying, 'what have you brought me here! This is not the valiant Johnson, the Champion of England. You have imposed upon me with a mere boy.' Egan continues: 'Tom's manly heart felt most bitterly this keen sarcasm and, bursting with indignation, instantly cried out, "By G—d! you shall soon know that Tom Johnson *is* here!" and directly made a *spring* at Perrins, and put in a lunge over the left eye that closed it up in a twinkling.' After sixty-two rounds lasting an hour and a quarter, the battered Perrins was dragged from the ring by his seconds.

Homer, Themosticles, Thucydides, Ovid, Virgil are all summoned up in the pages of *Boxiana* to underline the heroism and doggedness of the British fighter. In Egan's eyes and in those of his contemporaries, the bravery of Lifeguardsman Shaw at Waterloo was in great part attributable to his training in the ring, and Belcher, Scroggins, Cribb, Randall and other 'heroes' of the ring were the living equivalents of Achilles, Hector and Ajax. 'There was undoubtedly a finished and perfect beauty in the finest performances of Mendoza for which one may now look in vain. He was the Virgil—or, perhaps, the Addison of his time. His battle with Humphries was perhaps superior to anything in the "Aeneid",' said *Blackwood's* in its series on *Boxiana,* thus echoing the mood and style of Egan. The same paper, in the same vein, found lessons and analogies closer to hand. When Slack defeated Broughton in 1750, Egan relates the sequel: 'His patron, the Duke of Cumberland, earnestly exclaimed, "What are you about, Broughton? *You can't fight! you're beat!*" To which question, Broughton instantly replied, "I can't see my man, your Highness; *I am blind, but not beat; only let me be placed before my antagonist, and he shall not gain the day yet."*' Despite Broughton's courage, Slack defeated him and the Duke, who had earned the disgust of the crowd by pushing on Broughton to fight when he was spent and had both eyes closed up, lost several thousands on the bout. 'His Royal Highness,' Egan tells us, 'instantly turned his back upon BROUGHTON, *and by the interference of the legislature, his amphitheatre was shut up!*' His comment on this mean action is given in the words of Shakespeare's Wolsey after his rejection by Henry VIII: 'So farewell to the little good you bear me!' And *Blackwood's,* for whom, of course, Cumberland was that 'mean, cowardly and bloody Butcher', said, after quoting with approval Egan's account of Broughton's fall, that the Duke 'felt the loss of that battle more than the defeat of Fontenay—and it may be questioned if the liberties of Britain ever received so fatal a blow as that inflicted on them by the shutting up of Broughton's amphitheatre'.[6]

How seriously we are to take such high-flown analogies is another matter. There is, often in *Blackwood's* and hardly less frequently in Egan, the suspicion of a twinkle in the eye, a suggestion that, while the writer half means it, he is expecting his readers to make the necessary qualifications, that it is, in fact, all part of the fun of the game. At the same time one can be in little doubt that to most of the Fancy, anyhow, pugilistic battles and their contestants *were* 'heroic' and the classical references were not inappropriate ones.

It is when Egan is reporting a match or describing the crowds going to one, or the negotiations before a fight, or the excitement of the anticipatory days before, or the bustle of preparations for the contest, or the officials 'whipping out' the ring to obtain space in the press of spectators for the boxers to engage that he moves from his 'literary' style to his slangy and colloquial vein. More of this later, but for the moment let us look at that method of reporting when, with a judicious use of slang, he gives a concise summary of the main movements of each round, enough to recall to those who were present their pleasure in the shifts of fortune and to give to those who could only read of the fights a colourful and fair report of what actually took place. Here are two typical descriptions of single rounds involving Molyneaux.

In the first, which was fought at Moulsey Hurst on 21 May 1811, the Negro was matched against Rimmer, a young bruiser from Lancashire. Egan's account of the final section of the bout is especially interesting in showing how he was alive to, not only the changing pattern of the fight, but also the reaction of the spectators and the social implications of the encounter. He delights in the crowd as a Fielding would and he sees the mêlée through the eyes of his admired Hogarth:

> Fourteenth: It was *all up* with Rimmer, who retreated to every part of the ring, followed closely by Molyneaux, who put in a dreadful stomacher, which *floored* him. A scene now took place which beggared all description, during which Rimmer lay prostrate on the ground; the ring was broken; owing it is said from the antipathy felt against a *man of colour* proving the conqueror—if it was so, the illiberal were disappointed by this manoeuvre, as those who had taken the odds gained nothing by the event.

Rimmer was completely exhausted—almost in a state of insensibility. It would have been a fine subject for the pencil of Hogarth to have delineated—here were *Corinthians* and *Coster-mongers* in rude contact; *Johnny Raws* and first-rate *Swells* jostling each other; PUGILISTS and *Novices*, all jawing, threatening, but not hearing—the confusion was beyond every thing, sticks and whips at work in all directions, ten thousand people in one rude commotion, and those persons in the interior of this vast assemblage suffering from their attempts to extricate themselves from so perilous and unpleasant a situation. Twenty minutes elapsed in this *chaotic* manner, till the Champion of England [Cribb], assisted by some brave followers, once more formed something like a ring. By the rules of fighting, if either of the combatants leave the ring, he is considered to have lost the battle. Molyneaux and Rimmer again *set to*, but it proved a short-lived advantage to the latter, notwithstanding extraordinary exertions were made to renovate Rimmer, to make him stand upon his legs. It was all in vain; during six more rounds Rimmer was so severely *punished* as to be unable to stand up, when he acknowledged he had received *enough!*

And here is how Egan saw two of the most critical rounds in the second fight between Cribb and Molyneaux on 28 September 1811. In the absence of crowd interference, he concentrates on the main events of the interchange and incidentally crisply analyses the different techniques of each boxer:

Third: In the last rally, the right eye of Cribb was almost *darkened*; and another now commenced equally as ferocious, after sparring to obtain wind, in which it was perceived the *Moor* was defective, when the *Champion* put in a most tremendous *doubler* in the body of *Molyneaux*, who, notwithstanding that he was *hit* away, to the astonishment of every one, renewed the rally in that determined manner as to create considerable agitation among those persons who had betted the odds. There was a marked difference in their method of fighting: *Cribb* hit right and left at the head and body, while the *Moor* aimed at the *nob* alone, and with much judgment planted several dexterous flush hits, that impaired the eyesight of *Cribb*, and his mouth bled considerably. This rally continued a minute, and in closing the *Champion* received a heavy fall. The superiority of the *Moor's* strength was evinced by his grasping the body of *Cribb* with one hand, and supporting himself by the other resting on the stage; and in this situation threw *Cribb* completely over on the stage, by the force of a cross-buttock. To those not *flash*, the mere appearance of things appeared in favour of the *Moor*; but the fortitude of the *Champion stayed* his friends, although the betting had got down seven to four.

Ninth: It was so evident which way the battle would now terminate that it was '*Lombard Street to a China Orange*', Cribb was the conqueror. The *Moor*, in running in, had his jaw broke, and he fell as if dead, from a tremendous left-handed blow of the *Champion*. Molyneaux did not come to his time by full half a minute—but *Cribb* wished that the Spectators should fully witness his superiority in giving away this *chance*—dancing about the stage, when he ought to have been proclaimed the conqueror: and went in again, knocking him nearly down, and then up again, and *levelled* him.

In these accounts and others, the almost surrealistic syntax to which Egan was prone in his reports seems to add to their breathless immediacy; it is as if we are hearing the frantic commentary of a radio announcer at a football match or race-meeting.

This, then, was Egan's first book, an immediate success, and the herald of a new age in sports reporting, bringing a fresh spirit of involvement and exultation with it. *Boxiana*, Vol. I, could not be said, however, to have made his name. It was not until six years later that he acknowledged a book as his own and, in his early forties, entered into his true period of recognition as the writer for his age.

❧ III ❧

The World of the Fancy

As Egan's contributions to the *Weekly Dispatch* were unsigned and as his peculiar reporting style took some time to evolve, it is not easy to say when he first began writing for that paper. We have the editor's testimony that he was reporting 'exclusively' for it in 1819, but it is clear that he had been engaged by the journal for some time before that. According to Stanley Morison,[1] no mean authority, Egan's association with the *Dispatch* began in 1816. Certainly up to 1810 the *Dispatch* printed little or nothing to do with sport. From that year the amount begins to increase until by 1814 there is a substantial quantity dealing with various kinds of sport, some of which could well be by Pierce Egan. Various turns of phrase in 1816 accounts leave little doubt that by that year he was well established on the paper. There is no evidence to support the *D.N.B.*'s suggestion that he obtained the *Dispatch* position in 1812.[2] What seems to me highly probable is that the continued success of the first volume of *Boxiana* led in time to his being offered a job as sporting reporter on the *Dispatch*. It was a wise move on the part of the proprietors, for Egan's contributions were among the chief reasons for the *Dispatch*'s greatly increased circulation as the second decade of the century drew on.

The art of self-defence was no new topic for newspapers. In the later years of the eighteenth century many periodicals contained reports of the main bouts, and it was from these that Egan and other historians drew most of their material. *The Gentleman's Magazine*, *The Flying Post*, *Woodfall's Daily Advertiser*, *The Daily News Letter* and *The*

Mercury featured pugilistic news and gossip, as did, on occasion, *The Times* and *The Globe*. Among the most reliable and consistent of them all were Captain Topham's *The World*, established in 1787, and the monthly *Sporting Magazine*, beginning in 1793, which covered most of the principal events in horse-racing, hunting, cock-fighting, pedestrianism and boxing. But the increase of interest in sport and especially in pugilism in the new century meant that few newspapers could afford not to devote some attention to such topics. Among the papers that took up the challenge were several associated with the name of Bell. As there were so many different Bells involved in journalism at the time, a little sorting-out becomes necessary at this point.[3]

The first and best-known Bell, John of that name (1745–1831), was printer, publisher, bookseller, journalist and type-founder. 'He had no acquirement, not even grammar', wrote Leigh Hunt, 'but his taste in putting forth a publication was new in those times, and may be admired in any.' Among John Bell's ventures were the newspapers *The Morning Post* and *The Oracle* and editions of Shakespeare, 'The Poets of Great Britain' and 'The British Theatre'. On 1 May 1796 he launched the first issue of *Bell's Weekly Messenger*, a Sunday newspaper whose sound reporting, wide coverage and pleasant make-up made it a success. By 1803 it had attained a weekly sale of 6,000 copies at 6*d*. each and it had become widely imitated.

In 1801 a Robert Bell founded *The Weekly Dispatch*. Not much is known of this gentleman. When he died in 1825, Pierce Egan was one of the few to note the fact. In a warm obituary,[4] Egan praises Bell's human qualities and ends:

> I knew him well, Horatio! and as it has fallen to the Describer of
> a horse-race, the Reporter of a prize-fight and the Tale-teller
> of the Canine fancy, to travel for once out of his line to enter
> the classic regions of taste and literature, it is trusted that the
> Critic will not only act in a generous manner upon this humble
> effort, but assist the *scribbler* in 'getting over the ground well'
> to prevent a man like the late Robert Bell from sinking silently
> into his grave! This opportunity, likewise, cannot be resisted of
> expressing an acute feeling for the loss of a once valued friend,
> and asserting that no one will drop a tear with a more unfeigned
> sincerity over his tomb than
>
> Pierce Egan.

Shortly after it was launched, the *Weekly Dispatch* changed its name to *Bell's Weekly Dispatch*, legitimately enough in a way, but obviously attempting to cash in on the success of *Bell's Weekly Messenger*. Both papers remained very similar in style and content, being concerned with general topics, but giving occasional attention to sport. Among the other Bells involved in contemporary journalism, adding extra confusion to the scene, were John Browne Bell, who started the short-lived *Bell's New Weekly Messenger* in 1831, Richard Bell of *Bell's Commercial and Agricultural Register* and Charles Bell of *The Times*.

Thanks, however, to Egan's reports, the *Weekly Dispatch*, which was radical in its politics, became in the second decade of the century the foremost pugilistic journal and remained so for the next ten years, when it was superseded by *Bell's Life in London*.

By 1814, before Egan began his permanent association with the *Dispatch* and while he was making occasional sporting contributions to various newspapers, he had set himself up as an independent printer and publisher in premises at 29 Great Marlborough Street. Here he joined the company of the Catnaches in issuing cheap reprints, broadsides and chapbooks. It was during this period, too, that he began his long and profitable association with two young rising artists and caricaturists, the brothers George and Isaac Robert Cruikshank. According to Blanchard Jerrold,[5] George etched for Egan 'The Entry of Louis XVIII into Paris' as a frontispiece to a chapbook published by Egan in 1814. During these years, too, Egan, thoroughly at home in the taverns and gambling-houses of the city, took the brothers with him on his various 'larks and sprees'. George, who was in later life to become fanatically puritanical and a passionate propagandist for teetotalism, was in his youthful days anything but prissy—so little, indeed, that as Jerrold also relates, 'Christopher North', who acknowledged the artist's gifts, admonished him in *Blackwood's* to cut himself down to one bottle at dinner and to put a brake on his dissipations. But out of the trio's exploration of the seamier side of London came that intimate knowledge which was to give such authenticity to their *Life in London* a few years later.

Egan was not long content with producing compilations and hackpieces by others from Marlborough Street; he soon issued a work of his own. This was *The Mistress of Royalty or The Loves of Florizel and Perdita, Portrayed in the Amatory Epistles between an Illustrious Personage and a Distinguished Female*. The title-page shows no author's name, but carries the imprint, 'Printed by and for P. Egan, 29 Great Marlborough', and sold by all booksellers. 1814'. It was twenty-nine years before Egan acknowledged his authorship of this satirical squib. He did not, in the intervening years, ever refer to it in his various proud proclamations of authorship beneath the titles of his new books nor in any of his advertisements. But the British Museum copy of the work has the following dedication and note in his handwriting: 'January 25, 1843. With the Author's best respects, to J. Richardson, Esq. If there is any merit attached to this little Book—it is from its *singularity*. The Author having, in the capacity of a Printer—composed the Types, and worked it off at the Press. Pierce Egan.' *The Mistress of Royalty* is a sufficient proof of Egan's skill at his trade; it is an attractively produced little volume, clearly and efficiently printed, free from misprints and thoughtfully spaced. And the contents themselves show a sophistication sometimes denied to those who deem him a mere journalistic hack.

The Mistress of Royalty is a satirical gibe in the manner of the day at the notorious love-life of the Prince Regent (Florizel), and especially at his well-known and scandalous association with the gifted actress, Miss Robinson (Perdita). The Regent's unfeeling treatment of his ex-mistress aroused considerable popular indignation at the time, and the Radicals in particular exploited the liaison for political purposes. Egan gives little evidence of firm political convictions, except for a vague, general liberalism. The one consistent feature of his writing after 1814 is an uncritical adulation of the Monarchy, the British Constitution and the common man. While he made no attempt to conceal the fact that he was the publisher of the book, he was prudent enough not to admit to its authorship at the time; later, when he came into Royal favour and had hopes of further favours from Crown and Government, he was at pains not to draw attention to it, hoping, perhaps, that it would be forgotten in the flood of satirical pamphlets, caricatures and books, many much more scurrilous than his own. Only when he was an old man, when the Georges had passed from the Throne, did he openly acknowledge his authorship—not that then, or perhaps at any time, anybody cared.

The exchange of fictional letters between Florizel and Perdita which make up most of the book still amuses. Egan shows a gift for phoney rhetoric and for irony and a sense of the ludicrous and the incongruous in his recounting of Florizel's persistent wooing of Perdita, her surrender, his inconstancy, her forgiveness, his tiring of her and his final abandonment of her as he falls into debauchery. Florizel dishonours his bond to Perdita, she is pursued by various gallants, goes to the Continent, becomes the mistress of a Colonel, gets rheumatic fever, is deserted by the Colonel and sinks to a sad end. The characters are very thinly disguised and immediately recognizable. Egan pays tribute to the Prince Regent's good qualities, but deplores his fickleness and feeble moral sense. The following brief exchange will give some idea of the tone of the work, and of its often wry humour.

Florizel to Perdita:

My Angel, I know not how to express myself upon the occasion. Language is set at nought—and words are incapable of expressing my ideas. Accept this from my heart—my soul— Will be with you at seven.

Florizel.

Perdita to Florizel:

Indeed, Florizel, I am now too well convinced, that gratification cloys. The honey-moon is not yet over, and you have been absent three whole days—three whole nights—Not a billet from you in all that time—No letters now signed with your *propre sang*—Alas! Alas! I may say with the song

> Man was born to be a rover:
> Foolish woman—to believe.

Give me back my heart—that heart which you still possess!— Give me back myself, in that purity in which you found me!— Give me back that tranquility of mind, which once possessed the

Lost Perdita

Florizel to Perdita:

What does my angelic Perdita mean by this accusation? Engagements, and a thousand avocations, have drawn me from you. But to be still more ingenuous, I got damnably d—— the night before last, with those bucks D—t and C—d, and my head has not been clear since. I narrowly escaped being demolished by a bull-dog that was let loose in C—'s yard, and have some marks of his claws upon me yet; and had not the groom rushed from the stables with a pitch-fork, I should never have been able to subscribe myself.

Yours most devotedly
Florizel.

Much later, Florizel to Perdita:

Dear Perdita,

You disbelieved me last night, but believe me now—I was never so happy in my life.

31

Angels were painted fair to look like you!

But it must be Perdita to give delight! exquisite delight! Oh! what rapture I found within those arms! arms which have almost destroyed the power of my hand. I am, however, capable of subscribing myself

> Yours till death
>
> Florizel.

Perdita to Florizel:

I cannot, my much admired Florizel, reply in your strain; as well might an Arne attempt to surpass an Handel. They were both great masters in the art, the science of music; but never reached you, in the art and science of love.

> Accept this from
>
> Perdita.

But, despite this intimacy, within twelve months, Egan writes, 'the charm that had hitherto bound the delighted Florizel was dissolved' and the trusting, ruined Perdita was on her way to perdition.

Florizel certainly does not come off lightly in this story, but, in tune with contemporary morality, much of the weight of blame falls on Perdita. For all her gifts of mind and character, she had one major drawback, says Egan, 'that the elegant, enlightened, interesting, beautiful Perdita was unchaste!' And he ends with a warning to women not to emulate her, to make sure that they 'are not destitute of the very basis of all female excellence—*Chastity*'. It was, of course, the public dissoluteness of the life of 'The First Gentleman of Europe', of which *The Mistress of Royalty* gives us a glimpse, that helped make Englishmen a quarter of a century later greet with pleasure the coming to the throne of a young, innocent and respectable Queen.

The next work from Egan's pen was the second volume of *Boxiana*, issued in April 1818, together with a reprint of Volume I, both now presented under his own name 'at the request of several distinguished persons in the sporting world', and revealing the printer, publisher, stationer, reporter and bookseller for the first time as an 'author', which title he preferred above all others. As he was to issue another volume of the first series of *Boxiana* in 1821, these two latter books may be conveniently discussed here. The three first volumes of *Boxiana* were published by Sherwood, Neely and Jones of Paternoster Row, with whom Egan's association was to continue for several years. Incidentally, the issuing of the new edition of Volume I by this firm, which has led some critics to imagine that this was its first appearance, disposes of the suggestion that Smeeton, the original publisher, was author or part author, as does the fact that Egan always claimed the three volumes as his own work.

Like the original *Boxiana*, the new volumes were originally issued in monthly parts, accompanied by copperplates of the pugilists, either in the frozen poses of sitters for a portrait or 'squaring up' in the ring, stripped to the waist. The stylized heads, idealized yet retaining something of the traits of the individuals, are more often than not fitted somewhat awkwardly on to stereotyped torsos, all much of a muchness and cast in a heroically muscular mould. Many of the plates were executed by the painter and engraver, George Sharples, who was in 1821 to complete the only extant portrait of Egan himself.

As Egan continues *Boxiana* he carries the history of pugilism right up to date and adds extra details of the careers of boxers treated in the first book. A good deal of the material is taken directly from his reports of bouts printed in the *Weekly Dispatch* and elsewhere, and in humour, sprightliness, thoroughness and detail outdoes the contents of *Boxiana*, Volume I. Now that he is not drawing in part from earlier records, but describing what he himself had witnessed in his tireless journeys throughout England, he writes with something of the spirit and élan of an eighteenth-century novelist.

Volume II, sub-titled 'Sketches of Modern Pugilism from the Championship of Cribb to the Present Time', is dedicated to the Earl of Yarmouth, one of the principal founders of the Pugilistic Club and a devoted patron of the sport, and Volume III, 'Sketches of Modern Pugilism during the Championship of Cribb to Spring's Challenge to all England', to another noble supporter, the Marquis of Worcester.

Throughout the whole chronicle Egan is sustained by his never-failing interest in people, in their variety, their differences, their quiddity. Whereas in other sporting writings of the time, the patrons, the bettors, the judges, the seconds and the pugilists are merely names, he characterizes them all with quick, light strokes. This is 'The Fancy' at its most likeable and liveliest, viewed with a universal tolerance that extends to the lowest in society. The bruisers of the day are still alive in Egan's pages. Here, for instance, is Ned Scroggins, the formidable light-weight:

The singularity of his person tended, in a great degree, to
procure him *notoriety* as a pugilist; his height does not exceed
five feet three inches, and under eleven stone in weight. His
appearance, when stripped, is not unlike the stump of a large tree;

and, from his loins upwards, he looks like a man of fourteen
stone. He stands firm upon his legs. His frame is round, hardy,
and capable of great exertions, either in *giving* or receiving
the blow, accompanied with a *nob*, which seems laughing at all
opposition. A projecting forehead too, which, in a great degree,
protects his *peepers* from being easily measured for a *suit of
mourning;* and he frequently attacks his adversary more like the
antics of a *merryman* than displaying the practical system of a
disciplined boxer. *Smashing* is his principal *forte*; and he appears
to fight more from the impulse of *feeling* than acting with the
coolness of judgment.

When Bill Nosworthy, a former baker, confronts the once unbeatable
Dutch Sam, Egan begins by sketching the difference in the condition
of the two contestants:

On the combatants approaching each other, and shaking hands in
the usual way, the *difference* of person was so manifest that an
ordinary unbiassed spectator must have given the preference
to the *Baker*, from the roundness of his frame, the firmness of his
step, and the cheerfulness of his countenance. He must have
been a *novice* indeed, not to have discovered the wretched
condition of Sam upon his throwing off his clothes. His ribs
were *spare* in the extreme; his face, which hitherto assumed such
a formidable aspect, and his fierce eyes that seemed upon all
similar occasions to have penetrated the very souls of his
opponents, darting looks of terror and confusion to their most
pointed efforts, now appeared clouded with doubt and anxiety.
It was altogether a different frontispiece. Dejection, arising from
debility, marked strongly its most prominent feature. As for his
legs (the general criterion of strength) as if Sam had anticipated
they might be viewed against him, he for the first time in his life,
preferred fighting in gaiters and breeches. The *tout ensemble*
portrayed in every point of view more that sort of character
which required the careful assistance of a nurse—than what
Sam was about to assume—namely, the hero entering the
prize-ring, fully prepared to vanquish youth, health, and strength.

Impressed by the spirit of sportsmanship exhibited by most of the
pugilists, Egan loses no opportunity to show it in action. After Jack
Randall, 'The Nonpareil', had, in a thirty-four-round bout lasting
two hours and twenty minutes, decisively beaten Ned Turner:

The first act of Randall, on being pronounced the victor, was to push the crowd away from him, and to clasp the hand of his fallen, brave foe, with much zeal and friendship; while *Turner*, nobly disdaining animosity, gently patted the *prime Irish boy* on his back, in token that he was the best man, and had won the battle nobly and in gallant style.

The same gallantry, Egan would have us believe, extended outside the ring. Not only were the masters of the art of self-defence able to protect themselves vigorously against roving bands of riotous swells or against the footpads and thugs that infested the metropolis, but they never lost an opportunity of coming to the defence of a lady in distress. Jack Martin, a baker—hence, in sporting parlance, 'The Master of the Rolls'—once encountered a gang of six dandies pestering a genteel young married woman:

He *let fly* with his right hand on the *nob* of the first that approached him, and the Dandy went down as if he had been *shot*; the second shared the same fate; the third was no better off; the fourth came in for *pepper*; the fifth got a severe *quitting*; and the sixth received for his *insolence* so strong a blow on his mouth as to dislodge some of his *ivory*. It was truly laughable to see the ridiculous way in which the *Dandies* appeared—the *claret* trickling down their cheeks, and holding their hands up to their heads; but when the *Swell* [who was accompanying Randall] observed, 'JACK MARTIN, give it them,' the name operated like a shock of thunder upon their nerves, and they all *bolted* like *racehorses*, or rather after the manner of the French *sauve qui peut*.

The audiences for the contests are described with almost as much care as the bouts and the boxers. Sometimes they were uniformly distinguished. Egan illustrates the status accorded 'the national sport' in his account of the exhibitions staged by Lord Lowther on 15 and 17 June 1814 in his house in Pall Mall to entertain the royal guests of the Prince Regent who were visiting him to celebrate the peace of Europe. Before the Emperor of Russia, the King of Prussia, the Prince Royal of Prussia, the Princes Frederick and William of Prussia, General Platoff and General Blucher and other eminent persons, Jackson, Belcher, Cribb, Richmond, Painter and Oliver engaged in set-tos which apparently both intrigued and delighted the assembly.

In contrast is his account of the mêlée which occurred on 26 May 1817, when Jack Scroggins met Ned Turner in a field near Hayes before a crowd of 30,000 (out of a British population, be it noted, of something like 9 millions). The whole episode shows the keenness of the amateurs, who cared nothing for the inconveniences of travel over crowded roads in any kind of conveyance, the chances of being trodden underfoot in the press of spectators, the possibility of having to move miles away to some fresh destination to see a fight at all, the likelihood of a drenching by rain and the danger of being set upon and robbed by the criminals the gathering attracted or, despite the vigilance of those ex-pugs employed to guard the spectators, of being bludgeoned and stripped or of being involved in a fracas with a drunken supporter. That boxing survived its official outlawing, its attendant inconveniences and its 'hole-in-the-corner' presentations shows the strength of the hold it had on Regency crowds.

Egan describes the Scroggins-Turner occasion thus:

The concourse of persons was so great, and their eager curiosity not keeping pace with the etiquette usual upon these occasions, that they pressed forward to the ropes—the ring was broken and all traces of the fight lost sight of, excepting to a few, who at the hazard of their lives were in front.

The men continued to fight for several rounds under this disadvantage—when the small ring was broken into, the posts knocked down, and the ropes trod under foot. It was now like a street fight, and the combatants had scarcely a yard of space to exhibit in. . . . Carter, Painter, Dolly Smith, Richmond, &c. exerted themselves with their horsewhips to beat out the ring, but all in vain, and nothing less than a troop of horse or a company of soldiers with charged bayonets could have attempted it with success, and both the men were taken from the ring. Mr Jackson immediately went round the ring, declaring all the bets to be null and void. At this period not less than thirty thousand persons were present, and the carriages estimated on the spot and along the road at eight thousand. The oldest pugilist does not remember anything to equal such a numerous collection of the Fancy as at the above fight. . . . During this interregnum of milling, the costermongers wished to clear their carts, but not being able to persuade their customers, who had paid 3*s.* a piece to see the sports of the day, to retire, actually took out their horses, and lifted up their vehicles, after the manner of shooting rubbish.

This mode of ousting people occasioned much laughter, and

a little extra boxing. At length, Mr Jackson appeared, when it
was understood the contest between Scroggins and Turner must
be decided at some future period; but thousands followed the
above gentlemen to Hillingdon, near Uxbridge, to see Randall
and Dick fight. The men, however, could not be got together,
and some hints were given that the magistrates would not
permit any fight to take place. In this anxiety and dilemma,
it was at length agreed upon, that Arlington Corner, near
Hounslow-Heath, should be the place, and Holt and O'Donnel to
be the pugilists who were to exhibit. Thither thousands repaired,
across the country, notwithstanding the heavy rain, and at
half-past five, in 'the pitiless pelting shower', the above boxers
entered the ring, to finish the sports of the day.

When Jack Carter and Tom Oliver battled at Gretna Green on 4
October 1816, 'During the day on which the fight took place, the
streets and houses of Carlisle and its vicinity were totally drained of
the male population—females only were left to conduct business—and
a horse, chaise, cart, or any sort of vehicle whatever, however dirty
and despicable, was not to be procured at any price.'

Not only was this sport a much-needed diversion in the midst of
social distress and post-war malaise, but it also provided some kind of
catharsis, draining away a good deal of the violence lurking in the
spectators and going some way towards insulating Englishmen from
the danger of Continental revolts. There is no doubt that the members
of the audience identified themselves with one or other of the fighters
and gave and felt each formidable blow. And when Egan translated
the contests into the violent language of the Fancy, they loved him for
it. 'Richmond planted one of his desperate right-handed hits upon
Carter's *upper-works*, that not only made a *dice-box* of his swallow—
produced the *claret—chanceried* him, but *floored* like a shot the late hero
of Aix-la-Chapelle.'

Nevertheless, Egan's presentation of the boxers as supermen and the
glamour he sees in the sport does not blind him to its dangers. He
does not share the feeling which animated many of the spectators—
the possibility of seeing some spectacular physical injury. Egan faithfully records the deaths of the ring, of which there were several, and
the sentences for manslaughter which often followed. When Ned
Turner, for instance, in 1816, after sixty-eight rounds, knocked Ben
Curtis out, the latter died. Turner was charged at the Old Bailey with
murder, but a verdict of manslaughter was brought in and he served

two months in Newgate. Similarly, Thomas Clayton, who killed Jem Betts in 1817 in a bout near Reading, spent six months in prison for the offence.

Knuckle-fighting was brutal, especially in the old days, when bouts were uninterrupted, before Broughton's rules brought in the concept of rounds. It is true that fewer blows were exchanged than became the norm in later days of glove-fighting, since not only could the bare fists produce greater surface injuries, but incessant and careless hitting and defending could break wrists and fingers and swell hands painfully. There was a good deal of feinting and evading, and wrestling holds were often resorted to in protection. At the same time, *Boxiana* is full of references to shattered fingers and wrists, fractured jaws, split lips and closed eyes, and flattened noses, while the claret from cut eyelids and 'peppered' noses gushes in torrents. In a contest with Belcher, Dogherty's face 'was materially altered, from one of his eyes being closed. His mouth and lips were so lacerated, that an opening was made nearly up to his nose, and the gash was so large, that it resembled what is termed "a *hare's* lip". Three of his teeth were completely knocked out from a tremendous blow of Belcher's. His appearance was truly piteous.'

It was no game for the timid. One of the fascinations of *Boxiana* is its witness to the gradual evolution of some form of science, as well as of order, in pugilism, as the new 16- or 18-foot ring (in place of the old 24- or 30-foot-square one) allowed for faster boxing, the rules became more systematic and contestants, instead of trying to batter each other into insensibility, learnt to evade blows and taught the spectators that this was not, as was once thought, cowardly, but skilful and sensible tactics. Bit by bit, parrying, blocking and feinting came to be accepted. Boxers learnt to judge distance and to wear down their opponent before moving in for the kill. Jem Belcher, one of Egan's heroes, introduced 'milling on the retreat', a method of retreating while counter-punching which brought some style into the game.

All of this Egan sets down in his inimitable manner, not glorying in the gore or the injuries, but accepting the gradual refinement of the sport with pleasure, praising the 'bottom' of the fighters and seeing boxing as at once a manly diversion, a guarantee against national decadence and 'effeminacy of habit' and as a safety-valve. ('It is only from open and manly contests in England, my lord, that the desperate and fatal effects of human passion are in great measure, if not totally, prevented.') There is, he declares 'lots of PHILOSOPHY even in prize-fighting', and with these sentiments a sizable number of his fellow-citizens agreed. *The Times* itself admonished the guardians of the law for trying to suppress a sport that had aroused more enthusiasm in England than anything else in the memory of living man. Also, at a meeting of the Society for Mutual Improvement, established under the patronage of Jeremy Bentham, held at 52 Great Marlborough Street in April 1820, the following question was discussed: 'Ought the Magistracy of England to be considered worthy of censure for a negligent execution of the laws against Pugilistic Contests, or of approbation for their prudence in not too violently opposing public taste and winking at what affords much amusement and keeps up the spirit and courage of the company' (which seems, incidentally, as loaded a question as was ever framed). By a majority vote, the members of the Society approved of the second alternative, and agreed with the sentiments of the Chairman who, after praising 'exhibitions of the arts of self-defence', concluded with words which Egan was not slow to reproduce at the end of Volume III of *Boxiana*:

> Nor do the heroes of the fist enjoy merely fugitive fame; like Achilles and Hector, they have attained their honour in that wonderful production of talent, the Biography of British Pugilists. *Boxiana* is a work which, in genius, is not inferior to the *Iliad* itself; for the great poet of the ancients has not given more pleasure and diversified descriptions of feats of arms and battles than has been done by the author of that work.

Egan was not able to bask in the success of the first two volumes of *Boxiana*. He does not seem to have been prudent with money; indeed, it appears that his writing brought him very little. Again and again he was to lament the meagre returns he received. Booksellers and publishers of the day were only too often sharks and exploiters of writers, whom they regarded as suppliers of the raw material from which they fashioned saleable commodities. They drove hard bargains, paid pittances and set impossible deadlines. George Borrow was later to tell of the grind and misery of hack-work and the lamentable pay he received for his laborious compilation of volumes of Newgate trials in 1825. Things were even worse in the earlier decade, and Egan suffered for it.

The truth of the matter seems to be that, up to 1821 at least, he regarded himself as primarily a bookseller and printer; from these activities he made his main income. Sport was his hobby; while he was paid, of course, for his contributions to newspapers and for the volumes of *Boxiana*, these were for him labours of love. There is evidence that publishers and editors took advantage of his enthusiasm to pay him expenses and a token sum only for his work. The litigation over later volumes of *Boxiana*, which is described later, bears this out, as does his changing of publishers. It was only when he saw booksellers and theatre managers becoming rich on the fruits of his talent while he scratched out a mere living that he began to complain of unfair treatment. At the same time, his frequent travels to distant parts of Britain and Ireland in pre-expense-account days to report horse-races and boxing contests and his unashamed love of dinners, convivial occasions and gin must have made heavy inroads on whatever money he earned at his trade.

It is no wonder, then, that he continued to turn to compilations and hack-work to augment his income. One of the earliest of such productions was *Walks Through Bath: describing Every Thing Worthy of Interest connected with the Public Buildings, The Rooms, Crescents, Theatre, Concerts, Baths, its Literature, &c. . . .* (1819), which was published at Bath, Bristol, Oxford and London. This is a guide-book of the conventional kind on the model of the several previous guides to the extremely fashionable spa, such as those by Cornelius Pope (1762), Richard Cruttwell (1770), J. Savage (1805) and C. Duffield (1813). Egan's differs from most of its predecessors in the fullness of the data supplied and in its provision of thirteen walks or excursions recommended to the visitor. He clearly knew Bath well; he may even have resided there for a time, although he appears to have left no traces in the records or literature of the city. He must often have visited the district, since Bristol, so close by, was one of the main centres of boxing, the home of several noted pugilists and a favourite location for sporting events. After London, Somerset was Egan's most favoured part of England. He was to make it the home of Jerry Hawthorn and to set a large part of *Finish to Life in London* there, and it crops up on several occasions in his other books.

So, while he quotes from earlier authorities in *Walks Through Bath* and draws frequently upon Anstey's burlesque poem, *The New Bath Guide*, Goldsmith, Sheridan, Gray, Peter Pindar and others to celebrate the glories of the city, most of his book derives from a close personal knowledge of Bath and its environs. Naturally, he devotes attention to the Race-ground and to Lansdown Fair, the scene of many pugilistic battles; naturally, too, Sterne's *Sentimental Journey* is quoted and he goes out of his way to tell us that the original of Squire Allworthy in *Tom Jones* was Ralph Allen of Prior Park. His special interest in paintings, to be a feature of later books, is forecast in his meticulous description of the collection at Corsham House. Of no special significance, save as a curiosity for the antiquarian, *Walks Through Bath*, despite its masses of detail and its factual character, is lively enough and not unamusing. Is it to find irony where none was intended that one pauses on sentences like these concerning Corsham House: 'If admittance to the Library can be procured (which is not always the case) it will be found worthy of the attention of the visitor. It is 45 feet long and 22 feet wide, and well filled with handsomely bound books; but those of a high classic description do not appear to predominate'? Egan would not have been incapable of a sly dig at the notoriously low literary taste—indeed, literacy—of many of the aristocracy of the time. But the passage in *Walks Through Bath* which most catches the attention in view of Egan's links with Dickens, which I shall be discussing more fully later, is the first appearance of the name 'Pickwick' in print, when Egan describes the tiny village on the way to Bath: 'Pickwick (97 m.). A degree of importance is attached to this small place, from its contiguity to Corsham House (1 m.) in the celebrated seat of Paul Cobb Methuen, Esq., whose superb collection of paintings are the theme and admiration of every visitor. . . .'

On 7 September of the same year (1814) Egan collaborated with Robert Cruikshank in one of his most characteristic works, which is hardly to be surpassed as an epitome of the sporting interests of the time and which is certainly one of the most remarkable *tours de force* of the talented illustrator. This was a panorama, inspired, perhaps, by novelties of a similar kind popular in France in the eighteenth century—a continuous strip of pictures 14 feet long by $2\frac{1}{2}$ inches wide wound on a spindle and enclosed in a little cylindrical, domed box, so that it could be rolled out and wound back. The whole would fit comfortably into the pocket of a Swell, who could produce it for the entertainment of his friends of the Fancy. On the box itself was a painted representation of a boxing match, presumably at the Fives Court.

The title given to the panorama was 'The Road to a Fight or Going to a Fight at Moulsey-Hurst or A Picture of the Fancy'. Egan, who was particularly proud of his part in the work, usually called it by the latter name. It was advertised as

> showing the Sporting World in all its variety of style and costume along the Road from Hyde Park Corner to Moulsey Hurst . . . containing numerous Original Characters, many of them portraits, in which all the Frolic, Fun, Lark, Gig, Life, Gammon, and Trying-It-On, are depicted, incident to the pursuit of a Prize Mill; dedicated, by permission, to Mr Jackson and the Noblemen and Gentlemen comprising the Pugilistic Club.

The British Museum Print Room copy of 'A Picture of the Fancy' is in very good condition and, fortunately, is one of the hand-coloured specimens (14*s*. plain; £1 coloured). Robert Cruikshank was never to be more inventive, spirited and amusing, but there is no doubt that the whole thing was Egan's idea. In his *Book of Sports* of 1832 he writes: 'Bob Cruikshank accompanied myself down the Road to Moulsey Hurst to accomplish the above picture.'

The strip begins in the Castle Tavern, Holborn, showing the Daffy Club, a special group of the sporting fraternity, enjoying themselves on the evening before setting out, then moves into an elaborate Panorama of a motley collection of amateurs on their way to Moulsey Hurst via Hyde Park Corner in every conceivable kind of conveyance, 'the *Swells*, *Nib Sprigs* and *Tidy ones*, in their Tandems, Gigs, and Trotters; the *Lads* in their Rattlers, Heavy Drags, and Tumblers, including the Bermondsey-boys and Tothilfields Costermongers, in all their gradations, down to the *Stampers*', to quote Egan's elaborate Key which accompanied the strip. There are donkeys, traps, bicycles, horses, overloaded carts, fights and misfortunes shown on the road. The procession extends through Bushy Park and past a favourite stopping-place, Lawrence's, the Red Lion, at Hampton, to the Thames, where the Fancy are boating or barging across with their horses and carriages, and up to the scene of the fight itself at Moulsey Hurst between Jack Randall and West Country Dick.

The bird's-eye view of the bout is one of the most valuable records of contemporary boxing practice in existence, since most surviving pictures of boxing show the contestants only or are indoor scenes. The betting stand is depicted in the background, the ring itself is on level grass, each fighter has two seconds, and umpires are close to the ring. There is an inner ring of gentlemen a short way away from the boxers, presumably officials of the Pugilistic Club and journalists, and some distance further back the large outer circle of spectators. Boxing was plainly not the only attraction on such occasions. A bull is on exhibition, men are drinking, a dog is setting on a tethered bull and another bull is tossing both a man and a dog. Dustmen and costermongers are egging on the dogs. Finally, the panorama ends at Tattersall's, the settling-up place, where a group of gentlemen are gathered in front of the drinking fountain to receive or pay their bets. It is such a remarkable revelation of the sporting life of the day that Egan could fairly claim, in his advertisement, that 'not a *pink* has been overlooked, not an *out-and-outer* forgotten', and the *Sporting Magazine* assert, in December 1819, that 'Nothing equal to this Picture has appeared since the inimitable Hogarth's "March to Finchley"'.

Unhappily, Egan's Key to the panorama has disappeared, but a lengthy extract from it, reprinted by him more than once in his various publications, will serve to show its style, to represent his copious use of slang and to introduce the Daffy Club:

Notwithstanding the writer of this article most anxiously wishes his KEY should *fit* well, and that every person who is in possession of it should be able, with the utmost ease, to *unlock* the door that affords a peep into the movements of the Sporting World; yet, rather than attempt to *gammon* any of his readers— *etymology* being out of the question—the only *definition* he can give to the term 'DAFFY' is, that the phrase was coined at the *Mint* of the *Fancy*, and has since passed *current*, without ever being overhauled as *queer*. The Colossus of literature, after all his *nous* and acute researches to explain the *synonyms* of the English Language, does not appear to have been *down* to the interpretation of 'DAFFY'; nor indeed does *Bayley* or *Sheridan* seem at all fly to it; and even *slang Grose* has no *touch* of its extensive signification. The *squeamish* fair one who takes it on the *sly* merely to cure the *vapours*, politely names it to her friend as '*white wine*'. The *swell chaffs* it as '*blue ruin*' to elevate his notions. The *laundress* loves dearly a drain of '*ould Tom*' from its strength to *comfort* her inside. The *drag fiddler* can *toss off* a quartern of '*max*' without making a wry mug. The *costermonger* illumines his ideas with a '*flash of lightning*'. The *hoarse cyprian* owes her existence to copious draughts of '*jacky*'. The *link-boy* and *mudlarks*, in clubbing their browns, are for some '*stark naked*'. And the *out-and-outers*, from the addition of *bitters*, in order to sharpen a dissipated and damaged *victualling office*, cannot take anything but '*fuller's earth*'. Much, it would seem, therefore, depends upon a name; and, as a soft sound is at all times pleasing to the listener—to have denominated this Sporting Society the 'GIN CLUB' would not only have proved barbarous to the ear, but the vulgarity of the *chaunt* might have deprived it of many of its *elegant* friends. It is a subject, however, which must be admitted has a good deal of *taste* belonging to it—and as a sporting man would be *nothing* if he was not *flash*, the DAFFY CLUB met under the above title.[6]

The Daffy Club, which features prominently in all sporting chronicles of the time, typifies the convivial gatherings of Regency sportsmen. The ancestor of both the football supporters' drinking clubs and the Savage

Clubs and Orphans Clubs of today, such bodies of like-minded amateurs met, more or less regularly, in one or other of the London taverns.
It was common for a retired pugilist to become a pub-keeper; it was
profitable for the owner to have a man behind the barrel who could
attract his own following. Tom Cribb's Pub, once the Union Arms,
still stands in Panton Street, off the Haymarket, and makes some small
attempt to record the glories of bare-knuckle days in its prints and
posters. Jack Randall kept the Hole in the Wall, Chancery Lane, Tom
Spring the Catherine Wheel in Little St James's Street, Frank Redman
the Swiss Cottage, St John's Wood, Jem Burn the Queen's Head,
Windmill Street, and Ned Painter the Anchor, Lobster Lane, Norwich,
to mention only a few. There were various branches of the Daffy Club,
such as that at the Horse and Trumpeter, Aldgate (Peter Pidgeon) and
that at the Guildhall Tavern, Bristol (Sam Patch), but the parent body
and the most celebrated gathering met at the Castle Tavern, Holborn,
kept originally by Bob Gregson, but passing to Tom Belcher, whose
genial presence made the Castle a warm, friendly spot for sportsmen.

The President of the Daffy Club was the 'eccentric' James ('Jemmy')
Soares (which means he was a 'character'), a distinguished follower of
the science, referee, time-keeper and stake-holder. 'A great lover of
harmony,' Egan describes him, 'yet no person fonder of making
mischief! In principle, independent to the echo. The Swell or the
Coster-Monger asking his opinion receives it without any gammon.
He is no *flatterer*—and his only *aim* appears to be to decide without
bias, and to do justice to all parties.' Egan was one of the founders,
leading lights and most popular members of the Daffy Club. We can
only guess at the amount of gin consumed by these worthies, at least
as much as that put away by ageing American female entertainers
today; it was an alcoholic age, and nowhere did the spirits flow more
freely than amongst the members of the Fancy.

The fullest contemporary description of the Daffy Club is that given
in *The English Spy* (1825–6) by 'Bernard Blackmantle' (Charles Molloy
Westmacott), a book whose form and style owe much to Egan's own
influence. The account is especially interesting as being one of the very
few contemporary descriptions of Pierce Egan in a typical setting and as
showing his position as a dominant element in the Club:

> The Daffy Club presents to the eye of a calm observer a fund of
> entertainment; to the merry mad-wag who is fond of *life*, blowing
> his *steamer*, and drinking *blue ruin*, until all is *blue* before him,
> a source of infinite amusement; the convivial finds his antidote

to the *rubs* and *jeers* of this world in a *rum chaunt*; while the
out and *outer* may here open his *mag-azine* of *tooth-powder*,
cause a *grand explosion*, and never fear to meet a *broadside* in
return. The *knowing cove* finds his account in looking out for the
green ones, and the *greens* find their head sometimes a *little
heavier* and their *pockets lighter*, by an accidental *rencontre* with
the *fancy*. To see the place in perfection, a stranger should choose
the night previous to some important *mill*, when our host of the
Castle plays *second*, and all the *lads* are mustered to *stump up*
their *blunt*, or to catch the important whisper where the *scene* of
action is to be (for there is always due caution used in the disclosure),
to take a *peep* at the pugilists present, and *trot off* as well *satisfied*
as if he had partaken of a splendid banquet with the Great Mogul.

The long room is neatly fitted up, and lighted with *gas*; and
the numerous sporting subjects, elegantly framed and glazed,
have rather an imposing effect upon the entrance of the visitor,
and among which may be recognized animated likenesses of the
later renowned Jem Belcher, and his daring competitor (that
inordinate *glutton*) Burke. . . . The long table, or the *ring*, as it
is facetiously termed, is where the *old standers* generally *perch*
themselves to receive the visits of the *swells*, and give each other
the *office* relative to passing events: and what set of men are
better able to speak of society in all its various ramifications,
from the cabinet-counsellor to the *cosey costermonger*? Jemmy
Soares, the president, must be considered a *downy one*; having
served five apprenticeships to the office of sheriff's representative,
and is as good a fellow in his way as ever *tapped a shy one* on the
shoulder-joint or let fly a *ca sa* at your goods and chattels. Lucky
Bob is a fellow of another stamp, 'a *nation good vice*' as ever was
attached to the *house of Brunswick*. Then comes our host, a civil,
well-behaved man, without any of the exterior appearance of the
ruffian, or perhaps I should say of *his profession*, and with all the
good-natured qualifications for a peaceable citizen, and an
obliging, merry landlord; next to him you will perceive the
immortal typo, the all-accomplished Pierce Egan; an eccentric
in his way, both in manner and person, but not deficient in that
peculiar species of wit which fits him for the high office of
historian of the *ring*. The *ironical* praise of Blackwood he has the
good sense to turn to a right account, laughs at the satire, and
pretends to believe it is all meant in *right-down earnest*
approbation of his extraordinary merits. For a long while after

his *great instructor's* neglect of his friends, Pierce kept undisturbed possession of the throne; but recently competitors have shown themselves in the field *well found* in all particulars, and carrying such witty and weighty ammunition wherewithal, that they more than threaten 'to push the hero from his stool'. Tom Spring, who is fond of *cocking* as well as fighting, is seen with his bag in the right-hand corner, *chaffing* with the Duck-lane doss man; while Lawyer L——e, a true sportsman, whether for the turf or chase, is betting the *odds* with brother Adey, *Greek* against *Greek*. Behind them are seen the heroes Scroggins and Turner. . . . Here, my dear Bernard, you have before you a true portrait of the celebrated Daffy Club.[7]

It was in such environments that Egan practised that talent which was so greatly to aid his personal popularity, his ability to write topical songs and poems, which he sang or recited to vociferous applause at gatherings of the Fancy. He had no illusions about the literary merit of his effusions. 'Pierce Egan's no poet,' he once wryly remarked.[8] His 'poems' are unashamed doggerel or 'crambo', as he himself called them, with the roughest of rhythms and, frequently, the oddest of rhymes, yet, like the calypsos they resemble in intent and at times in form, having both vitality and a certain naïve charm. Several of his songs were taken up by other sporting writers of the time and quoted without acknowledgment right up to late Victorian days. Hardly a major pugilistic contest went uncelebrated in metre by Egan; many of such pieces he printed in appendices to the various volumes of *Boxiana*, together with similar effusions by Charles Sloman, William Leman Rede, W. Lawrence and other laureates of the sporting fraternity. These 'Chaunts for the Fancy' constitute an invaluable record of the attitudes and sentiments of contemporary sportsmen and a more authentic, if less polished, reflection of their tastes and preferences than the sophisticated prose and poetry dealing with sport produced by Byron, Thomas Moore, J. H. Reynolds and Hazlitt, who were, compared with Egan, mere dilettantes.

Egan wrote the official song of the Daffy Club:

> Bring the Daffy,
> Let's be happy,
> Life, you know, is but a span:
> No melancholy,
> All be jolly,
> Smoke your pipes and fill the can!

> Sure as a button,
> Though a prime glutton,
> By Old Time you will be scor'd:
> Then kiss your lass,
> Enjoy your glass,
> Daffies all, before you're floor'd.

Another of his most gleefully received efforts was 'The Lads of the Fancy', which began:

> You lads of the Fancy, who wish to impart
> The tokens of friendship and soundness of heart,
> To Belcher's repair, at the Castle so strong,
> Where he'll serve you all well, and you'll hear a good song.
> The company's cheerful, and Sporting's the go—
> Though milling's the theme, you'll not meet with a foe;
> But each in good humour, enjoying his pipe,
> With tales of the Fancy—and knowledge of life!
> > Then let us be merry,
> > While drinking our sherry.
> For friendship and harmony can't last too long—
> > Be still our endeavour
> > That nothing shall sever
> The Lads of the Fancy at the Castle so strong!

The names of other Egan compositions give a fair idea of their sub-ject-matter: 'Milling Near Carlisle', 'The Prize Ring in 1819', 'The Pugilistic Feats of Jack Scroggins', 'Cribb and the Black', 'Prime British Boxers'. From such songs at Daffy Club and other gatherings as much as from the broadsides of the day arose in time the music-hall songs and the popular entertainments of Victorian and Edwardian times.

With his social life, his active participation in pugilism, his book-selling and publishing business and his miscellaneous sporting journal-ism, Pierce Egan was a busy man between 1818 and 1820. He was still the leading sports reporter for the *Weekly Dispatch*, but other journals were only too glad to print his by now completely idiosyncratic boxing accounts. The *New Times*, for instance, regularly featured Egan's milling descriptions, including vivid reports of the Oliver–Shelton bout on 14 January 1820 and of the great fight between the Gas Light Man and Neat on 11 December 1821. All the same, in the former year he found time to complete two more books for his avid public.

47

The first of these, which appeared in early 1820, was *Sporting Anecdotes, Original and Selected, Including Numerous Characteristic Portraits of Persons in Every Walk of Life who have acquired Notoriety from their achievement on The Turf, at the Table and in the Diversion of the Field, with sketches of various Animals of the Chase, to which is added an account of noted Pedestrians, Trotting-Matches, Cricketers, &c., the whole forming a complete Delineation of the Sporting World.* Much of this is Egan's own work; the rest, showing his copious reading in sporting literature, consists of lively extracts from memoirs, hand-books, newspapers and so on. Boxing, surprisingly enough, plays a comparatively minor part, while much attention is given to horse-racing, wrestling, archery, pedestrianism, equestrian performances, shooting, fox-hunting, cricket and angling. There are excellent brief memoirs of Captain Barclay, Major Topham, Colonel Thornton, Tom Cribb, John Cavanagh, the famous fives player, and Captain Francis Grose, the antiquary. There are statistics, natural history notes on fish and game and various accounts of big-game hunting in other lands, much on the care and training of dogs and a generous number of sporting songs and poems. The range of the material indicates the catholic tastes of Regency amateurs and the strength of the hold sport of all kinds had upon them. Egan's wit, or what passed for it, his colloquial energy and his journalistic eye for a good story make *Sporting Anecdotes* still most entertaining reading and an admirable dipping book. It is a pleasure to meet the Rutlandshire clergyman who was so passionately fond of the hunt that 'he has been known several times, when at prayers, to leave the congregation and join the hounds, when they chanced to pass in full cry; and once when he was marrying a couple, left them in the middle of the service, and told them he would finish it the next morning'; to learn of the cricket-match between a Hampshire eleven and a Surrey eleven, arranged by two noblemen for 500 guineas a side, both teams consisting of women, with the best runner and bowler one Ann Baxter, sixty years of age; to read of the lord of a manor who 'having brought an action for shooting upon his land, imagined himself to be addressed from the desk, one Sunday, in these words—"O Lord, forgive us our trespasses", and, rising in fury, swore *he would see him damn'd first!*'; to note the popularity of pedestrianism and the feats like that of Foster Powell of Yorkshire, who walked 100 miles in twenty-two hours; to encounter Major Baggs, the inveterate gambler, who once won £17,000 at hazard by throwing on fourteen successive mains and who, when he was so ill that he could not get out of his chair, would be brought to the hazard-table where the rattling of the dice revived him—as well as many more substantial pieces of information about the sporting life of the day.

Sporting Anecdotes was a distinct success. *Baldwin's London Magazine* said of it: 'It is a happy composition, full of whim and particular phrases, with a slip of morality in it, like a bit of lemon-peel in one's punch, and delightfully flavoured with the choicest lime-juice of slang.' A second, enlarged edition was published in 1825, including some characteristic plates by Robert Cruikshank, one of which, 'Monday after the Great St Leger', recalls the Tattersall's scene in 'A Picture of the Fancy' and another, a fold-out plate, 'A Visit to the Fives Court,' showing Spring and Neat in action and a group of spectators, mostly drawn from life, depicts several members of the Fancy, as well as the Cruikshank brothers and Egan himself.

Egan's other publication of 1820 is one of his most hasty pieces of hack-work, rushed out as soon as possible after the death of King George III in January. Its short title is *A Concise Biographical Memoir of His Late Majesty, King George III*, but only some fifty pages are devoted to a scanty life of the monarch, while over seventy are occupied with a lengthy description of his body lying in State at Windsor and the procession and solemnities at his funeral; anecdotes of the king and poems of mourning take up another 100 pages, including a section on 'His Late Majesty as Sportsman' from Pierce Egan's *Sporting Anecdotes,* 'recently published'. It is all rather like the script for a modern television coverage of such an event, fill-ins, background and all. But it hardly deserves hard covers, being a hastily-flung-together piece of journalism. Egan was clearly not proud of it. Despite the fact that his name at that time was enough to sell almost anything, he issued the *Memoir* under the name of 'E. Pierce, Esq.', letting whoever cared make the connection.

If he did not acknowledge such a work openly—and there may well be several similar compilations which will never be identified as his— he was at great pains to stake his claim to his next book, which brought him even more kudos that he had received for *Boxiana* and carried his reputation, for good or ill, far beyond the circles of the Fancy. This was *Life in London.*

✣ IV ✣

Enter Tom and Jerry

In September 1820 appeared the first number of a monthly publication, with text by Pierce Egan and hand-coloured illustrations by George and Robert Cruikshank, which was to take the town by storm. This was *Life in London or The Day and Night Scenes of Jerry Hawthorn, Esq., and his elegant friend Corinthian Tom, accompanied by Bob Logic, the Oxonian, in their Rambles and Sprees through the Metropolis*. It was dedicated to His Most Gracious Majesty King George the Fourth, whom Egan addresses familiarly in his preface, since a short time previously he had been presented to the sport-loving monarch at Court as the celebrated author of *Boxiana*. Both in its monthly numbers, several times reissued, and in the numerous editions of the bound book which followed its first appearance as a volume in July 1821, *Life in London* outdid *Boxiana* in popularity and was to make Egan as well-known an author on the vulgar level as Scott was on the polite one.

The genre to which *Life in London* belongs has a long history, going back, in modern times at least, to Elizabethan days, when writers like Greene in his *Coney-Catching Tracts* and Dekker in his *Gull's Horn-Book* exposed the tricks of contemporary rogues and shysters and warned 'Johnny Raws' from the country against the sophisticated sharks of the town. The influential *The English Rogue* (1665), begun by Richard Head and continued by Francis Kirkman, delved further into the London underworld, pretending an authenticity that rarely extended further than some graphic surface detail. Defoe and less reputable writers continued the tradition of 'true' life-stories of criminals and pictures of the seamy side of metropolitan life. But it was Ned Ward who, in his *London Spy* (1698–1700), produced the real ancestor of *Life in London.*

Instead of the sensational, racy tales which Head and Kirkman had used as their framework, Ward hit upon the device of having a Londoner take a visitor to the city around the various quarters, respectable and otherwise, dispensing with the crude narratives of earlier books and focusing interest on the actual places, people and customs of the city. Tom Brown, doubtless taking hints from Ward, issued his *Amusements, Serious and Comical* in 1700, which also exploits the facts of London life as shown on a tour by an American Indian. The eighteenth century saw a spate of similar books, cheap and often cheaply produced, while after *Life in London* the genre continued with renewed vigour.

Between *The London Spy* and *Life in London* there were such books as *A Trip Through London* (1728), *A Ramble through London* (1738), *Tricks of the Town Laid Open; or a Companion for a Country Gentleman* (1747); *The Country Spy or a Ramble Through London* (1750); *The Devil upon Crutches in England or Night Scenes in London* (1755); *The Midnight Spy or . . . London from 10 in the Evening until 5 in the Morning, exhibiting a Great Variety of Scenes in High Life and Low Life* (1766), a title which it is interesting to compare with that of *Life in London, The Countryman's Guide to London or Villainy Detected* (1780), *The Complete Modern London Spy* (1781), *London Unmasked or The New Town Spy* (1784?), and many others. Smeeton, as we have already seen, issued *The Stranger's Guide or the Frauds of London Detected* in 1808, and in 1816 Jonathan Badcock had published *Letters from London: Observations of a Russian during a Residence in London of 10 Months*, allegedly translated from the original manuscript of one Olaff Napea. The fact that this latter work attracted little attention may have been one of the reasons for Badcock's virulent attacks on Egan after *Life in London* was issued.

Most of these books wanted to have it both ways, adopting, like modern sensational newspapers, a tone of high-minded indignation at the vices of London while at the same time titillating their readers with details of roguery, prostitution, drunkenness and gambling. They borrowed shamelessly from each other. Their general theme was much the same—the moral perils and the physical dangers of the metropolis, the exotic character of its night life, the different types of crooks and prostitutes and their tricks, the curious sights, the strange characters and the atmosphere of the underworld. Sometimes the material was woefully out of date; sometimes it was taken in part from

French sources; more often than not it pretended to be translated from the diary of a visitor from a distant land.

Egan clearly knew this kind of book well; he may even have helped prepare more than one for the press. There was, indeed, little original in the basic concept of *Life in London*. Its superiority lay in its style and handling.

Nor was the number form in which it was first issued at all new, although it was the signal success of Egan's work which was to give serial publication its greatest impetus and help establish it as a staple way of Victorian publishing and the regular method employed by Dickens. The high price of books in Regency times, when powerful booksellers were exploiting for all they were worth the new voracious reading public and novels were expensively padded out by overwriting and printers' dodges, meant that there was a ready-made public for any cheaper way of presenting fiction. Number publication owed much to the first Dr Syntax book, *The Tour of Dr Syntax in Search of the Picturesque* (1812), the versified burlesque written by William Combe in prison, illustrated with hand-coloured engravings by Rowlandson and published by the enterprising Rudolph Ackerman, who did so much to develop the art of English engraving. In the 'Invocation' to *Life in London*, Egan pays tribute to both author and publisher of the Syntax chronicles:

> Ackerman, if ever thou didst *value* the Tour of Dr Syntax, I
> call upon thee now to lend thy friendly assistance and protection
> to Corinthian Tom and his rustic protégé poor Jerry. Present a
> copy of their Sprees and Rambles to the learned Doctor, and his
> 'Picturesque' brain will be all on fire for another tour, from the
> new scenes it will develop to his unbounded thirst for enterprise
> and knowledge.

Two of the three later 'Tours' of the Quixotish Syntax coincided with the publication of *Life in London*. Of course, during 1812 and 1813 the separate numbers of *Boxiana* had appeared, although with un-coloured illustrations. In any case, *Life in London* was one of the earliest of the new style, the first work of prose fiction to be so published and certainly the most widely read and imitated.

When we turn to consider the idea of this book and the general direction it took we come at once up against the notorious proclivity of George Cruikshank in later life to lay claim to being the inspiration for a considerable number of works of literature and a guiding force behind them—Dickens's *Oliver Twist*, for one—a claim which few take seriously today in respect to major writers, but which still in some quarters appears to be believed in respect to Egan.

The biographers of the Cruikshanks are at odds on the matter. Blanchard Jerrold,[1] for instance, quotes Percy Cruikshank, the son of Robert, as saying, on his father's evidence: 'The wonderfully successful Tom and Jerry, or *Life in London*, although ostensibly Pierce Egan's idea, was universally given to George Cruikshank, whereas the original notion and the very designs were mostly Robert's.' He conceived the notion, Percy said, and planned the designs, while showing a brother-in-law, just returned from China, some of the 'life' which was going on in London at the time. George, still according to Percy, said to him before his death: 'When your father proposed Tom and Jerry to me, I suggested that it should be carried out in a series of oil paintings, after the manner of Hogarth, but he objected, considering etchings were safer, and more rapidly converted into easy money.' On the other hand, as Blanchard Jerrold points out, 'in those days, the Cruikshanks were not in a position to command Pierce Egan.' But George continued to spread the story that he was the inspirer and guiding hand, taking in such contemporaries as 'Cuthbert Bede', for instance. Even a recent authority, Dr Dorothy George, in her *Hogarth to Cruikshank*,[2] says: 'The text was written for the plates.'

William Bates, in his life of George Cruikshank (1878),[3] has another tale to tell:

> The story is, as he has often related it to me and others, that George who was even then a moralist, either had misconceived the object of the author, or saw that his designs were used for a purpose he had not contemplated; and finding that the book ... was a guide to, rather than a dissuasive from the vicious haunts and amusements of the metropolis, retired from the firm, in which, from relative age, he figured as junior partner.

George, it seems, told whatever story suited him at the time, since two rejected sketches for the *Life in London* frontispiece in the British Museum Print Room are headed in George Cruikshank's hand: 'Frontispiece to "Life in London", the ideas and characters of which work originated from me, George Cruikshank' and 'Frontispiece for Life in London which originated from me, George Cruikshank'. The matter is further complicated by the fact that, in tiny lettering at the foot of the frontispiece to *Finish to Life in London*, Robert Cruikshank, this time, has added to the plate: 'Fair play: Robt. Cruikshank Invt. et Fecit. Original Suggester and Artist of the 2 Vols. Adieu'!

We may fairly quickly dispose of the Cruikshanks' attempts to appropriate *Life in London*. They made no pretence to be the originators of the work when it was first published, the whole tone and atmosphere of the work are characteristically Egan's, and it is a logical development from *Boxiana* and his other sporting publications, much of the text is quite independent of the plates, and 'Christopher North', always on the look-out for a phoney and an admirer of the Cruikshanks' work, makes no bones about accepting the book as Egan's brain-child. In *Blackwood's* for July 1823 he wrote of George:

> But what a start did he make when his genius had received a
> truer and a diviner impulse from the splendid imagination of an
> Egan! How completely—how *toto coelo* did he outcruikshank
> himself when he was called upon to embody the conceptions of
> that remarkable man in the designs for Tom and Jerry? The
> world felt it—and he himself felt it.

Moreover, Egan himself wrote in *Life in London's* 'Invocation':

> In all the varied portraiture of the interesting scenes of Life, let
> me invoke thy superior talents, Bob and George Cruikshank
> (thou *Gillray* of the day and of *Don Saltero* greatness) to my
> anxious aid. Indeed, I have need of all thy illustrative touches;
> and may we be hand-in-glove together in depicting the richness of
> nature, which so wantonly, at times, plays off her freaks upon the
> half-famished bone-rakers and cinder-sifters round the dust-hill,
> that we may be found, *en passant*, so identified with the scene
> in question as almost to form a part of the group. . . . But,
> before I dismiss thee to thy studies, bear it in remembrance,
> 'nothing to extenuate nor set down aught in malice'.

This should leave nobody who reads the work in any doubt as to who was the inspirer, the controller of the project and the source of the plan and the development of the book.

Moreover, in Chapter XII of the published volume, Egan offers a short digression addressed to subscribers to the numbers, explaining that he had got drunk recently with Bob Logic and in consequence had lost his 'Reader' or pocket-book containing his notes and part of the text for No. 5 of January 1821, and thus could offer only one sheet of letterpress this time: 'I therefore trust, under all the circumstances of the case, a liberal allowance will be made, when it is recollected that such Rambles and Sprees first gave the Author an idea of detailing some of the "*rich scenes*" which are only to be found in LIFE IN LONDON.'

The truth of the matter, I have no doubt, is that Robert, who did the greater number of the thirty-six plates, and had collaborated with Egan before, as we have seen, and to a lesser extent George, made suggestions in the course of the numbers as to details and incidents, some of which Egan adopted, some of which he rejected. In their frequent excursions through the metropolis together, the trio must have had experiences which went into the *Life in London* stock-pot. It was widely believed at the time that Tom, Jerry and Logic were modelled upon George, Robert and Pierce Egan. Moncrieff, one of the dramatizers of the book, used to assert this. Physically, perhaps, the trio served as models for the characters in the plates, but there was little of a country sportsman about Robert and even less of a true Corinthian about George. Bob Logic is another matter. In this fun-loving character, fond of gin and of convivial company, always ready for a ramble or a spree, the constant promoter of another lark, the initiator of many a practical joke, a dab hand at a song or the piano, and a perpetual fount of terrible puns, Egan seems to have put a great deal of himself. And he was later to impersonate Logic on several occasions in the various plays based on the book. It would be just like Egan to make Bob Logic an Oxonian; always conscious of his own scanty education, he valued very much the enormous success of *Boxiana* with the Fellows and students of Oxford and Cambridge, and attended many a rowdy, liquorish evening at both universities.

If we view *Life in London* as showing a special rapport and close collaboration between author and artists, but with Egan as the guiding spirit and shaper of the work, we shall have a fairly clear idea of its genesis. In more than one way posterity has been less than just to Egan, tending to minimize his achievements and to take it for granted that the chief interest of *Life in London* resides in the plates. Thackeray, perhaps, has been unwittingly to blame here. In one of his *Roundabout Papers*, 'De Juventate', he tells of reading *Life in London* in his childhood and of going as an adult to the British Museum to look at it again. He found it

> not so brilliant as I had supposed it to be. The pictures are
> just as fine as ever. . . . But the style of the writing, I own, was
> not pleasing to me; I even thought it a little vulgar—well! well!
> other writers have been considered vulgar—and as a
> description of the sports and amusements of London in the
> ancient times, more curious than amusing. But the pictures—oh!
> the pictures are noble still!

It is true that, after quoting passages from Egan's text, he adds: 'How nobly those inverted commas, those italics, those capitals, bring out the writer's wit and relieve the eye. They are as good as jokes, although you mayn't quite perceive the point.' But the suspicion he leaves is that the text is a mere inferior appendage to the plates.

The pictures are unquestionably fine, but they are not one whit less original or spirited than Egan's prose. This is not to claim *Life in London* as a literary *tour de force*. It has wit, interesting detail, charm, personality and drive, but it also has its *longueurs*, most notably in Egan's disquisitions in the manner of Sterne, its frequent catalogues, and the deplorable Gothic tale with which he pads out the final number. At times, too, a disordered sentence, a solecism or a syntactical chaos betrays the speed at which the material was written. Nevertheless, the book is extraordinarily fresh and original, standing head and shoulders above its chapbook predecessors, and affording an invaluable insight into Regency London life, high and low, and into the values and attitudes of the time.

In the lengthy opening 'Invocation' Egan calls to his aid such 'shades of departed talent' and living spirits as his beloved Sterne, Fielding, Smollett, Byron and Moore, the great reviews, especially *Blackwood's*, and reviewers, such as 'Old Christopher North', whom he challenges to the scratch, publishers such as Colburn, Humphreys and Murray, artists such as Flaxman, Fuseli and Turner, and Townshend, the 'renowned hero of the police'. He ends: 'if I cannot command success, at least it shall not be averred that I did not exert myself to deserve it'.

Then he passes to a 'camera obscura' view of the Metropolis, a general conspectus of the city as seen through the eyes of a Regency man of fashion:

LONDON is the looking-glass for TALENT—it is the faithful emporium of the enterprising, the bold, the timid, and the bashful individual, and where all can view themselves at full length. . . . The EXTREMES, in every point of view, are daily to be met with in the Metropolis; from the most rigid, persevering, never-tiring industry, down to laziness. . . . The most bare-faced villains, swindlers, and thieves, walk about the streets in the day-time, committing their various depredations, with as much confidence as men of unblemished reputation and honesty. . . . Yet . . . there are some of the worthiest, most tender-hearted, liberal minds, and charitable dispositions, which ornament London, and render it the delight and happiness of society.

This introduces what is to be one of Egan's guiding principles and delights, the contrasts and paradoxes of life in London, the 'diversity', the extraordinary mingling of good and bad, the contact between different social levels at sports and amusements. 'The contrasts', he says, 'are so fine and delightful—so marked with light and shade—and, upon the whole, offer such an extensive volume of intelligence, that the peruser must be ignorant indeed if something of importance does not fasten upon his mind.'

At length he comes to Corinthian Tom, the archetype of the well-to-do idler of his time. He was not a Dandy, although he dressed well and fashionably; neither was he a Grandison, a Lovelace nor a Joseph Andrews. Left a wealthy orphan at the age of twenty-five, he was 'not vicious from principle, although it might be urged his morals would not bear the strictest investigation of propriety'; he was 'polite, generous and good-humoured'; he was popular with women and fond of their company; he was a first-class boxer, fencer, hunter, driver; he gambled on races, dog-fights, boxing matches, but eschewed the gambling-houses. 'Pleasure and novelty were his constant pursuits by day or by night. . . . In short, Tom was *born* to be a happy fellow, if the enjoyment of the "good things" of this world could have made him so.'

The chief companion of Corinthian Tom in his sprees is Mr Robert Logic of No. 9, Albany, who, it is said, had 'rather been sent to Oxford to have the *character* of the thing, than to *astonish* the world at any after period with any great works of intellectual profundity'. Logic was fast compensating for his *dry* study of the Classics by an endless round of fun and games in London:

> In the *Kingdom of Sans Souci* he proved himself a *brilliant* of the first water; and from the figure he had cut in the *Province of Bacchus* and the *Dynasty of Venus*, Logic had been pronounced a hero. . . . His knowledge of *Navigation* was so good, that he had been enabled to steer clear of the shoals and rocks of *Dun Territory* and the *River Tick*. . . . Logic had been '*on the town*' for several years; and no person had been more industrious towards *destroying* a fine constitution, or endeavouring to reduce a long purse, than he had.

Egan makes play with the contrast between the two. This 'was so great, and the attractions so powerful, that Tom might be said to be placed between two magnets'—that is, the manly, moderate advice of his father and the seductions of the ebullient Logic. When his father dies, Tom accepts Logic's philosophy and becomes known to the Beau

Monde for his elegant manner and fashionable clothes and for his frequenting of Newmarket, Epsom, Tattersall's, the Fives Court, Moulsey Hurst and the Dog Pit, as well as for being a favourite of the ladies, none of whom he values as much as the lovely, accomplished Catherine, who in consequence is known as 'Corinthian Kate'. But Tom's pursuit of pleasure takes toll of his health and he is forced to visit Dr Pleas'em, who is described, with a characteristic dash of Egan irony, thus:

> His penetration and knowledge of characters was so extensive, that he could distinguish with the utmost facility, from a touch of the pulse, between a vulgar plebeian habit of body, and the imaginary, refined, elegant creature of the upper circles of society. . . . He well knew that, in the upper circles of society, *illness* is perfectly necessary towards health; and that it would be quite *barbarous* to deprive any fashionable lady of the enjoyments resulting from an *elegant* indisposition.

Pleas'em recommends a few days' rustication; fortunately having received an invitation from his uncle, Jeremiah Hawthorn of Hawthorn Hall in Somerset, Tom says goodbye to Corinthian Kate and sets off for the country. There he and we meet the third member of the trio, Tom's cousin, Jerry Hawthorn, as accomplished at sports as Tom, a dab hand at hunting, shooting, riding, cudgelling and the art of self-defence. Without the metropolitan polish of his cousin, Jerry, although somewhat shy, 'was not *sheepish*'. He was 'no *Johnny Raw* either—he was not a staring, gawky, grinning country bumpkin, who laughs at he cannot tell what; and who is *astonished* at everything he sees!' 'In short,' writes Egan, 'he was the very *double*, or *counterpart* of Corinthian Tom.'

The two men get on famously together, and it is inevitable that Tom should invite Jerry to return to London with him to repay his hospitality by introducing him to the true life of the city. After a jolly evening at Hawthorn Hall during which the company say farewell to Tom in a scene of hearty jollification which looks forward to similar scenes in the novels of Surtees, the cousins leave for London and the comparatively brief Part One ends with a lengthy doggerel song, beginning

> London Town's a dashing place
> For ev'ry thing that's going,
> There's *fun* and *gig* in ev'ry face,
> So natty and so *knowing*

and set to music by A. Voight, the music being printed on a fold-out sheet in the book.

Despite occasional flashes and the entertaining 'Invocation', the first part of *Life in London* is the least interesting and most tedious portion of the book; it is repetitive and discursive and serves little more purpose than to introduce the main characters and set the scene, which any of Egan's admired eighteenth-century novelists would have done in a third of the space. I have the impression that much of it was written hastily after the numbers had appeared, to bulk out the volume. This is impossible to prove in the absence of any copies of the original parts. That some sections of Part One did appear in the numbers is shown by a review of the first three numbers in the *European Magazine* for November 1820, which quotes extracts, all of which come from Part One. On the other hand, the plates, the earliest of which is, nevertheless, dated 21 August 1820, do not begin until Chapter VIII, about a third of the way through the book. Since the nature of the work demands text and plates in close association, and since Egan, as already mentioned, invokes the aid of the Cruikshanks at the very beginning, it is difficult to believe that there could have been so great a quantity of bread to so little sack in the first numbers. The only conclusion I can come to is that the number text was padded out for the bound volume; certainly, it shows every sign of inflation.

At the same time, these first chapters are rich in one of Egan's favourite devices, the expanded footnote, sometimes flooding over several pages, almost in the manner of the *Variorum Shakespeare*, leaving a tiny shoal of text isolated at the top of the page. These notes are full of diverting details of contemporary social life, scandalous anecdotes, glosses on slang, character-sketches and home-spun eighteenth-century philosophizing and jokes. There is a long section on Junius, a eulogy of R. B. Sheridan, a description of Dutch Sam, a pugilist of note, a biography of the genteel pickpocket, George Barrington, a blistering attack on the Duchess of Macclesfield for her desertion of her son, the unfortunate poet, Savage, a splendid account of the place of pawnbrokers in the economy of the poor, praise for the industry of Mr Thrale and Mr Rothschild and a contemptuous comment on Dandies. ('The Dandy was got by *Vanity* out of *Affectation*—his dam, *Petit-Maitre* or *Maccaroni*—his grandam, *Fribble*—his great-grandam, *Bronze*—his great-great-grandam, *Coxcomb*—and his earliest ancestor, *Fop*. . . .')

Life in London begins for Jerry in Chapter VIII, where he is introduced to the elegance of Corinthian House, which is described room by room in the manner of *Walks Through Bath*. Tom advises him on the prime requisites of deportment and *ton*, and the multitude of polite accomplishments in conversation, behaviour and outlook expected of a true Corinthian. One of the first requirements is fitting attire. Dickey Primefit, the celebrated apparel-furnisher, is summoned to measure the robust rustic frame of Jerry for the latest rig-out of a Swell, and in due course Jerry discards his country garb for top-boots, white cord breeches, a green coat with brass buttons, a neat waistcoat and stock, and a light upper Benjamin, an 'elegant metamorphose'.

In the meantime, Jerry has been introduced to Bob Logic and the three agree to ride together in 'the *Show-Shop* of the Metropolis— HYDE PARK'. Jostling together there, the astonished countryman sees 'the NOBLEMAN and the *Yokel*—the DIVINE and the *Family-man*—the PLAYER and the *Poet*—the IMPURE and the *Modest Girl*—the GRAVE and the *Gay*—the FLASH COVE and *Man of Sentiment*—the FLAT and the *Sharp*—the DANDY and the *Gentleman*—the out-and-out SWELL and the *Groom*—the real SPORTSMAN and the *Black Leg*—the HEAVY TODDLERS and the *Operators*—the dashing BUM TRAP and the *Shy Cove*—the MARCHIONESS and her Cook—the DUKE and the *Dealer in Queer . . .*' and many more. Tom presents Jerry to the Duchess of Hearts, a reigning beauty, and points out to him the Marchioness of Diamonds, the best-dressed lady in town. Logic and Tom also draw their companion's attention to other figures, giving a potted biography of each— Old Evergreen, 'the most systematic debauchee in the town', Bill Dash, a well-breeched swell, 'Fond of joking, but as coarse as a fishwoman at Billingsgate', the Honourable Dick Trifle, one of the 'Tribe of Fops, Got 'tween sleep and wake!', an idler, a smatterer and a dandy, Plausible Jack, a beautifully dressed card-sharp and gambler, on the look-out for '*pigeons*', and a rosy-faced middle-aged female and three attractive young girls, whom Jerry is much taken by, until Logic identifies the woman as a well-known Madame and the ladies as 'Cyprians' or fashionable prostitutes, favourites of 'some of the *tender* part of the Peerage'.

With such experiences, the rusticity of Jerry begins to wear off and he starts to acquire some sophistication, although he remains still much baffled by Logic's slang. Tom and Jerry set off for the theatre; 'Logic (who was a great lover of the bottle) was too *bosky*, as he termed it, to accompany them'. Not caring for the entertainment offered at Drury Lane, they move off to Covent Garden, where it is not the play that catches their attention, but the hordes of gay Cyprians, their protectors and customers, who infest the place. The ladies press their cards upon

Jerry, who, innocent at first of their profession, is 'astonished that such dashing females should keep *shops!*' Fanny, one of the girls, points out a gentleman who has a passion for slaveys (which Egan, putting the word in print for the first time, glosses as 'a *slang* term for servant maids: being servants of all work; and also in allusion to their laborious employment and hard work').[4]

The two next go slumming in a 'Sluicery' or gin-shop, where they encounter such characters as Old Mother Brimstone, Fat Bet, Gateway Peg and Swipy Bill. Mother Brimstone, 'an old *cadger* and a *morning-sneak* COVESS,[5] who is pouring some *blue ruin* down the baby's throat to stop its crying, has borrowed the kid in order to assist her in exciting charity from the passing stranger in the street'. Even more vividly than Cruikshank's graphic illustration to this scene, Egan's text summons up the misery, degradation and pathos of the contemporary gin-shops, where the wretched poor sought an anodyne. 'It is, however,' he says, 'LIFE IN LONDON.' But Tom and Jerry find the coffee-shop they next visit still more chaotic and vicious than the sluicery, with a motley lot of depraved, drunken and unfortunate characters brawling and scuffling. Some of the 'kids', 'anxious for a *lark*', determine to serve out the two swells and start a fight with them. Just as Tom and Jerry are getting on top of their opponents in the street, the Watch is summoned and the Charleys, as the incompetent, bumbling predecessors of Peel's police force were called, overpower the two and drag them to the watch-house.

Bail is allowed them and they return the next morning to Bow Street. Here they witness the plight of an unfortunate young woman, charged by a coachman with underpaying him. When the driver hears her pathetic story of seduction and desertion told to the magistrate, he returns part of the fare. 'It was a fine scene altogether,' writes Egan. 'Sterne would have made a complete chapter of it.' When Tom and Jerry are called to defend themselves against the charge of Barney O'Bother, the watchman, their plea is nullified by the performance of the old hand, who has skilfully got himself up as a most injured party:

> *Barney*'s head was tied up with a handkerchief; in his right hand
> he held a broken lantern, a sort of stage property, that had been
> brought forward on many similar occasions; and in his left a
> damaged *rattle*, also an old performer at Bow Street. A thread-
> bare coat, torn in slits, likewise ready for any emergency,
> completed the denouement.

Tom and Jerry get off with a bill for damages.

Other experiences follow thick and fast. At a Masquerade Ball at the Opera House, amidst the drinking and the revelry, Logic plays pranks on his friends by changing his costume and misleading Tom as to the mask Corinthian Kate is wearing. Jerry, meanwhile, has been smitten by a lady dressed as a nun, whom Logic later reveals as Lady Wanton, the wife of a rich old nobleman. There is eating and drinking and dancing and, for extra entertainment, several ballads and songs, among them one which several later writers picked up from Egan:

> O slumber, my *Kid-wy*,[6] thy *dad* is a *scamp*,[7]
> Thy mother a *bunter*,[8] brush'd off on the *tramp*;[9]
> She's sold all her *sprats*, and left nothing for thee,
> And got *lushy*[10] with *daffy*, and out on a *Spree*!
> Then, rest thee, *Kid* rest thee, *Kid*, *snooze* while you can,
> If you open your *peepers*, you'll go without *scran*![11] . . .

Next day, while the three are on their way to Gentleman Jackson's rooms in Bond Street, Logic draws attention to a former actress, now happily married to a banker, who is a famous Lady Bountiful, set only on doing good to all in need. His praise of her character is in contrast to his flippancy about the Cyprians and his mocking of the Dandies. In the Bond Street room Tom engages in a sparring bout with the celebrated Commander-in-Chief, while Jerry weighs himself, watched by Bob Logic wearing his green spectacles and carrying his furled umbrella with both of which he is always identified. Their next call, in the evening, is to Tom Cribb's pub. Here, while supping their *heavy wet*, they meet the Champion of England, admire the cup presented to him by 'the Sporting World' in 1811 and *blow a cloud* with the pugilist.

They are enticed to a dog-fight at the Westminster Pit, where the celebrated real-life Italian monkey, Jacco Maccacco, defeats yet another dog three times his weight and wins some *blunt* (money) for the trio. The evening develops into a pub-crawl in the neighbourhood of Tothill Fields, where they see, among other sights, soldiers and their *trulls* tossing off the *heavy wet*, *cadgers* enjoying a good supper and *prigs* with their *blowens* spending the produce of the day; at one public-house, a dustman's wedding is being celebrated. By this time, the trio have taken several *flashes of lightning* (glasses of gin). Bob gets lost and Tom suggests to Jerry 'getting the best of a Charley', in revenge for their experience at Bow Street. This was a favourite Corinthian sport —overturning the sentry-box in which the watchman sat dozing and leaving the occupant imprisoned face downwards. The two have no trouble in finding a victim in Temple Bar and roar with laughter at the subtle prank as they scamper away, followed by the noise of another scout's alarm rattle.

Jerry, now a thorough Londoner, has reversed his country habits, sleeping by day and rising by night, but he is able to get up at one in the afternoon. A chastened Logic joins the cousins and they set off for Tattersall's, where Tom intends to buy a *prad* (horse) on Jerry's advice. Tattersall's, says Egan 'gives a *tone* to the *sporting* world, in the same way that the transactions on the ROYAL EXCHANGE influence the mercantile part of society'. Jerry persuades Tom against purchasing a horse. Tom takes his friends to meet Corinthian Kate and her friend, Sue. The result is a pleasant social evening, with Logic playing waltzes at the piano while Tom and Kate take part in 'the *lascivious* dance' and the girls singing duets. Jerry is much taken with Sue.

Next day, while leaving the Fencing-rooms in St James's Street, where Tom has exhibited yet another skill, that in the 'ornamental parade of quarte and tierce', the men see Kate and Sue hurrying along. They follow them to a fortune-teller's, where they interrupt the session and the girls fly in confusion. Caught up, they agree to accompany the trio to Carlton Palace. In this building Egan falls into his guide-book style, giving a virtually foot-by-foot description of the 'NE PLUS ULTRA of Life in London', room by room, picture by picture, carpet by carpet, the whole suffused with his exaggerated praise of the British monarchy. Even Logic's puns are subdued in this environment.

In contrast, as the pattern of the book demands, the next place visited is the condemned Yard at Newgate, which Tom deems essential to Jerry's education. Here they see the condemned prisoners having their chains knocked off in preparation for hanging, and receiving religious consolation from the Rev. Mr Cotton, Chaplain at that time and a friend of Egan's, who had on more than one occasion dined with the clergyman at Newgate. Logic's visit is not one of curiosity; he is there at the request of one of the condemned men, Lively Jem, an old Oxford companion, to take a farewell message to his woman.

A visit to the Royal Exchange is followed by a trip to All-Max in the 'back-slums', the latter another word printed for the first time in *Life in London*[12] and glossed by Egan as 'low, unfrequented parts of town'. All-Max, in the East End, is one of Egan's special delights, a gathering-place and drinking spot for some of the most colourful and out-of-the-way characters of London's low life. Here Max, Mr Lushington, blue ruin—in other words, gin—is consumed in huge quantities by a motley group indeed—Lascars, blacks, jack tars, coal-heavers, dustmen, women of colour, old and young and a sprinkling of the remnants of once-fine girls. While Tom chats to the female proprietor and Jerry feeds gin to the fiddler, Bob Logic enjoys the chaste salutes of Black Sal on one knee and Flashy Nance on the other. Attention in the accompanying plate is focused upon Nasty Bob, the coal-whipper, and African Sal dancing a spirited duo. These two characters were to become among the most popular in the dramatizations of the book. Logic disappears again, but not before saying to Tom, in words which echo much of Egan's own attitude:

> It is . . . the Lower Orders of Society who really *enjoy*
> themselves. They eat with a good appetite, *hunger* being the
> sauce; they *drink* with a zest, in being thirsty from their exertions,
> and not *nice* in their beverage; and as to *dress*, it is not an object
> of serious consideration with them. Their minds are daily
> occupied with work, which they quit with the intention of
> *enjoying* themselves, and *enjoyment* is the result; not like the
> rich, who are out night after night to *kill time*, and what is worse,
> dissatisfied with almost everything that crosses their path from
> the *dulness* of *repetition*.

At three the next day the cousins lift their damaged heads from the pillow. Tonight, says Tom, is the night at Almack's. 'The contrast will be delightful.' The fashionable assemblies at Almack's, representing the most wealthy, elegant and superior of London society, were, indeed, as far from evenings in a coal-heaver's pub as could be imagined. Egan enjoys both equally and enjoys as much the extent to which they differ and are yet, in a way, the same—as he makes Tom say:

> Far be it from me, Jerry, wantonly to *satirise* any of the classes
> of society, from the highest to the lowest of mankind; as I am
> perfectly convinced, in too many instances, that both of them
> have been traduced and libelled, by numerous persons, who
> have had no opportunity of judging of either of them but at a
> distance of *extreme* PERSPECTIVE.

When Tom and Jerry go to the great ballroom, Logic is not with them. 'The Oxonian does not like *etiquette*. He is too fond of *fun*.' Tom takes the occasion to give Jerry a lecture on deportment and to decry scandal, cant and gambling. During the evening he has several times to say 'Lethe!' to Jerry, a signal agreed upon by them should the latter forget his 'p's and q's' and verge on a *faux pas*. But the ball passes off well, although Jerry is disappointed again in seeing Lady Wanton but being unable to talk to her.

Cock-fighting is next patronized in the Royal Cockpit, Tufton Street, Westminster, after which two swell, broad coves who have lost money in the pit against Tom and Jerry invite the two to dine near St James's Park. Here the four play whist, and Tom and Jerry are cheated by various devices. A visit to the Grand Carnival at the English Opera House follows with Logic as Dr Pangloss, Tom as Rover and Jerry as Hodge, then a meeting with the actors playing *Don Giovanni* in the Green Room at Drury Lane. In the latter scene, Egan shows his special interest in the stage by putting into the mouth of one of the players some pertinent observations on the art of natural acting and on the many hazards of a theatrical career, as well as on the ephemeral character of the actor's art. 'The *fame* of an actor is likewise composed of the most perishable materials; and his *talents* are entirely left to the *recollection* of his audience to be preserved from oblivion.'

After tasting wine at the London docks, where Tom's wine-merchant does his business, they move to the Italian Opera. Egan devotes equal attention to the glittering spectacle, the audience, including Dick Trifle and the Marchioness, and the bustle at the exit, where the various coachmen jostle and fight their way towards their passengers.

No tour of London would have been complete without a visit to Vauxhall Gardens, that 'festival of LOVE and *harmony*'. The trio decide to go the next evening, but first get rid of an hour or two before dinner with 'a *turn* or two in Bond Street—a *stroll* through Piccadilly— a *look in* at Tattersall's—a *ramble* through Pall-Mall—and a *strut* on the *Corinthian Path* (Regent Street)'. The evening at Vauxhall really crowns Egan's exhibition of the contrasts and paradoxes of Regency London, with its 'happy mixture of society', all classes mingling together in exploring the illuminated walks, the rotundas, the gardens, listening to the music and watching the entertainment and drinking the burnt-wine and eating the ham-shavings. Logic ('Mr Green Specs') becomes involved in a fight with an insulting dandy, and knocks him down, afterwards disappearing into the crowd.

Jerry's time in the city is drawing to a close and the friends undertake their final excursions. The first is a look at the exhibition of pictures at Somerset House, 'the best shilling's worth in London'. The next is an evening visit, in the guise of beggars, to the slums of 'the Holy Land', where they venture into a resort of the Cadgers, the numerous cheats, impostors, fakers and charlatans who begged or extorted money in the London streets. Here, with relish and knowledge, Egan depicts a collection of mock cripples, fake blind men, women pregnant with the help of a pillow, the genteel-looking crossing-sweeper, women with hired children, hymn-singing hypocrites, all squandering the day's takings in gin and revelry.

Tom and Jerry do not see Logic again for three days. At length they learn that he has been *'blown up at Point Non-Plus'*—in other words, he is broke and the bailiffs are in. Bob, like Mr Pickwick after him, is lodged in the Fleet and the cousins, visiting him, meet his

> fellow-collegians—the *cleaned-out* Gambler—the *dissipated* Spendthrift—the Debauchee—the *extravagant, dishonest, fashionable* Tradesman—the *pretended* Merchant—the *pettifogging* Lawyer—the *fraudulent* Bankrupt—the *bold* Smuggler— the *broken-down* Captain—the *roguish*— the *foolish*—the *schemer*—the *swindler*—the *hypocrite*—and the *plausible*—the *poor gentleman*—and the really well-meaning but *unfortunate fellow.*

On the way home Jerry contracts a chill in a rain-storm; Dr Pleas'em tells him that he has been *'trotting* too hard' and needs the country air of Hawthorn Hall. As Egan is running out of material, Tom leaves Jerry to read in bed a perfectly dreadful romantic melodramatic tale, 'The Hero of the Cavern', which fills up several pages. On his feet again, Jerry catches a coach from the White Horse Cellar, Piccadilly, where, after good-byes from Tom and Logic and warm thanks from Jerry with a promise to return, the trio go their separate ways, Tom to Corinthian Hall, Logic back to the Fleet and Jerry to Somerset. For the time being *Life in London* concludes.

Although it is in the *London Spy* tradition, Egan's book has a character of its own. It is hardly to be called a novel; it has no plot to speak of, and promising fictional leads, such as Jerry's confrontation with Lady Wanton or Sue or the relations between Tom and Kate, remain quite undeveloped. If it were taken as the first part only of a book which includes *Finish to Life in London*, where such leads *are* followed up and incidents more neatly linked, a case could, indeed, be made out for it as a work of fiction in a more traditional sense. As *Life in London* stands, the construction is loose and primitive and the circumstances—hardly to be called a plot—serve merely as an excuse for presenting a series of pictures of city life. Egan lacked the imaginative power necessary to transform his material into an integrated work or to contrive incidents and characters which transcend the observed. But he was a superb reporter, and, for all the touches of caricature and the simplifications, he does present a faithful and detailed picture of the Regency scene, of the life and habits of a typical man about town, of fashionable life and low life in particular.

Life in London is no mere miscellany, as earlier books of its type had been. As we have seen, it works quite skilfully in terms of contrast, and the alternating scenes of low life and high life, of places of culture and places of amusement, of respectable pursuits and disreputable ones, of country ways and town ways, used systematically, although not mechanically, give a sense of structure and purpose to the whole. This form is not arbitrary; it is related to Egan's philosophy and moral outlook. George Cruikshank's frontispiece, apart from its delineation of 'the varieties of LIFE IN LONDON', shows also the 'UPS and DOWNS'. At the top of the Corinthian column is the King and his nobles 'the ROSES, PINKS, and TULIPS: the *flowers* of SOCIETY', next the 'respectable', the merchants, then in the centre, Tom, Jerry and Logic drinking (Logic the worse for it)—all of them the UPS; and at the bottom the DOWNS, the mechanics, the humble labourers and the human vegetables. Egan describes the gradations thus:

> The NOBLE (high birth; on such good terms with himself that if a *commoner* accidentally touch him in crossing his path, he looks down, with a sort of contempt, muttering, '*D—n you, who are you?*'), the RESPECTABLE (the merchant &c., their *stilted* place in life acquired by talent, or from lucky circumstances, with more *upstart* pride than the former character, and fastidiously squeamish in mixing with any but *upper* customers), the MECHANICAL (honest, industrious, merry, and happy, if not more so in London, perhaps, than the other two classes put together, and so independent in mind as to *chaff* 'win gold and wear it'): and the TAG-RAG and BOB-TAIL *squad* (who do not care how the *blunt* comes or how it goes. *Togs* or no *togs!*, but, nevertheless, who must live at any price, and see a *bit of life*, let the world jog on how it will; yet who can drop a *tear* upon a sorrowful event—*laugh* heartily at fun—*shake* with cold—*perspire* with heat —and go to *roost* much sounder upon a dust-hill than many of the *swells* can *snooze* upon their *dabs*; likewise, in comparing *notes*, feel happy in the presumption that there are hundreds worse off in society than themselves.)

These characters are set in the 'angles'; the Corinthian capital itself, which sustains them all, contains the King and his Court and the Corinthians.

All of this sums up Egan's own outlook. The Corinthian is always to be differentiated from the dandy or the snob, those with a contemptuous attitude towards other classes; he is a true gentleman who respects and delights in the diversity of society and who sees it as a hierarchy whose base is the honest working man. Each class has its own duties, its own pleasures, its own problems. Egan views all this with a generous tolerance, without a trace of social indignation or indeed any awareness of the extent of the misery and poverty of his day. For him the contemporary order of society is a natural one. His indignation is reserved for the snob, the affected, the effeminate, the tricks of thieves, con-men and fakers, the wiles of prostitutes, the seducers of women, the evils of excessive drinking and gambling. In his portrayal of London life he is not too far from Henry Mayhew. Many of his anecdotes are true and given in the words of the original teller. He does not hesitate to show destitution, although for him it is circumstance or character that is to blame rather than society. He is all the time certain that the poor have at least as much fun as the rich.

Little place is given to the middle class in *Life in London*. Certainly, there are occasional references to merchants and bankers, but in general Egan does not separate upper and middle classes. He is more at home among the sporting fraternity and the lower orders, he knows All-Max more intimately than Almack's, yet his virtual ignoring of the all-important class of Victorian society gives a fair indication of the way his contemporaries looked upon this stratum; the middle class in Egan's day were neither as pervasive nor as influential as they were very soon to become. Inevitably, there is little about work in *Life in London*. Tom and Jerry are wealthy idlers, as are most of their acquaintances. Logic is a spendthrift. Those who do work for a living in the book are engaged in such occupations as cater for the needs and pleasures of the Fancy and the nobility. It is a very different world from that of Carlyle!

In contrast, too, with the sprawling, often Gothic, London of Dickens's *Nicholas Nickleby* and *Little Dorrit*, Egan's London is a minute area; it lies in fact within a mile radius of Piccadilly; the suburbs and outer areas might not exist. This London of an eighteenth-century adopted Cockney is even narrower than that of Pope's *Dunciad*.

The amazing popularity of the book can be attributed to several factors. There is no doubt that in its scenes of both high and low life, its concern with sport, its *News of the World* treatment of crime and vice it hit off the taste of the times. Its unquestioned raciness also appealed. But its truth to life was its major recommendation. Many of the humbler members of society saw themselves portrayed for the first time in a book more or less as they were, and both rejoiced in this fact and approved of the correctness of the picture as they had approved of the accuracy of *Boxiana's* reports.

And then there was Egan's remarkable style. Here at last was a master of cant, not a writer who had mugged up a sprinkling of words from slang glossaries to give colour to his work, but one *fly* to all the subtleties of thieves' slang, sportsman's lingo, 'St Giles's Greek', and fashionable vernaculars, and, while capable of impressive oratorical flights—impressive, that is, to those who had not read the major eighteenth-century prose writers—also able to write passages like this:

> Tom is *sluicing* the *ivory* [giving drink to] of some of the
> unfortunate heroines with *blue ruin* [gin] whom the breaking-up
> of the SPELL [the prostitutes' parade at Covent Garden] has
> *turned-up* [disappointed] without any *luck*, in order to send them
> to their *pannies* [apartments] full of *spirits*. Jerry is in *Tip Street*
> upon this occasion [paying for drinks] and the *Mollishers*
> [prostitutes or low-class women] are all *nutty* [very fond] upon
> him, putting it about, one to another, that he is a *well-breeched*
> *Swell* [with his pockets full of money].

Or like this, from a graphic piece of narration by Chaffing Peter, which anticipates some of Dickens's Cockney monologues:

> 'Come, *Lummy*, von't you stand a *drap* of *summut*, as you are in
> luck, and it's a wicked *could* day?' 'No', says I, my Lord, 'I
> vasn't a going for to pass you'. 'Vell', says *Jem* to me, 'I have got
> a *duce* [twopence]—I suppose as how, my Lord, you knows what
> a *duce* is—and Tom's got a *win* [a penny]—and *Dirty Suke*
> can flash a *mag* [a halfpenny], and I dares to say ve can make it
> out amongst us to have a *kevarten* or two of gin, before we does
> part. Come, *Lummy*, let us *toddle* to the *Pig and Tinder-Box*
> [Elephant and Castle], they have got a *drap* of *comfort* there, I
> knows.'

Inevitably, a good deal of the slang Egan uses has faded away and his book has paid the price for its topicality in this respect, but, on the other hand, *Life in London* helped to preserve, pass on to other writers or catch in print for the first time a surprising number of words which are still in wide use, either as slang or as ordinary colloquialisms in Britain and Commonwealth countries. Among these are *bruiser* (fighter), *bunch of fives* (fist), *chopper* or *chops* (mouth), *clout* (blow), *conk* (head), *done over* (thrashed), *game* (brave), *gob* (mouth), *grub* and *scran* (food), *ivories* (teeth), *up to scratch* (fit and ready), *mug* (face), *nob* (head), *peeper* (eye), *pins* (legs), *sneezer* (nose), *tile* (hat), *topper* (hat), *upper story* (head), *white feather* (cowardice), *toddle* (walk) *raise the wind* (get money), *Uncle* (pawnbroker), *up the spout* (pawned), *tick* (on credit), *born with a silver spoon in his mouth, a screw loose* (not quite normal in the head), *making a dead set at somebody, dead beat, cross* (a fixed fight), *leary* (cautious), *lumbered* (arrested or found out), *bilked* (cheated), *keep mum* (keep silent), *filly* (young girl), *nutty* (infatuated), *lark* (an adventure), *lush* (drunk or a drunkard), *fancy-man* (pimp or protector), *chaffing* (talking or making fun of), *gammon* (*n.* nonsense, *v.* deceive someone), *coves* (men), *a trump* (a good sort), *lugged off* (dragged away), *to try it on* (attempt deceit), *decked out* (dressed up), *traps* (policemen), *snooze* (sleep), *deep* (clever, cunning), *green* (innocent), *glim* (light), *down* or *downy* (wise to tricks)—to list merely a few. Rather more than half the slang and cant, exotic to many of Egan's contemporaries, and thus obligingly translated in footnotes, is wholly unintelligible to the modern reader, however. But Egan owed much of his reputation for being a *fly cove* to the complete ease with which he was able to manipulate so many private languages.

The excellent plates of the Cruikshanks, perhaps the first full flowering of their talent for illustration, also played their part, of course, in establishing the *Life in London* vogue. A perfect match for Egan's text, they are rich in closely observed detail, animated and lively, without the stiffness of so many eighteenth-century engravings, Hogarthian in their revelation of low life and their crowded abundance, and expressing a comic sense and an impish wit as well as sardonic and pathetic touches. Observe such things as the pose of the young man awaiting execution and praying with Mr Cotton contrasted with the arrogant disdain and defiant bearing of the other criminal having his chains struck off for the same purpose (Thackeray especially admired this), the mixture of irritation and pleasure on the face of the beggar scratching himself in the 'Holy Lands' scene, the intentness of the spectators at the fight between Jacco Maccacco and the dog, the vigorous design of the 'Boxing a Charley' plate, the wonderful Rowlandson magistrate at Bow Street, the frieze effect of the Vauxhall scene, the individualized 'supers' at All-Max and the virile line of all the drawings. It is no wonder that George, who did only a few of the plates, was anxious to maintain his stake in the work.

Those who reacted against *Life in London* did so mainly on the score that it was 'vulgar' and that it set a bad example in teaching, or at least tolerating, vice. This attitude was expressed mainly by the Evangelicals, who were increasing in numbers and power, and who were among the most militant opponents of pugilism. The whole world of *Life in London*, with its idle Corinthians, its emphasis on the enjoyment of novelty, frivolity and liquor, its acceptance of the fact of prostitution, of brutal sports and of betting, and its partiality for low characters, was at odds with the nascent world of *bourgeois* respectability, propriety and decorum. Since the widespread acceptance of the work made it impossible to be ignored, it was often savaged in such terms as those of W. F. Deacon, who called it 'a curious specimen of the most singular and superlative stupidity that the thrice-sodden brains of a hireling scribbler ever yet inflicted on the patience of the public'.[13] The journal *Town Talk* in 1822 lamented that the 'glowing descriptions' which Egan had given of low life had led to the London theatres being filled with 'vivid representations of the vilest practices of the blackest sinks of iniquity', and concluded: 'All this is Pierce's fault; it is really a pity that a decent man like Pierce should have done so much mischief.'

Yet, far from being a round of debauchery, Tom, Jerry and Logic's forays into London are astonishingly innocent, especially if compared with the secret life of many a Victorian paterfamilias or the public life of many a modern beatnik. Whatever Logic gets up to whenever he is separated from the cousins Egan leaves to the imagination of his readers. The trio get drunk now and then, they sing and dance with coal-heavers, negresses and beggars, they turn over a watchman's box in retaliation for a dirty trick by one of his tribe, they watch a dog-fight, they play whist. For the rest, they attend balls and parties, they go to the opera and the ballet, they look at paintings and visit places of cultural and historical interest and they enjoy the society of the nobility as much as they enjoy that of All-Max. Throughout *Life in London* Egan seldom loses an opportunity of setting out his distaste for dissipation and debauchery: Jerry decides early in the book what 'life' in London is not:

> it was not to agree with every disposition, and conform
> with every species of behaviour totally inconsistent with the tenets
> of reason, prudence, and good manners; neither was it to ridicule
> all sober, well-disposed persons, as persons wholly unfit to live in
> the world. .... It was not that '*sort* of LIFE' that encouraged
> individuals to drink very hard—to swear a good round hand—to
> sing an indecent song—or to be *smutty* and fulsome in discourse. ....
> It was not to be loose in morals, wanton in debauchery, and
> horrid in imprecations; to appear *learned* in everything allied to

obscenity and lewdness, and in everything else to appear as
ignorant as a person might please. . . . It was not to go to taverns,
coffee-houses, and places of ill-fame, to commit every sort of
outrage and disorder. . . . It was not to frequent places of
fashionable resort, and to *keep it up* all night in drinking, swearing,
and singing; and when fair morn makes her approach, then
heroically to sally forth into the street, *reel* about like a RAKE of
the first magnitude, insult all you meet, knock down an old woman
or two, break a few windows, stagger to another tavern for a
fresh supply of the juice of the grape, and finish your glorious
frolic in being sent home in a hackney-coach, senseless,
speechless and motionless, more like a beast than a rational
human being.

Egan is no teetotaller and he enjoys a 'lark'; but for those seeking
details of Regency vice he is as disappointing as any respectable Victorian novelist. It was his disclosing of and lack of condemnation of aspects
of contemporary life which the respectable preferred to pretend did not
exist that made him an object of disdain to some. But he had his staunch
defenders. The *Sheffield Independent* of 12 April 1828, for instance,
speaks of Egan's having invented a language for the sporting fraternity,

and enriched it with terms which *flash* on the dullest and put the
lowest *up*! In doing this, he observed a moral syntax; and some of
his happiest efforts betray a strength of sense, and an inclination
to support honour and correct feelings, which we have not
particularly observed in the lucubrations of his successors
and imitators.

It was, indeed, the many who cashed in on the success of *Life in London*
who often deserved the strictures of its critics rather than Pierce Egan
himself.

❦ V ❦

The *Life in London* Furore

To say that *Life in London* was a phenomenal success is not to exaggerate. So great was the demand for copies of the numbers that the printers, Sherwood, Neely and Jones, could hardly keep pace with it, and whole armies of women and small boys, employed to colour the plates, were worked to exhaustion. The numbers were again reissued from the start in 1821, overlapping with later numbers of the original issue,[1] and once more in 1826.[2] A large, paper edition came later, and in 1830, concurrently with the publication of Egan's *Finish to Life in London*, Virtue put out yet another set of numbers. As the Abbey catalogue remarks, 'That a book reprinted in large numbers for ten years should stand a fresh printing in 12 parts at 3/- each is a strong proof of its amazing popularity.'[3] The complete volume of *Life in London*, after its first appearance in 1821, was reprinted in 1823, 1830, 1841, 1870 and 1904, to note merely the editions that have been traced. It is an extraordinary thing that all copies of the numbers seem to have vanished. Even in early Victorian times writers were bemoaning the difficulty of locating copies of them. Thackeray was unable to find a copy of the volume in the British Museum on his first search, but discovered one there some years later. Today first editions and early editions fetch ridiculous prices on the London book mart. So, too, do imitations and plagiarisms of *Life in London*.

And these were innumerable. In the first chapter of *Finish* Egan declares that almost everybody has made money out of *Life in London* except himself: 'We have been *pirated*, COPIED, *traduced;* but, unfortunately, not ENRICHED by our indefatigable exertions; therefore NOTORIETY must satisfy us, instead of the smiles of FORTUNE.' He goes on to list over sixty derivations, including books, dramatizations, newspapers, song-books, games, street ballads, drinks, printed tea-trays and so on. Some of these are trivial enough, but the Tom and Jerry mania, which extended to snuff-boxes, painted fire-screens, shawls, handkerchiefs, fans, cushions, and dress-stuffs marked with the images of the two heroes and Corinthian styles from tailors, bootmakers and hatters, as well as a rash of babies named Tom or Jerry (in one case, at least, Tom Jerry!) can be paralleled perhaps only by the extent to which modern advertising techniques have succeeded in selling objects labelled with Walt Disney characters.

The earliest attempt to cash in on the success of Tom and Jerry was a work in 6*d.* numbers by an anonymous author, which began appearing before the numbers of *Life in London* had been completed. This was *Real Life in London; or The Rambles and Adventures of Bob Tallyho, Esq. and his Cousin, the Hon. Tom Dashall, through the Metropolis,* published by Jones & Co. of Finsbury Square. Egan calls this 'a bare-faced piracy', as indeed it is. Yet it is also a clever, vivacious piece of work, superior in sophistication and in constructive ability to Egan's original, as well as being less clogged with guide-book detail and padding. But it lacks Egan's originality, his intimate knowledge of low life and his command of the vernacular, and the illustrations, clever enough, by Alken, Heath, Dighton, Rowlandson and others, have not the wit, the detail and the consistency of style and purpose of the Cruikshank plates. One of the illustrations is a blatant imitation of 'A Picture of the Fancy'. The author remains unknown. Some catalogues attribute it to Egan,[4] but this is impossible, in view of the difference in style and his own vehement denunciation of it. A possible candidate is Jonathan Badcock, or 'Jon Bee', Egan's bitter rival; another is William Combe, the creator of 'Dr Syntax'. Badcock's own books include *Living Picture of London* (1818) and *Slang* (1823), and he was the editor of *Annals of Sporting* and *The Fancy Gazette,* in most of which publications he snipes at 'Fancy's Child', claiming that he himself is the real originator of the *Life in London* idea,[5] and that he is a far more accurate reporter than Egan. Badcock may have written *Real Life*; certainly he is an admirer of Alken's work and Alken is to the fore as illustrator of the book. Also *Real Life* contains sporting and boxing knowledge and an insight into the ways of the Fancy such as Badcock possessed. At the same time, Badcock, who had many chances to do so, never acknowledged the book, despite constant Cruikshank-like claims to have originated much else.

Real Life was only the first imitation. David Carey's *Life in Paris; comprising the Rambles, Sprees, and Amours of Dick Wildfire, of Corinthian Celebrity, and his Bang-Up Companions, Squire Jenkins and Captain O'Shuffleton* (1822) takes its characters on a Tom and Jerry tour of the French capital, with considerable humour and much English fun at the expense of the French language and French pugilism. Unlike most of the copyists of *Life in London*, Carey is careful, in his preface, to acknowledge his original: 'Life in London has justly received the approbation of the public; to seek to match such a work, by confining description to London, notwithstanding no field is so ample for collecting the materials for humour, would have appeared slavish and Quixotic in any person but the author of that work.' George Cruikshank's illustrations to Carey's book give the lie to his story about being too nice-minded to continue with plates for Egan's work. Not only is Carey's book considerably more indelicate than *Life in London*, but at least one illustration, 'Dick and Jenkins engaging in a frolic in the Cafe d'Enfer', is much more suggestive than anything relating to Tom and Jerry. Carey's book ran through several editions and had a sequel. *Real Life in Ireland; or the Day and Night Scenes, Rovings, Rambles and Sprees, Bulls, Blunders, Bodderations and Blarney of Brian Boru, Esq. and his elegant friend Sir Shawn O'Dogherty . . . By a Real Paddy* (1821) took copies of Tom and Jerry on a tour of the Emerald Isle. This is very close to Egan in spirit and style; there is an excess of frantic English patriotism (King George's visit to Dublin in 1821 is described in terms as swooning as a teen-age magazine's account of a pop concert), much horse-play and a surplus of guide-book information. By 1829 *Real Life in Ireland* was in its fourth edition, and it was reissued as late as 1904.

In 1823 *Life in London* was paid the compliment of a French translation, published by Baudouin Frères as *Diorama Anglais ou Promenades Pittoresques à Londres* and ascribed to M. S. The Introduction acknowledges the realism and accuracy which were felt to mark Egan's picture of London:

> La peinture des moeurs de toutes les classes ne pouvait manquer d'y exciter un vif intérêt. L'auteur a parfaitement justifié son titre, car il conduit successivement son héros depuis le palais du roi jusqu'au dernier cabaret où s'assemblent les mendiants et la lie du peuple . . . le fond de cet ouvrage offre un attrait réel, parce qu'il sert à mieux connaître la capitale d'Angleterre.

Despite his enthusiasm for the book, the translator was forced to cut it severely, excising most of the footnotes and the digressions. He also confesses that he found the slang exceptionally difficult to understand, and thanks a friend who has lived in England for his help in interpreting some of the lingo. All the same, although M.S. omits a number of the more exotic locutions, he has managed to find clever and apt equivalents for a suprising number of Egan's individual turns of phrase. The work, which reproduces the Cruikshank plates, appears to have been very popular and much discussed in France.

George Smeeton's *Doings in London or Day and Night Scenes of the Frauds, Frolics, Manners and Depravities of the Metropolis,* illustrated by George Cruikshank (1828), has Peregrine Wilson, the son of a retired merchant, being shown the by now predictable London sights by his father's former confidential clerk, Mentor. By 1849 this had reached its tenth edition. Smeeton's work was only one of the flood of books which continued to flow in Victorian times from the spring of *Life in London.* Many of them were related to the previous 'London Exposed' genre from which Egan's own book stemmed, but almost all reveal the impact of *Life in London,* often by direct imitation or plagiarism. Among these were *Life in London or The Metropolitan Microscope and Stranger's Guide,* by Two Citizens of the World (1828); *London and All Its Dangers,* by a Man about Town (1835); *A Peep into the Holy Land or Sinks of London Laid Open* (1835); *London by Night or the Bachelor's Facetious Guide to all the Ins and Outs and Nightly Doings of the Metropolis* (1857); *The Tricks and Traps of London* (1868); and the much reprinted *Sketches of London,* by James Grant, 'containing exact descriptions and amusing Anecdotes of its Beggars and Begging Imposters, Gaming Houses and Gamblers, Debtors and Debtors Prisons, Police Officers, etc.'

Even polite literature was not free from the direct influence of *Life in London.* When Fanny Burney published her *Evelina* in 1821, at the height of the Tom and Jerry craze, it was almost inevitable that she should give it the sub-title of 'Female Life in London'.

One of the most impudent derivations came from the egregious Jemmy Catnach, who brought out a broadside or 'whole sheet' called *Life in London or the Sprees of Tom and Jerry.* It comprised wretched woodcuts plagiarized from the Cruikshanks' plates, some doggerel songs and a versified summary of the plot of Egan's book. With astonishing gall, Catnach headed the 2*d.* sheet with a warning to still lesser fleas: 'This is to give Notice that those persons who are in the constant habit of pirating my Copyrights that if they dare to print any part of this sheet, they shall be proceeded against according to law.' The piracy sold in its thousands, edition after edition. There were also many songs and parodies directly inspired by the vogue—*The Corinthians'*

Song Book, Tom and Jerry's Collection of Songs, Logic's Song Book, Bob Logic's Memoranda, An Original Budget of Staves and *The New Harp Song Book* among them. But the most widespread imitation of *Life in London* and the source of its most pervasive influence was in the theatre.

In those days there were in London just two 'official', 'major' or licensed theatres, Sadler's Wells and Covent Garden, the only two houses at which straight drama could be performed, and consequently the home of Shakespeare and the chief stamping-ground for Kean and Macready. The other, 'minor', theatres, of which there were many, were permitted to present merely 'musical entertainments'. Although, in time, the law about music came to be very laxly interpreted to mean a modicum of inserted song or of orchestral accompaniment to almost any play, reduced in later Victorian times to a few token opening chords on a piano, in the early decades of the century the material seen in the minor theatres was usually fairly generously musical—burlettas, musical plays, melodramas with songs and choruses, variety and so on. The English theatre was then in one of its frequent troughs of decadence; the bulk of the material supplied was, in Tennyson's phrase, 'brainless pantomime', hasty and crude dramatizations of novels, translations or adaptations of French or German plays, Gothic melodramas, 'epics' about brigands, pirates, sailors, gipsies, eye-rolling foreign villains, persecuted maidens and cutlass-wielding heroes.

Since the minor theatres were well-attended places of entertainment, there was a very large turn-over in pieces, so that dramatists were always on the look-out for grist to the adaptation mill. *Life in London's* popularity made it an obvious choice and the hacks descended upon it like vultures. The first stage version appeared shortly after the publication of the volume, from the pen of W. Barrymore, who flung it off in three days. Egan, who was friendly with Barrymore, assisted at the rehearsals, and *Life in London*, 'an entirely New, Whimsical, Local, Melo-Dramatic, Pantomimical Drama', opened at the Royal Amphitheatre on Monday, 17 September 1821. Edward Stirling, one of the original cast, gives us a brief idea of the form of the entertainment in his memoirs:

> I played the Hon. Dick Trifle in the then great attraction of the day, Tom and Jerry . . . first produced at Astley's in an equestrian shape with real horses, donkeys, etc. The renowned pugilists, Tom Cribb and Spring, boxed in the circle. Tyrone Power (an unrivalled Irish comedian) was the original Corinthian Tom. This extrordinary piece made the fortunes of half the managers in England.[6]

The next version followed rapidly. Also called *Life in London,* or *The Larks of Logic, Tom and Jerry,* it was the work of Charles Dibdin, first performed at the Olympic Theatre on Monday, 12 November 1821. The floodgates were opened, and there was hardly a theatre in London that did not have its own 'Tom and Jerry'. During the summer of 1822 no less than five theatres were playing versions simultaneously. By no means everyone approved of the furore. The young James Robinson Planché viewed it all with lofty distaste:

> I entered into an agreement with Messrs Jones and Rodwell, the
> then proprietors of the Adelphi, to write only for that theatre,
> but cancelled it after a few months, rather than soil the stage
> with the production of 'Tom and Jerry'. A newly married man,
> the engagement was of consequence to me; but I can safely say
> that I never suffered pecuniary considerations to influence my
> conduct where the higher interests of the drama appeared to be at
> stake. Moncrief [*sic*] was not so fastidious. The piece was
> woefully dull and was ill received on its first presentation, but
> the fun and spirit gradually introduced into it by Wrench,
> John Reeve, Keeley and Wilkinson kept it on its legs, till by
> degrees the town took to it.[7]

Thomas Dibdin expressed, in a more moderate and less self-congratulatory way, some of the reservations he, too, had about the subject:

> Although I finally quitted the Surrey in March, it was part of
> our arrangement (which I fulfilled) that I should write a comic
> piece on the strangely popular plan of 'Tom and Jerry'; but it
> was to be a distinctly original disposition of those three eccentric
> characters; it was in three acts, containing about 40 songs, or
> rather *chansonettes,* and as I am informed, was fortunately well
> received; my brother, at the same time, wrote one for the
> Olympic Theatre; Astley's had produced one prior to the Adelphi;
> and every minor theatre had a 'Tom and Jerry' of its own. I
> have to confess what if a fault (and a great one) I cannot now
> help; that is, that I was offered the plan of the 'Great
> Adelphi' Tom and Jerry before any piece of the kind had
> appeared, and the assistance of the original artist, Mr
> Cruikshank, in producing it; but I could not prevail upon myself
> to approve the subject; and, pitifully erroneous as I was,
> imagined the public would do anything but patronize what I

conceived would be a marked disrespect toward them, and one which would deprive me of that good opinion which the magistrates had yearly honoured me with in expressing their praise of my theatrical administration.[8]

Tom Dibdin, as he acknowledges, was proved wrong. The public flocked to the stage versions. In addition to the dramatizations of the Dibdins and of Barrymore, there were pieces by Tom Farrell and Douglas Jerrold; records survive of *Tom, Jerry and Logic* at the Royalty Theatre in April 1822, *Tom and Jerry in France or Vive la Bagatelle,* by G. McFarren, at the Royal Coburg in December 1822, *Tom and Jerry or Life in London* at David's Royal Amphitheatre also in 1822, *The Treadmill or Tom and Jerry at Brixton,* played at the Surrey, *Our Future Fate or Tom, Jerry and Logic in 1845* at the Royal Coburg in 1823—to mention only London presentations.

By far the most successful play based on the book, however, was that run up by the ubiquitous W. T. Moncrieff, a tireless adaptor of novels, later to pillage Dickens for dramas, and one of those who did a great deal with plays like *Jack Sheppard* and *Eugene Aram* to establish a tradition of roguery in the theatre. His *Tom and Jerry* opened at the Adelphi on 26 November 1821, and had a quite extraordinary run, playing for ninety-three nights in its first season, and resuming to complete a total of 300 nights, making a profit of £10,000 and setting the new Adelphi, which had opened in 1820, firmly on its feet. There were some who declared that Moncrieff, not Egan, was the main originator of the material in the Adelphi version. William Clark tells the following story, which he admits is probably apocryphal, in his *Every Night Book* (1827), another work, incidentally, which owes much to *Life in London.* Egan, he relates, meeting Moncrieff after the success of *Tom and Jerry,* had a 'verbal turn-up' with the dramatist whom Egan accused of purloining his scenes wholesale from the pages of *Life in London.*

'No, by the mass!' exclaimed Moncrieff. 'Not so, Sir! not at all —I'll tell you what, Pierce, Rodwell sent me the books to read— I did so—but they pozed me for a month. I could neither make head nor tail of them. So what did I do, Sir? Why, d—e, wrote my piece from the inimitable plates—Cruikshank's plates—and boiled my kettle with your letter-press—that's the plain fact.'[9]

It is a good story, but unfortunately does not square with the facts. The published version of Moncrieff's play shows that he drew heavily on

Egan's text for plot, characters and dialogue. It follows the main lines of Egan's narrative, plunders the text wholesale for speeches, and uses all its major scenes. On the other hand, Moncrieff stiffens the plot by giving Logic a female companion, Jane, identifying Kate, Sue and Jane with the Misses Trifle and making the pursuit of the young men by the young women a major element of the story. Also, from a mere hint in Egan, he introduces the London gull, Jemmy Green, and makes into lively, colourful characters Little Jemmy, Dusty Bob and African Sal, whom Egan only names. The roles of Corinthian Tom and Jerry made the reputations of Wrench and Reeve, Bob Keeley was a terrific hit as Jemmy Green, but the public's affections fastened on Walbourn as Dusty Bob and Sanders as African Sal, and their comic *pas de deux* was one of the major attractions of the piece. When Walbourn retired to take over a public house at Battle Bridge, George Cruikshank painted an inn-sign for him showing Walbourn in his Dusty Bob character.

'Little Jemmy' Whiston had been a familiar figure begging on Blackfriars Bridge as he propelled himself along in a small box on wheels by means of two miniature crutches. A genuine cripple, deformed in his legs, he was notorious for his cadging and his frequent bouts of drunkenness. When completely intoxicated, he was often carried home on the shoulders of coal-heavers. One night in 1826 'Little Jemmy' was so taken home, this time head downwards, but was found to be dead on arrival. During the run of *Tom and Jerry* at the Adelphi he was in high spirits, since his impersonation on the stage greatly increased his beggar's takings. Another real life character whom Moncrieff introduced into *Tom and Jerry* was Billy Waters, reputed to be an African prince, certainly a former slave, who was a clever fiddler and, despite a wooden leg, an accomplished dancer. He, too, was a familiar street cadger, known to all and sundry as 'The King of the Beggars'.

The play, of course, owed much of its success to the skilful dramatic sense of Moncrieff and to the racy cant songs he inserted into his 'new Classic, Comic, Operatic, Didactic, Aristophanic, Localic, Analytic, Panoramic, Camera-Obscuric Extravaganza Burletta of Fun, Frolic, Fashion and Flash'. But perhaps its greatest appeal lay in the introduction to the stage not only of representative London types, but of actual characters known to many as belonging to the London underworld. In an age when the overwhelming majority of plays were unrealistic melodramas or Gothic thrillers, as far removed from life in setting and story as could be imagined, Moncrieff brought a sense of truth to the stage. Idealized in some respects the picture may have been, but at least London audiences were seeing on the boards characters they knew and a story not at all improbable in plot, and hearing references to places and things that were part of the daily life of many of them and language which, far from being the inflated fustian of melodramas or the high poetry of Shakespeare and the Elizabethans or the mock-Shakespearean of such contemporary wind-bags as Sheridan Knowles, was the actual lingo of the sporting world, the poor, the beggars. Some of the audience were seeing themselves on the stage, in fact, for the first time. And the sense of reality was greatly enhanced by the backcloths, after the plates in *Life in London,* which were designed by Robert Cruikshank and the painting of which was supervised by him. Contemporary reviews especially praise this feature of the production; the interior of Cribb's pub and of Gentleman Jackson's rooms were among the most admired. The tradition of realism in the theatre, which was later to develop in the respectable theatres in the 1880s with the advent of Pinero and Jones, had begun some sixty years before in the despised minor theatres with *Tom and Jerry.*

The Methodists, in particular, were active in attacking the immorality of Moncrieff's play and demanding its withdrawal; some of the Press took up the cry. However, the Lord Chamberlain and the Chief Magistrate both came to see it and approved of it, the Chamberlain returning with his wife for a second visit. When Moncrieff published his version in 1825 he dedicated it to the Duke of York, reminding him that he had been the first member of the Royal Family ever to attend a minor theatre when he came to see *Tom and Jerry* at the Adelphi and expressed his high approbation of it to Moncrieff.

Not all the 'respectable' visitors were so approving. In her journal, Mrs Arbuthnot, wife of the Rt Hon. Charles Arbuthnot, M.P., and a friend of the Duke of Wellington, records her own impression of the play. Her comment is particularly interesting, not only as showing a 'polite' response to this 'low' presentation, but also as revealing something of the reaction to it of the popular audience:

February 20, 1822—Went to the Adelphi Theatre to see a new farce called 'Life in London'. I never had been at the place before; it is a very pretty theatre, but beyond anything vulgar I ever saw. It was crowded to overflow, the people were hollowing and talking to each other from the pit to the gallery, and fighting and throwing oranges at each other. The play itself was a representation of all the low scenes in London, such as the Watch House, spunging and gaming houses and the rendezvous of beggars. In short, it was a sort of very low Beggar's Opera,

but it is impossible to describe the sort of enthusiasm with
which it was received by the people, who seemed to enjoy a
representation of scenes in which from their appearance, one
might infer they frequently shared.[10]

To such criticisms, Moncrieff replied ringingly in his preface to the
published play. He claims for *Tom and Jerry* 'a sensation, totally
unprecedented in Theatrical History', recording that seats were sold
weeks in advance, that every theatre in the United Kingdom, and several
in the United States, enriched its coffers by performing it, and that it
established the fortunes of most of the actors playing in it. 'The success
of "The Beggar's Opera", "The Castle Spectre" and "Pizarro" sank
into the shade before it. In the *furore* of its popularity, persons have
been known to travel from the furthest parts of the kingdom to see it,
and five guineas have been offered for a single seat.'

He goes on to defend the play against the Evangelicals, the Watchmen,
the clergymen and the magistrates who have charged it with immorality:

So far from being immoral, if the Piece be fairly examined, it
will be found to be as correct in its tendency as any production
ever brought on the Stage. The obnoxious scenes of life are only
shown that they may be avoided; the danger of mixing in them is
strikingly exemplified; and every incident tends to prove that
happiness is only to be found in the domestic circle . . . To
those venerable noodles who complain that I and my prototype,
Pierce, have made this the age of *Flash*, I answer—any age is
better than the AGE OF CANT!

Moncrieff did not exaggerate the success and influence of his play.
According to *Blackwood's* of 11 March 1822, 'the proprietors of the
Adelphi have already realized £12,000 by its representation and are
likely to get a great deal more'. It adds that, although the piece, with its
'amazing truth of slang and blackguardism', has run upwards of 100
nights to date, 'it is yet an affair of peril to squeeze your way into the pit'.

Provincial theatres were quick to cash in on the metropolitan vogue.
At the Theatre Royal, Brighton in 1822, in Liverpool at the Royal
Amphitheatre in the same year, and later in 1826 and 1828, at the two
theatres in Edinburgh, the Theatre Royal and the Caledonian, in 1822–3,
and at other theatres throughout Britain, Moncrieff's version did
excellent business. Even in Dublin the sporting trio made their mark.
In April 1822 *Tom and Jerry* began 'an enormous run', as the *Annals of
the Theatre Royal, Dublin*[11] put it, partly helped by the nightly 'set-to'

2 A Visit to the Fives Court

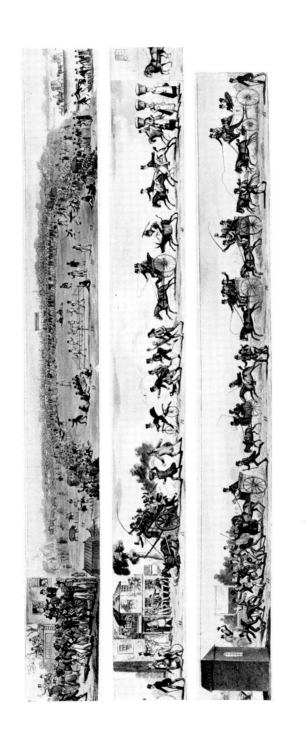

3 Strips from a Road to the Fight or a Picture of the Fancy by Robert and George Cruikshank

by celebrated amateur practitioners of pugilism, an attraction frequently associated with the piece. There was even a children's version of the play performed and published[12] and it took its place in the children's toy theatre, 1*d*. Plain and 2*d*. Coloured. As Egan himself relates in *The Pilgrims of the Thames*, 'Muster' Richardson, the well-known show-man of Bartholomew Fair, made more money out of *Tom and Jerry* in his travelling theatre than out of any other play he staged.

Nor did the plays based on *Life in London* die with their age. In London and the provincial theatres one or other version was revived as a main attraction or as an afterpiece regularly up to the 1850s. As late as 1868, Moncrieff's play was produced at the Victoria Theatre, London, under the title *Tom and Jerry or Life in London Fifty Years Ago* and ran for nine weeks, inspiring imitations and revivals at the Grecian Theatre, the Surrey Theatre and the Britannia Theatre. E. L. Blanchard saw the Victoria version in March 1870, and speaks of a 'careful revival' to a 'tremendous house'.[13] In 1886 J. A. Cave, who had brought the play to the Victoria, reproduced it at the Elephant and Castle (Grand) Theatre with the decidedly misleading sub-title of 'Life in London 100 Years Ago'. In the United States pirated versions were played at Charleston in 1824 and at New York and Baltimore in 1825; licit and illicit dramatizations continued to be presented for decades in these and such other centres as New Orleans. The play gave its name to a well-known American drink (a hot concoction of rum and water, spiced and sweetened) and from this, no doubt, came the name of the admirable cartoon characters, cat and mouse, whose never-resolved warfare still delights audiences throughout the world. Indirectly, but still genuinely, the modern Tom and Jerry derive from *Life in London*.

By 1823 London had become so saturated with Tom and Jerry plays that Tom Greenwood, a friend of Egan's, mildly satirized the craze in his *The Death of Life in London or Tom and Jerry's Funeral*, first performed at the Royal Coburg in 1823 and revived for the Adelphi in 1824. A brief rhymed skit, it opens with the announcement by Logic that both Tom and Jerry are dead; widespread mourning follows, leading to a funeral procession, crowned with the revelation that the whole thing has been a hoax and the two heroes are still very much alive. This much disconcerts the Charlies, who, on hearing of the cousins' deaths, have uttered 'dismal yells of demoniac joy, in a dreadful parody of the Witches Chorus in Macbeth'. Hardly in the nicest of taste, perhaps, Greenwood's piece is nevertheless amusing and lively. It contains some pleasant burlesque of current bombastic styles in the major theatres, such as Kate's lament:

Hung be the heaven with black, henceforth be seen
Yon azure firmament in bambazeen;
Ye summer clouds assume a grimmer shape,
And let your edges all be trimmed with crape;
Gone to that bourne from whence no soul returns,
To cheer the hapless, weeping o'er their urns.
Thou might'st as yet—the reck'ning Death have scor'd
And not the best of Toms—untimely floor'd.

Tom's supposed Will, as read by Logic, goes:

I will and bequeath to the girl I adore
My estate in the county of Ballynapore.
I give to Bob Logic, when I'm in the dust,
My new *Lilly Topper*, and best *upper crust*.
My courage I leave to the lads of the *ring*
And my *mufflers* (three pair) to Neate, Randall and Spring;
Item, I bequeath, as 'twill be a dry job,
A bottle of *daffy* to young *Dusty Bob*.
To the Charlies, new words—to the ancient *Te Deum*,
My *Sketches by Cruiks.* to the *British Museum*;
I leave poor *John Bull*, who talent espouses
Some *blunt* to improve *Minor Managers' Houses*.
I leave to Pierce Egan, lest his muse should be undone,
An *unfinished sketch* for a new *Life in London*.
My *Tattler* I leave to my laundress, sweet Nancy,
And my *coinage of words*, in a lump, to the Fancy.

What had Pierce Egan been up to while all and sundry in the theatrical world were exploiting his book and the fashion it had started? Had things gone right for him, he may well have anticipated Moncrieff's success, although, as we shall see later, he had even less than Moncrieff's literary skill in the theatre and very little of that dramatist's practical know-how. Five days after the first dramatic version of the book, Barrymore's, opened at the Royal Amphitheatre, Egan wrote on 21 September 1821 to Harris, then Manager of Covent Garden, offering him a Tom and Jerry play of his own. Harris replied favourably, and Egan made proposals for a pantomime. As Harris preferred a 'comic opera', Egan prepared an elaborate outline for such a version in twenty-three scenes, incorporating the main incidents of *Life in London*, but rounding the work off neatly.

On 4 December, after considerable delay, Harris rejected Egan's play with the following note:

Sir—The subject of Life in London has now become so hacknied by its production at the Minor Theatres, that I should despair of its proving successful with us, particularly as, according to your sketch, I perceive it must take nearly the same feature. I return it, therefore, with my thanks, and I am,

Your obedient servant,
H. Harris.

As Egan remarks in the opening of *Finish*, 'After the above unexpected disappointment, well might the *poor scribbler* exclaim—where now are all my flattering dreams of joy?' By December, of course, several versions were already on the boards and Moncrieff's piece had begun its sensational run. Harris, incidentally, while rejecting Egan's burletta, had meantime no scruples about staging Moncrieff's in Dublin. As the theatrical season was ending, Egan's version failed to reach the stage until 1822, when Egerton, the manager of Sadler's Wells, accepted it. On 8 April 1822, Egan's *Tom and Jerry* opened at 'the Wells'; after a lengthy season, it was transferred to the Olympic, where on 2 January 1823 it ended a very respectable run of 191 nights. One of the ironies of this incident is that seven years later Covent Garden presented *Tom and Jerry* with considerable success and much to Egan's disgust.

Unfortunately, his burletta was not published. To judge from the reviews of it and the songs, which did find their way into print, it seems to have been a respectable enough piece of work. The *Morning Herald* of 9 April praised Egan's enriching of his book with new scenes and humour and the play's impressive moral lesson on 'the folly and danger to health and reputation attending the nightly sprees and profligate adventures which young men of fortune are too much in the habit of encountering'. On 11 April it returned to the play to laud its superiority in plot to the other 'unconnected extravaganzas' and its excellent scenes of low life, concluding: 'we do not think that the cause of morality can suffer anything from the pictures of vice and folly which it presents'.

Egan, in fact, had spared no effort to introduce novelty into the bur-letta. It ended with Tom and Jerry at the Grand Sweepstakes, 'for which purpose a commodious course by means of platforms over the orchestra (completely railed in) has been constructed, passing into and round the Pit, giving the audience a perfect and safe view of the whole race'. Several pony races began from the stage into and through the pit, concluding with the 'Grand Sweepstakes', in which six ponies raced three times round the auditorium to the winning post on the stage. The playbill contains the following warning:

The eagerness of several Ladies and Gentlemen to Promenade
the Course during the Race having at times produced a
temporary delay and inconvenience, they are respectfully
entreated to observe the directions of the Clerk of the Course
(Dusty Bob—Walbourn), who will attend with Mrs Dusty Bob
(African Sal) in their Carriage from *Murder Lane, Battle
Bridge,* for the purpose of preserving order.

Robert Cruikshank did a special engraving of this final scene, which
appears on the programme. It is interesting to note that when Sadler's
Wells mounted a '1683–1969' exhibition in the latter year this Cruikshank engraving was chosen to appear on the poster. The pony races
and the exhibition of the art of self-defence in the scene in Jackson's
rooms indicate that Egan's piece relied at least as much upon the appeal
of such entertainments to the Fancy as it did upon its presentation of
London life.

Before the Tom and Jerry craze hit the British stage, Egan had displayed a special interest in the theatre, as is shown by the attention given
to drama and acting in *Life in London.* But there is no doubt that the
great financial success of dramatized versions of his book developed in
him a veritable passion for the stage, as well as the idea that he could
make a good deal of money from drama. He could see no reason why
managers and slapdash hacks should grow fat by exploiting his ideas and
he be left with the mere scraps of regard and rewards. Nor could he see
why, since he was already well known as an entertainer, he should not
take a direct part in the performance of the plays.

Thus on 24 February 1822, the *Weekly Dispatch* contained the following notice: 'Adelphi Theatre. *Tom and Jerry or Life in London.* Pierce
Egan respectfully informs his numerous friends and the sporting world
that his Night takes place in the course of a fortnight, when the part of
Bob Logic (at the particular request of several of his patrons) will be
most humbly attempted by the Original Author.' The benefit and Egan's
dramatic debut were a decided success. The *Weekly Dispatch* of 17
March devoted most of its review to an analysis of Pierce in his new role.
It began by confessing fears as to his adequacy:

> We will readily admit we heard of Mr Egan's Thespian
> undertaking with notions of acute apprehension for his dramatic
> fame, not that these notions were the creation of a moment's
> doubt as to his perfect comprehension of the Oxonian's character,
> but we held in our mind's eye the vast difference between the
> just *conception* of a part, and the due *histrionic development* of it.

But it goes on to praise his 'chaste and sinewy piece of acting'.

It was not within the power of gratification to have *dished up* a
more attic treat than we partook of in witnessing the respectable
Author of *Boxiana* in one of the happiest characters of his own
ingenious modelling. So intense had been the interest created in
the sporting circles to behold Pierce's *debut* at the dramatic
scratch, that for days previous to the *noon of his glory*, not a single
seat could be procured (for love or *blunt*) and long before the rise
of the curtain, the house overflowed almost to suffocation. Many
of our readers will no doubt have heard the *uproarious*
applause that occasionally bursts from a ring during the gallant
struggle within it, and to such welkin shouts only can we
assimilate the peals of approbation that greeted Mr Egan on his
appearance last Monday.

Pierce, the *Dispatch* does not fail to note, had at times some difficulty in
knowing what to do with his hands,

and had it not been for the friendly shelter of his *off side* breeches
pocket and the still more effective agency of his *spread* [umbrella]
we are free to think his *maiden* essay might not have appeared so
unequivocally graceful. Taking it as a whole, however, we
assuredly were never better pleased with an evening's
entertainment . . . . When the curtain fell but *one opinion* seemed
to represent the feeling of the house and, as delighted spectators
ourselves, we heartily congratulated Mr Egan upon his creditable
Identity with [one of his own] characters.

Of course, the Daffy Club was there in force, as was the Metropolitan
Ring Society, with Gentleman Jackson at its head. The success of Egan's
initial histrionic venture gave him a taste for the boards. He was to play
Bob Logic many more times, as well as other roles in his own pieces.

It says much for Pierce Egan's stamina and resource that he was able,
when almost fifty, to add acting in the professional theatre to his already
multitudinous activities, and, at an age when many men were, in his day,
slowing down, to seek fresh avenues for self-expression. By this time he
had become one of the most celebrated of London personalities. His
name crops up in all kinds of contexts. *Blackwood's*, of course, continued
to take frequent notice of his doings. More often than not it was 'Christopher North' himself who held the pen, as in the 'Open Letter to
Pierce Egan' in the issue of March 1821, which, in the usual half-
mocking Wilson way, after mildly chiding Egan for reproducing a

Cockney article in his *Sporting Anecdotes*, praises his 'striking volumes' and his role as 'the great lexicographer of the Fancy'. Wilson, too, had spoken in *Blackwood's* of occasionally dining in Egan's company at the One Tun, and of being allowed to admire his cast of Jackson's arm. On one occasion, the *Blackwood's* fraternity of authors sent out a jesting letter to Egan, facetiously inviting him to attend an *Edinburgh Magazine* dinner. To their surprise and pleasure, he turned up for the evening and joined in their convivialities.[14]

The gifted young John Hamilton Reynolds paid his special tributes to Egan in *The Fancy: A Selection from the Poetical Remains of the late Peter Corcoran, of Gray's Inn, Student at Law*. This delightful collection of parodies, which gave enormous pleasure to the Fancy, was fathered on an imaginary law-student who, by a strange coincidence, had the same name as a celebrated pugilist and who became, as Reynolds himself did, an addict of the ring and a frequenter of the Castle Tavern, passing his days in bed 'or over *Boxiana*'. In one of the poems, 'The Fields of Tothill', a Byronic imitation, there is a cynical definition of 'the Fancy':

> Fancy's a term for every blackguardism—
> A term for favourite men, and favourite cocks—
> A term for gentlemen who make a schism
> Without the lobby, or within the box—
> For the best rogues of polish'd vulgarism,
> And those who deal in scientific knocks—
> For bull-dog breeders, badger routers—all
> Who live in gin and jail, or not at all.

Egan himself receives a different treatment. In 'Stanzas to Kate on Appearing Before Her after a Casual Turn Up' there are these lines:

> Forgive me—and never, oh, never again,
> I'll cultivate light blue, or *brown* inebriety;
> I'll give up all chance of a fracture or sprain,
> And part, worse than all, with Pierce Egan's society,

to which Reynolds appends a note:

> The author of *Boxiana*—a gentleman of considerable talent and unassuming manners. His writings are replete with gaiety, information, and spirit; and there are few authors who have made history the vehicle of so much life and charm as Mr Egan. He is an intelligent man in conversation, a clever pedestrian, and a pleasant singer. That man is no contemptible caterer of joy in

life's feast, who can walk about and collect knowledge, write poetry on what he has seen—and sing it with a cheerful and good voice to his friends. Mr Egan deserves this note and it is devoted to him.

The Fancy ends in the almost obligatory fashion for such books at the time with a glossary of slang terms, including 'Fancy—Life preserved in spirit', 'Half-and-half—3 quarters of porter and one quarter of ale (Exquisite at Belcher's)', and '*Boxiana*—The Lives of the Pugilists in 2 volumes'.

Egan was 'Glorious Pierce' and 'Fancy's Child' to the Fancy and 'Pip' or 'Pippy' to his friends (several letters to the editor of *Pierce Egan's Life in London* newspaper are so inscribed). Both groups were proud to hang upon their walls the engraving published from 71 Chancery Lane by Egan in February 1823 from Sharples's oil portrait of him, which had been exhibited at the Royal Academy in 1821. This very popular engraving was reissued in 1832.

Egan's main activities at this time, despite his new interest in matters theatrical, were concerned with the ring. The prominent part he played in arranging bouts, holding stakes, organizing the articles, selecting places for contests, refereeing, bringing pugilists together and presiding over inquiries into the conduct of bouts shows the esteem in which the sporting fraternity held him. He was the witness to an agreement between William West and Thomas Spring on 12 March 1822 to fight for £200. On 23 October of the same year he was voted into the chair at a meeting at the One Tun, Jermyn Street, to investigate an allegation of a cross in the fight on the previous day at Moulsey Hurst between Ward, 'The Black Diamond', and Abbot, when Ward went down. It was decided by the meeting that the bout had indeed been fixed. On 5 February 1823 there was a display of boxing at the Fives Court by Spring, Cribb, Belcher and others in aid of the widow and children of Tom Hickman, 'The Gas Man', who had been killed in a drag-cart accident. Egan made the appeal from the stage and later gave thanks to the sportsmen for 'shelling out their blunt' to the tune of £136. He was one of those who attended the funeral of Hickman. He also collected from the stage of the Surrey Theatre in 1824 at a similar exhibition raising money for the Irish Champion, John Langan.

In November 1823, at a meeting of the Partiality Club at the Blue Anchor, Smithfield, Egan proposed, seconded by Tom Owen, that a silver cup to the value of 100 guineas be presented to Josh Hudson, 'The John Bull Fighter', 'for the courage displayed by him at all times in the prize-ring'. On 6 May 1824 Hudson was presented with the cup at a Partiality Club dinner; it was filled with bottles of port and placed on display in front of the Chairman—Pierce Egan. According to the taste of the day, it was a magnificent object, in the shape of a heart and inscribed with these deathless lines by the author of *Boxiana*:

> John Bull in the ring has so oft played his part,
> The form let it be in the shape of a heart—
> A true British one! at its shrine take a sup.
> Can a more noble model be found for a cup?

And so it was to be for the next few years. Again and again Egan's name keeps cropping up in the annals of the ring. At a dinner at Ben Bunn's, Great Windmill Street, on 21 October 1824 he was in the chair when a quarrel broke out between Cribb and Tom Belcher, the brother of Jem and also a pugilist, over stake-money held by Cribb; Cribb struck Belcher, who brought a charge of assault. This was heard in December and the jury awarded Belcher £100 in damages. When Josh Hudson fought Tom Cannon for £1,000 at Warwick in November 1824 it was Egan who superintended the erection of the stage. In February 1825 Jem Ward, challenging Tom Cannon for £1,000, gave Egan authority to make the match. Egan attended the funeral of Ned Turner on 23 April 1826 at Aldgate Churchyard, riding in the first coach with Turner's relatives. He held the deposit and nominated the place of fighting for a bout between Ned Neale and Philip Sampson on 12 December 1826. On 26 July of the same year he presided over a meeting of the Fancy in the King's Head, Birmingham, after the fight between Pat Magee and Jem Burn. He was the stake-holder for the bout on 23 January 1827 at Monmouth Gap between 'Young Gas' Bissell and Robinson, and chaired the convivial meeting at Spring's pub in Hereford the night before the fight. On 26 June 1827 he placed £20 in the hands of the chairman at Belcher's as a deposit on a £300-a-side contest between Ned Brown and Jem Ward. He presided over the celebration of Ned Neale's defeat of Jem Burn at the Bull's Head, Saffron Hill, on 27 November 1827, and proposed a 100-guinea cup for Neale, opening the subscription himself. He also spoke at the Tennis Court on 21 July 1828 at Neale's benefit and presented him with the cup. In May 1828, when Neale fought Ned Baldwin, Egan chose the ground. As late as 4 January 1829 he witnessed the articles of agreement between Tom Brown and Isaac Dobell to fight for £550. These are only a handful of his pugilistic activities as recorded in *Boxiana* or in the various newspapers of the time.

It is impossible to imagine boxing in its palmy days without Egan.

Short of taking part in bouts himself, he seems to have performed almost every function a devotee could, and to have been regarded by all and sundry as oil in the machine. His 'eccentric' ways, his vivacity, his enthusiasm, his sense of fair-play, his expert knowledge, his drive, his ability to make a friendly evening 'go' made him, after Gentleman Jackson, the most celebrated boxing personality of his age. It cannot have been easy or always pleasant to have been so closely engaged in the business of pugilism. The boxers and their supporters, euphoric from victory or morose from defeat, and inflamed by copious draughts of porter, gin, brandy and beer in smoke-filled, noisy taverns, were quick to use their fists in an argument, and often heads and feet as well. While most of the social gatherings appear to have been little less decorous than a Buffaloes' 'smoke concert', sometimes violence erupted, oaths and fists flew freely and not even a peace-making chairman was spared. More than once Egan arrived home slightly damaged from such a mêlée or, if physically whole, in a state of advanced intoxication. His loss of his 'reader' while 'under the weather' during the course of *Life in London* has been noted. In his recollections, a contemporary[15] tells of another occasion in which 'Fancy's Child' had been attending a masquerade organized by the Fancy, and at the end of the evening was in a temporary state of collapse. He was put into a cab, 1s. 6d. was placed in his pocket and the cab-driver told to be careful of his load, since his burden was none other than a visiting foreign nobleman. On arriving at the given address near Soho Square, the driver found ten door-bells and pulled them all. Since it was four o'clock in the morning, the result was to produce ten indignant heads. 'I have a foreign nobleman in the cab,' said the cab-driver. 'No nobleman, foreign or domestic, lodges here,' answered the best-informed occupant, 'and the sooner you move off the better.' 'I'm positive he's a foreign nobleman,' said the driver. 'He's got money in his pocket.' This produced a sensation and a crowd collected around the cab, attracting the attention of a policeman. Egan, still insensible, was extricated from his recumbent position at the bottom of the vehicle 'rolled up after the manner of a hedgehog at the approach of winter, owned by the affectionate partner of his sorrows and his joys, conveyed upstairs with some difficulty, put to bed, and attended with conjugal solicitude. He arose the next morning like a "giant refreshed with wine", and made his appearance at his usual haunts unscathed by the effects of his nocturnal indulgence and ready to commence *de novo*. He was accustomed to relate the story with great good humour.'

There were other hazards, too, in the kind of life Egan was living, of a more dangerous kind. It was not wise to be too close to the ring, for instance, when spectators, enraged by a seeming cross, flooded violently in to form a struggling, cursing, brawling mass, sweeping officials and reporters before them, or when an enthusiastic boxer hurled his opponent into the nearest crowd of watchers. During the bout between Barney Aaron and Dick Curtis on 27 February 1827, on a stage behind the Queen Charlotte at Andover, Curtis

> by a sudden impulse, gave Barney a hoist between the ropes, and he would have fallen at least six feet from the ground, which in all probability might not only have put an end to the contest, but might have cost the Jew his life. Fortunately for the Star of the East, a waggon had been placed near to the stage for the accommodation of the Reporters, Umpire and Referee; whence Pierce Egan and another scribbler caught hold of him by the arm and his leg, and rescued the Jew from his perilous situation.[16]

Egan was, of course, used to this sort of thing. But positions so close to the ring were not for the squeamish. Charles Knight, the well-known publisher of cheap and informative literature and friend of Dickens, tells us in his memoirs:

> The only exhibition of pugilism I ever saw was perfectly unmolested by justice or constable. It was on Maidenhead Thicket, where the renowned Pierce Egan, with a considerate regard for a brother of the Press, got me a good place, out of which I escaped as fast as I could when I saw Young Dutch Sam fall across the ropes with a broken arm.[17]

❦ VI ❦

Jack Thurtell and Others

Egan's close association with pugilism, involving as it did frequent journeys often far out of London, did not interfere with his other pursuits. He was still the boxing correspondent of the *Weekly Dispatch* and was producing sporting paragraphs for other newspapers as well, and he had opened a 'tiny crib' at 71 Chancery Lane as a sporting bookseller. His shop was not only a show-place for the many sporting books, prints and newspapers of the time and a bureau for tickets for benefits and exhibition bouts, but also a main clearing-house for information about the sport. As soon as the word got around that there was to be a contest between two giants of the ring, Egan's shop would be besieged by hundreds of members of the Fancy seeking details of the venue. None of this could have been bad for business.

Egan gives an interesting portrait of himself as he was at this time (1822)—interesting because it is the only personal description in all his writings (and, characteristically, it takes the form of an enormous foot-note) and because of the detailed impression it presents of the man both in his everyday working attire and in his Fancy rig-out. The passage describes his first encounter with the young artist, Theodore Lane, who was later to work closely with Egan as an illustrator:

> Strange to say, instead of exploring the classic regions as a mart
> for his talents—instead of making his bow to Mr Murray, or
> offering his designs to the 'all-publishing' Mr Colburn, as a
> decided proof of his ignorance in these matters, not to say bad

taste, he [Lane] knocked at the door of the humble *domus* of the
scribbler of 'Life in London' in the year 1822, between the hours
of eight and nine o'clock in the morning, in Spann's Buildings,
St Pancras. 'Admit him!' was the cry, something similar to the
rough accent of the most noble grand of a lodge of Odd Fellows,
when the heavy chain behind the door of the lodge is thrown down
for the entrance of the novice, and Lane ascended into the
presence of the *slang* writer he had heard so much talk about. It
is most true that Theodore Lane did not exclaim, nor start after
the highly-finished manner of the late John Kemble—

> Angels and ministers of grace defend us!
> Be thou——?

neither did he 'run away' like Monsieur Tonson, but he appeared
very much surprised, as if he had mistaken the apartment, on
beholding a person busily employed in writing, whose head
appeared to him like the rough hedgehog, with a beard of nearly
four days' growth—a waistcoat which had seen much better days,
discovering a part of his naked breast—aged pantaloons, that
would have puzzled any draper as to their original colour—a coat
or rather a part of one, that might once have been the pride of a
Snyder as to its fashionable recommendation, but then reduced to
a worn-out thread-bare remnant—and with slippers to correspond,
the sad relics of better days. The *tout ensemble* like one of the
members of the Bampfylde Moore Carew Club, well dressed for
the part, although put on without the aid of a reflecting mirror—
worn only for ease, and without a single thought as to the value of
appearance. The dress bad enough (according to the accepted
term of 'First Impressions') and the *ad*-dress, merely exempt from
rudeness, perhaps in perfect *keeping* with the other parts of the
character. Lane, not exactly recovered from his surprise, observed,
'I believe I am speaking to Mr Egan?' 'Most certainly, sir. Pray
be seated; but I shall be candid with you, as *time* is on the wing
with me; I am compelled to finish a few lines for the press—my
prad is at the door, and as I must have two-pen'north of decency
before I start for the *mill*, while I am togging myself, I can listen
to you with every attention; therefore, if you will have the
kindness to get over the ground as fast as you can, I shall feel
very much obliged to you.' Lane, with considerable modesty,
presented to my view, six designs, observing at the same time—
'Sir, if you will undertake to write a work to accompany these

illustrations, it will be of great service to me, and I assure you
Mr Ackerman or Mr Sherwood will purchase the manuscript.'
'But have you any material, Mr Lane?' 'None, sir! But I have no
doubt with your intimate acquaintance with so many theatrical
persons, and your knowledge of the stage, it will be a matter of
little, if any, trouble to you to prepare the work in question.' 'To
deal fairly with you, Mr Lane, my *upper works* at the present
moment are so overcharged with the *Fancy*, that I cannot lose the
time to spare a single thought upon the *imagination*; and
therefore, I am sorry to say, that I must decline your offer.' By
this time the *barbatic* had changed the appearance of that face
which at first had caused him to start, ten to one, more in favour
towards the *agreeable*; the comb had also given a more decent
appearance to the *nob*, and the fretful porcupine quills had been
reduced to something like order; the white *cameza* gave that sort
of improvement to the figure, like a dirty room that has
experienced white-washing; the Belcher *Fogle* round the squeeze
did not only add to but improve the *look*—the white cords and
top boots were also an improvement—and the Witney upper
Benjamin, decorated with large mother o' pearl buttons, now
encompassed the frame—the *castor* (one of Perring's lightest, but
knowing) covered the knowledge box!—the gloves on—the
persuader in the hand—and 'time' called to mount the *drag*, to
bear in mind that 21 miles must be accomplished before one o'clock.

Hear it not, Mr Northcote—do not listen to it, Sir Martin Shee,
Knt., that instead of a classical hero being called upon to do
justice to the drawings of the enterprising Theodore Lane—just
upon entering one of the most arduous and difficult professions
in life, instead of having to encounter the microscopic eye of the
critic—the rigid pause—the slow, half-suspended sentence
from the man of judgment—which so often makes tyros wince
again, and proficients tremble—the hopes and fears on all sides
attached to merit—behold *One of the Fancy* selected to give an
opinion—with 'Ya! hip!' escaping from his lips, anxious to 'push
along and keep moving' until the grand object in view—the prize
ring—appeared in sight! 'Good by, my dear fellow' (giving Lane's
talented bunch of fives a friendly shake), 'come and see me as
often as you think proper; tho' I do not possess the vanity to set
myself up as a judge in these matters, believe me, I always feel
myself honoured by the *call* of a man of talent.' Poor Lane
seemed sadly disappointed with the termination of the interview

—the chance was lost—not only as to his appearing before the
the public as an artist—but his designs, at least for some time,
were nothing more than waste paper as to the production of the
cash (always so much in request by the *needy* artist) and he
'toddled off' with a countenance more in sorrow than in anger!
The *prad* on feeling the whip was off in prime style, displaying
fine action like a first-rate player—and in less than an hour I had
joined the bustle on the road with lords and commoners—and
'seven to four, you don't name the winner' soon *distanced*
Theodore Lane and his drawings completely out of my mind.
Such is the fate of genius![1]

Despite Lane's disappointment on this occasion, the work he had
proposed to Egan was, in fact, as we shall see, to be accomplished
two years later.

Much of Egan's energy during this year was taken up with his
venture into the theatre, but he found time for something new again.
This was his first excursion into 'rogue literature' with his account of the
Life and Adventures of Samuel Denmore Hayward, the Modern Macheath,
which originally appeared in instalments in the *Weekly Dispatch* and was
later published as a book by Sherwood, Neely and Jones. As has been
mentioned, stories and ballads of rogues, highwaymen, tricksters and
murderers were much in demand at the time; plays dealing with eighteenth century and more recent criminals, such as Dick Turpin, Jonathan
Wild, Sixteen-String Jack and others, crowded the stage, contemporary
murderers were celebrated in tracts and broadsides, and Jemmy Catnach
and his kind poured out thousands of copies of the alleged 'dying
speeches' of executed rogues. Egan had already had a thorough experience of such publications, both during his period working for Smeeton
and as a publisher himself of popular material. To a certain extent, too,
Life in London, in so far as it portrayed aspects of low life, impinged upon
current criminal literature. It was almost inevitable that sooner or later
he would write something dealing with a contemporary real-life rogue.
In fact, the Hayward book was only the first of several such works which
were to come from his pen.

Because of its sub-title, *The Life and Adventures of . . . Hayward* has
been assumed by some commentators to be the tale of a highwayman.[2]
Actually it is the cautionary account of the career of a petty swindler
and impostor who preyed upon women. Hayward, the son of a poor
journeyman currier, learned to ape the appearance and manners of a
gentleman while in the employ of an antiquarian and a military captain.

He then began to live upon his wits, obtaining credit by lies, forging banknotes and gambling. The military appearance he affected and his smooth manner gained him access to fashionable society, where he met his victims. He had especial success with women, and for a time lived off the mistress of a rich old man. On one occasion two prostitutes fought over him, like Polly and Lucy over Macheath in *The Beggar's Opera* (hence Egan's somewhat strained sub-title). 'Their clothes were literally torn off their backs, their pretty faces, also, were scratched, their eyes damaged', writes Egan. Hayward almost married a well-to-do young woman on the Isle of Wight, but was recognized in time by a sportsman as a passer of false cheques. He took money from a woman with eight children, and when he was arrested later, over 300 letters from various female conquests were discovered in his trunk.

Hayward soon overplayed his hand, however, and gradually became known throughout London society as a cheat and a fraud. He was reduced to petty theft and to bilking prostitutes. Eventually he joined a gang of house-breakers, and was caught by the watchman while robbing the house of a Mrs Stebbings. At his trial his elegant dress contrasted with the shabby appearance of Elkins, one of his confederates, and Hayward declared he was of noble parentage, until his real father, hearing of his fate, came to see him in prison and this lie was exposed. Hayward was found guilty and executed on 25 November 1821 at the age of twenty-four.

Egan's account of Hayward's life and trial is efficiently carried out and salted with sprinklings of his characteristic style: 'The game was now drawing fast to a *close*; our hero had played nearly all his best *cards*: and he could no longer follow *suit* (i.e. *tip* the *blunt*), so as to prevent his pillow from being a *restless* one, or to make his home a place of safety.' The whole purpose of the book, Egan asserts in Defoe-like manner, is to warn 'the genteel and higher classes of society to be more on their guard in future, respecting the too careless mode of introducing young men into the bosom of their families, as if nothing else was necessary than an outward appearance', and also to remind the youth of England 'that, in all situations of life, and under every difficulty, it will be found that *Honesty is the Best Policy*'. *The Life and Adventures of . . . Hayward* was popular; it ran into a second edition in the same year, and to this were added a facsimile of Hayward's handwriting and a miniature of the criminal etched by Robert Cruikshank.

Egan dedicated the work to Hayward's defence counsel, the most volcanic criminal lawyer of the day, James Harmer, who was to acquire the *Weekly Dispatch* in the 1830s and make it the leading ultra-Radical journal in England. Harmer's dynamic personality had a particular appeal for Egan, although he could share nothing of the lawyer's reformist outlook. Harmer was a doughty fighter for changes in the criminal law of the time, especially with reference to capital punishment. He was also a fierce opponent of the Establishment in Church and State and an assiduous smeller-out of unsavoury scandals among the wealthy and the titled. By its vigorous attacks on the Government, its accounts of goings-on in high society, its reformist politics, its coverage of the prize-ring and other sports and its stories of Newgate characters, the *Weekly Dispatch* greatly increased its circulation under Harmer's control, rising from 30,000 in 1836 to 60,000 in 1840, a remarkable figure for the time. Harmer, a 'hope of the hopeless' for criminals, was making an income of some £4,000 a year when he retired from his solicitor's practice in 1833; when he died he left an estate of £300,000, a great deal of it from the *Weekly Dispatch*. But all this was to happen some years after Egan and Harmer first became acquainted during the Hayward trial.

In 1822 Egan managed to put out still another book—one of some importance in its influence. This was his version of the well-known *Classical Dictionary of the Vulgar Tongue*, by Captain Francis Grose, first issued in 1785. In his 1963 edition of Grose, Eric Partridge, mis-dating Egan's book as 1823,[3] chides the latter for describing his edition as the third, whereas it was, in fact, says Partridge, the fifth, and also for claiming to refine Grose, while actually excluding hardly anything indelicate. On the first point, Partridge is technically correct. Egan seems to have been unaware of the fact, or considered it unimportant, that there were three editions by Grose himself—1785 and 1788 and 1796. In any case he used only the last of these. This he carefully collated, however, with the curious version called *Lexicon Balatronicum: A Dictionary of Buckish Slang, University Wit, and Pickpocket Eloquence*, by 'a member of the Whip Club [H. Clarke], assisted by Hell-Fire Dick and James Gordon, Esqrs. of Cambridge, and William Soames, Esq., of the Hon. Society of Newman's Hotel'. The *Lexicon* adds to Grose a good number of words and phrases from sport and from upper-class slang.

> Our Jehus of rank [says the preface], have a phraseology not less peculiar to themselves than the disciples of Barrington. To sport an Upper Benjamin and to swear with a good grace are qualifications easily attainable by their Cockney imitators; but, without the aid of our additional definitions, neither the cits of Fish-street, nor the boors of Brentford would be able to attain

4 Tom and Jerry getting the better of a Charley by Robert and George Cruikshank

5 Tom, Jerry and Logic at 'All Max' by Robert and George Cruikshank

the language of whippism. . . . They may now talk bawdy
before their papas, without fear of detection, and abuse their less
spirited companions, who prefer a good dinner at home to a
glorious *up-shot* in the highway, without the hazard of a
cudgelling.

Egan's edition was attacked in its own day by his tireless adversary,
'Jon Bee'. In his *Slang: A Dictionary of the Turf, The Ring, The Chase,
The Pit, of Bon-Ton and the Varieties of Life* (1823) Badcock alleges
that Egan's work was undertaken in haste so as to forestall *Slang*, which
Egan had somehow learnt was in preparation, so that he did not have
time for the necessary research, and merely added copious extracts from
the *Lexicon* to Grose, embellishing these with 'the introduction of
several inventions of the editor's own manufacture'. Neither Badcock's
waspishly jealous criticisms nor the strictures of Partridge ('his additions
are typically Regency slang, and he inserted a great deal of self-advertisement') are just to Egan's very interesting and skilful work.

A comparison of Egan's edition, Grose's 1796 version and the *Lexicon*
shows that Egan had very carefully collated the two latter, dropping
some of Grose's entries as obsolete and taking over some of the Whip
Club's slang. He also added many new entries, by no means all of them
Regency slang, amounting to over a sixth of the total, expanded explana-
tions and illustrations greatly and often modified the original definitions.
For instance, Grose's and the *Lexicon*'s' 'Abbess or Lady Abbess: a bawd,
the mistress of a brothel' becomes in Egan 'Abbess or Lady Abbess:
The mistress of a house of ill fame'. Several of the terms for the male
and female sexual organs and the sexual act itself in either or both Grose
and the *Lexicon* Egan suppresses, e.g. 'Bite: A cheat, also a woman's
privities' and 'Arbor Vitae: A man's penis'. Occasionally he tempers a
definition in the following amusing way: Grose and the *Lexicon* give
'Notch: The Private parts of a woman', but Egan puts it : 'Notch: The
monosyllable'. On the other hand, he sometimes adds 'obsolete' to
words found in both Grose and the *Lexicon*, such as 'Gregorian Tree:
The gallows', or to words found in Grose alone (which, by the way,
indicates the collation referred to above), such as 'Alsatia the Higher:
White-friars, once a place privileged for arrests for debt'. While some of
his alterations indicate a less direct and robust attitude than the eighteenth century found acceptable, Egan is no prude. He adds such items
as 'Blow: A prostitute' and 'Fancy Man: A petticoat pensioner; a fellow
kept by a prostitute'. (The *Lexicon* has for the latter 'A man kept by a
lady for secret services'.)

The main value of Egan's edition, however, lies in the additional matter, both in the new words and phrases he includes and in his expansions. It is again surprising to find how many of the terms he prints are still in general use, some having acquired respectability over the years. Among these are 'Racket', which he defines as 'Some particular kinds of fraud and robbery are so termed'; 'Hell or Hells: Gambling houses at the West End of the town'; 'Blow the Gaff: a person having any secret in his possession or a knowledge of anything injurious to another, when at last induced . . . to tell it openly to the world . . . is said to have blown the gaff upon him'; 'Bounce: To bully, threaten, talk loud, or affect great consequence'; 'Dandy: That's the dandy, i.e. the ton, the clever thing'; 'Throw Off: To talk in a sarcastical strain, so as to convey offensive allusions under the mask of pleasantry'; 'Yarn: Yarning or spinning a yarn is a favourite amusement among flash people, signifying to relate their various adventures, exploits and escapades to each other'. One wonders if there is any moral to be drawn from the fact that in Egan's day 'Bingo' was a term for brandy or other spirituous liquors.

His expansions of the other editors' definitions frequently swamp the original. For instance, the *Lexicon*'s three lines defining 'Swell' become twenty-eight in Egan; its two and a half lines for 'Square' become nineteen. His additions and amendments quite often reflect changes in social manners and outlook. Where both Grose and the *Lexicon* have 'Corinthians: Frequenters of brothels. Also an impudent, brazen-faced fellow', Egan, naturally, defines 'Corinthian' as 'The highest order of swells', and adds three lengthy verse quotations in illustration.

His own long definitions are, in fact, miniature essays in the style of his footnotes to *Life in London* on various aspects of contemporary manners, on the habits and mentality of sportsmen, criminals, the poor, the tricksters and the 'swells'; they provide a fascinating picture of further aspects of Regency life, and they show again Egan's remarkably intimate knowlege of low life. Three examples should suffice to indicate this:

Fakeman-Charley, Fakement: As *to fake* signifies to do any act, or make any thing, so *the fakement* means the act or thing alluded to, and on which your discourse turns; consequently any stranger, unacquainted with your subject, will not comprehend what is meant by *the fakement*; for instance, having recently been concerned with another in some robbery, and immediately separated, the latter taking the booty with him, on your next meeting you will enquire what he had done with *the fakement?*

meaning the article stolen, whether it was a pocket-book, piece of
linen or what not. Speaking of any stolen property, which has
a private mark, one will say, there is a *fakeman-charley* on it; a
forgery, which is well executed, is said to be a *prime fakement*; in
a word, any thing is liable to be termed a *fakement*, or a *fakeman-
charley*, providing the person you address knows to what you
allude.

The *Lexicon* gives 'Down: Aware of a thing, knowing it'. Egan continues:

Sometimes synonymous with *awake*, as when the party you are
about to rob sees or suspects your intention, it is then said that
the *cove is down*. A *down* is a suspicion, alarm, or discovery, which,
taking place, obliges yourself and *palls* to give up or desist from
the business or depredation you were engaged in; to *put a down
upon* a man, is to give information of any robbery or fraud he is
about to perpetrate, so as to cause his failure or detection; to
drop down to a person is to discover or be aware of his character
or designs; to *put* a person *down* to any thing, is to apprise him
of, elucidate, or explain, it to him. To *put* a *swell down*, signifies
to alarm or put a gentleman on his guard when in the attempt to
pick his pocket, you fail to effect it at once, and, by having touched
him a little too roughly, you cause him to suspect your design,
and to use precaution accordingly; or, perhaps, in the act of
sounding him, by being too precipitate, his suspicions may have
been excited, and it is then said that you have *put* him *down*, *put*
him *fly*, or *spoiled* him.

Accommodate or Accommodation: In the Sporting World, it is
to part a Bet, or to let a person go halves (that is, to *accommodate*
him) in a bet that is likely to come off successfully. It is, also, in
an ironical manner, to *believe* a person when you are well assured
he is uttering a lie; by observing you believe what he is saying,
merely to *accommodate* him.

The book contains a valuable study of Grose's life and character, from
which many later writers, including Partridge, have drawn. In his
Preface Egan says, after indicating that he has excluded some indelicate
expressions and softened others:[4]

If any apology is requisite, the subject in question must be viewed
as a *compilation* of sentences collected from the lower walks of
society, in which a scrupulous attention to *nicety* of expression is

neither expected nor looked for; the persons alluded to, from whose lips they have escaped, not being *'partiklar* as to a *shade'* in colouring their *lingo,* or displaying their *taste* for *erudition—* their only object being *effect.*

Grose's Classical Dictionary of the Vulgar Tongue became one of Egan's most popular publications. Its greater fullness, comprehensiveness and liveliness won it wider acceptance than any of the other many slang and cant glossaries circulating at the time. It was reprinted again and again until late in Victorian times, and became a popular source-book, together with *Life in London,* for such novelists as Ainsworth, Bulwer Lytton and Disraeli seeking for some authentic phrases with which to pepper their novels of low life or with which to define a criminal character.

The year 1823 began quietly enough for Egan. *Life in London* was reissued in parts and, as the vogue continued, quickly sold out. He published a trivial *jeu d'esprit, The Fancy Togs' Man versus Young Sandboy, the Milling Quaker,* a facetious description of a trial of 24 April in the court of Common Pleas, in which Mr Gore, a tailor or 'fancy togs' man', was the plaintiff and Edmund Foster, claiming to be a minor, the defendant. In July of the same year it was Egan himself who was the defendant in another case, playing a leading role in what must have been one of the most extraordinary cases ever to be heard in that home of extraordinary cases, the court of Chancery.

What happened was this: Egan was naturally eager to continue his successful series of *Boxiana* by adding more volumes. For some reason or other, he decided to publish a fourth book on his own account, instead of with Sherwood, Neely and Jones, who had issued the first three. Sherwood's applied for an injunction restraining Egan from publishing or selling a Vol. IV of *Boxiana,* declaring that, as he had done the previous volumes for them and as they held the copyright, he was not entitled to use the same name for a book to be published by himself. The case was heard from 24 July to 26 July before Lord Eldon, the Lord Chancellor, with Messrs Shadwell and Kennersly for the plaintiffs and Egan appearing on his own behalf. The result was a remarkable exchange, with Shadwell, Egan and the Lord Chancellor involved in a series of pugilistic puns and slang comments that reads like a passage from *Life in London.* The report has it:[5]

The Lord Chancellor said, that he had a very *long arm* in granting injunctions, but he doubted much whether, from what he had heard, the defendant came within his *reach.* His lordship had heard before of boxers getting each other 'into Chancery', but this, he believed, was the first time they had made their appearance in that Court.

Mr Pierce Egan then said, that he did not wish to occupy his lordship's valuable time with a waste of words; as the matter before the Court related to the art of *self-defence*, he might, perhaps, be pardoned, if, for once, he *took his own part*. The learned gentleman, his opponent, had doubtless made a great *display*, and been extremely *striking*: but, in his opinion, with all his *science*, he had not made one single *hit*.

Mr Shadwell—I find that I have now got into *Chancery* myself, but I hope Mr Egan will not *fib* me. [In boxing slang 'in Chancery' was to have one's head under an opponent's arm while he punched it; 'to fib' was to hit.]

Mr Egan—No: the learned gentleman, he believed, understood the art of fibbing infinitely better than himself. He should be perfectly satisfied by *flooring* a few of his assertions, and of satisfying his lordship that the present motion was a mere *feint* to induce him, the defendant, to *give in*.

The Lord Chancellor—Come, I think there has been quite enough *sparring*.

The argument proceeded with Egan, 'though he was no lawyer', challenging Sherwood's to produce the assignment of the copyright of *Boxiana*. Shadwell admitted that no legal deed existed, but contended that the payment of the consideration by the firm to Egan established them as holders of the copyright in equity. Egan further argued that, when he had expressed dissatisfaction with the sum offered him by Sherwood's for Vol. III, they had referred him to Longmans to see if he could get a better price, thus admitting that he possessed the copyright. After examining the volumes of *Boxiana*, the Lord Chancellor said: 'The *title* was of little object to Mr Egan, as his name would sell the work', and sent the parties off to try to agree on his suggestion of 'New Series of Boxiana' as Egan's title. 'Mr Egan then thanked his lordship for the attention he had paid to his remarks, bowed, and left the Court, in a whole skin, without either being *fibbed*, *scratched*, or *floored*; and remarked to a sporting wig, that it was only a little bit of *chaff-cutting*.'

The next day, however, Shadwell announced that the firm could not accept the Lord Chancellor's suggestion of a title for Egan's proposed work, and the Chancellor said he would give his judgment in the morning on the injunction. On 26 July the case was settled. Lord Eldon based his judgment on the fact that there had been no legal assignment of a copyright. Hence Egan was fully entitled, as author of the first three volumes, to continue the work on his own behalf, and thus the Lord Chancellor felt he must refuse the injunction. Egan left the court in triumph, firing a parting shot at Sherwood's: 'Although I sold the plaintiffs my book, I did not sell them my brain.'

What followed from this Chancery case adds even more confusion to Egan bibliography. In 1824, Sherwood, Jones and Co. published *Boxiana ... containing all the transactions of note connected with the Prize Ring during the years 1821, 1822, 1823*, dedicated to Colonel Berkeley. The advertisement on pp. vii-viii says:

> On the publication of a New Volume of *Boxiana*, the
> Proprietors take occasion to allude to the changes which it has
> been necessary to make in the Editorship, since the publication of
> the preceding volumes. In making this change, they have been
> induced to avail themselves of a gentleman of good practical
> knowledge and judgment on all parts of the subject, whereby
> they have been enabled to introduce much improvement, both
> in the plan and execution of the work.

No author's name is given, and the Dedication is signed simply 'The Editor'. But internal evidence strongly suggests that the author of Vol. IV of *Boxiana* was none other than Jonathan Badcock, Egan's enemy, and one of the few contemporaries whose knowledge of pugilism almost matched Egan's own. Despite these facts, Vol. IV is quite often bound in with Egan's third volume and the four parts attributed to Egan himself.[6]

Perhaps because Sherwood's got out their book so quickly, Egan postponed the publication of his own for five years, although he continued to issue the work in parts. When his *New Series of Boxiana* came out in 1828 it had a cock-a-hoop and effusive dedication of thanks to the Earl of Eldon, late Lord High Chancellor, in which Egan says, with typical impudent assertiveness:

> Unlettered, untutored, unaided and unadorned, I appeared in
> the Court of Chancery, most respectfully, before your Lordship,
> to take *my own part*—
>
> > True hope ne'er tires, but mounts on eagles' wings;
> > Kings it makes God, and meaner creatures kings!

Your Lordship's well known love of FAIR PLAY was nobly
developed in acting as *referee* on that occasion; it enabled me to
meet my adversary without *shifting*—parrying off his scientific
attacks with effect—hit him to a *stand-still*—ultimately *floor* the
Crown Lawyer, and enjoy the proud triumph of *winning* the GAME.

Before 1823 ended Pierce was in Court again, but this time as
reporter, not defendant. He was recording the sensational trial of
John Thurtell, William Probert and Joseph Hunt for the murder of
William Weare. The case, which was tried at the Hertford Assizes
beginning on 4 December, was the most-discussed trial of the day,
one which aroused extraordinary public interest and attracted the
fascinated attention of many distinguished writers of the age and later,
Borrow, Hazlitt, Lytton, Lamb, Scott, De Quincey and Carlyle among
them. In themselves, neither the crime nor the trial had any remarkable
features. The murder was a clumsy, brutal act of violence, easily detected, and there was no doubt as to the identity of the perpetrators. The
fact that it stirred up so much interest was almost certainly due to, on
the one hand, the increasing role of newspapers as reporters of criminal
proceedings and, on the other hand, the connection of John Thurtell,
the First Murderer, with the world of the Fancy and, in a minor way,
with the world of the theatre.

Thurtell, born in 1794, was the son of a prosperous Norwich merchant. He had held a naval commission and, after marrying in 1824,
had been set up by his father in business as a bombazine manufacturer.
But the attractions of sport, especially pugilism, and of London low
life interfered seriously with his business activities and he became a
familiar figure in flash circles.

I first became acquainted with John Thurtell [Egan wrote] by his
occasional visits to the metropolis about the years 1818 or 1819,
by accidentally meeting with him amongst the sporting characters
at the various houses in London kept by persons attached to
the sports of the field, horse racing and the old English practice
of boxing. . . . He was viewed as a young man of integrity.

But Thurtell's character deteriorated with his increasing dissipations.
He became suspected of dubious business practices and also of arson
for insurance, his business failed and he was forced to take the licence
of a tavern, The Black Boy in Long Acre. Here he kept a mistress and
entertained so many rough, brawling companions that he soon lost his
licence.

Then Thurtell moved into the fringes of the Fancy, where he became known as a hanger-on of pugilism, a small-time trainer and backer of boxers and a promoter. But his reputation was anything but good. He was known to have arranged crosses and also to be a coward. Although he posed as a fighter himself, he never met anyone of quality in the ring. Once he challenged Tom Belcher, but quickly withdrew when Belcher took up the gauntlet. Likewise, when challenged by Josh Hudson for some slighting comments on the John Bull Fighter's prowess, Thurtell declined to meet him. Just before the murder of Weare, then, Thurtell had become a typical member of the disreputable elements who haunted the resorts of the Fancy and lived on the margins of sport. He made his living by gambling, fraud, hazard, billiards and arranging crooked fights. At the same time he had a considerable conceit of himself and affected the style of a man of taste and talent. He had a theatrical manner and a gift for rhetoric, and was known in the taverns he frequented, such as the Brown Bear and the Army and Navy, for his imitations of Kean. Egan tells us how he used to recite speeches he had learnt off, and inquire of the listeners 'if that were not delightful?'

Like others of his kind, Thurtell was always short of cash, especially after one of his gambling sessions. Among his gambling companions was William Weare, an ex-waiter, billiards-sharp and expert gamester; the two often played at Wade's Mill in Hertfordshire, where pugilists were trained. Thurtell, a reckless player, frequently lost heavily. In October 1823 he was in particularly desperate straits when Weare returned from a most successful foray at the St Leger meeting at Doncaster. The latter was seen in the billiards saloon of the Coach and Horses, Conduit Street, with Thurtell, his brother, Tom Thurtell, a shady bankrupt, Joseph Hunt, an ex-convict, former manager of the Army and Navy Tavern and a chucker-out from gambling hells, and William Probert, another bankrupt, the burly son of a farmer and a hanger-on of the Fancy. On this night Weare, who was supposed to have been carrying a large sum of money, disappeared. The Thurtells, Hunt and Probert were quickly arrested by Bow Street Runners. Tom Thurtell was released for lack of evidence, then Hunt turned King's Evidence, blaming John Thurtell for the murder of Weare, whose body in a sack was then recovered from the green slime of Hill's Slough, Elstree, not far from Probert's cottage at Gill's Hill Lane.

The trial opened on 4 December at the Hertford Assizes before Mr Justice Park, and was later adjourned to 7 January 1824. Evidence at the trial, in which both Hunt and Probert tried to fix the primary guilt on Thurtell, resulted in a true bill against Hunt and Thurtell, with Probert named as accessory. Probert was acquitted, only to be hanged in the following year for horse-stealing. Hunt, sentenced to death, was reprieved and transported to Botany Bay. Thurtell was condemned to death and, in the speedy manner of those days, executed on 9 January 1824. One irony of the whole affair is that the murderers had found only a few pounds on Weare's dead body.

Both the trial and the execution of Thurtell became events of prodigious national interest. Thousands of people crowded into the little town of Hertford to witness the entertainment in the court-room or to glean gossip from the taverns. No previous criminal trial had been given such extensive coverage in the Press. The newspapers maintained express-riders in the town to rush the reporters' dispatches to London. One penny-a-liner declared that he had made £70 by his accounts for the journals. Here was a case that combined a sporting interest with a savage murder, and the newspapers had a field day. So free in fact were the Press comments that Mr Justice Park protested against such reports as those of *The Times* as biased and prejudging the case. The Thurtell trial was indeed the first trial by newspaper, as, despite the law, it was not to be the last.[7]

Even more flagrant anticipation of the jury's verdict was to be found in the theatre. Before Thurtell had been indicted, Mr Williams of the Surrey Theatre presented a cobbled-up piece entitled *The Gamblers*, in which the whole story was enacted, with Thurtell as chief murderer. Williams had enterprisingly bought the chaise in which Thurtell had driven Weare to the scene of the murder and in which he had first unsuccessfully and bunglingly tried to shoot him (he had to pursue the wounded man out of the chaise and finish him off). This play was halted by an injunction after criminal information was laid against Williams, but put on again following Thurtell's conviction. A second dramatization of the crime also played at the Royal Coburg.

Egan's report of the trial, which appeared as a booklet early in 1824, is the most comprehensive imaginable, a verbatim record of the proceedings, in addition to full descriptions of the principal figures and woodcuts of the scene of the murder and of the gig. It must have sold in huge numbers, for *Pierce Egan's Life in London* newspaper for 1 February advertised the thirteenth edition of *Pierce Egan's Account of the Trial*. Jemmy Catnach likewise did well out of Thurtell's misfortune, making some £500 out of penny broadsides on the affair.

More personal and more individual than the *Account* is Egan's separate booklet *Recollections of John Thurtell*, which quickly followed.

Here Egan drew upon his acquaintance with the murderer to give a rounded picture of his personality and considerable biographical detail. A particular feature of the *Recollections* are reports of two interviews Egan had with Thurtell in his cell on 4 December and 5 December. Such verbatim reports, especially of interviews, were most unusual for the day. So far as I can tell, they are among the first interviews with a criminal to appear in a newspaper, anticipating similar popular Press reports in Victorian and modern times. In the first interview the following exchange took place:

> Thurtell: But you are come down to Hertford to take a few minutes about me. I suppose (smiling).
>
> Egan: Yes, to cast my eyes around: to report what is going on: you know my forte.
>
> Thurtell: Yes, I have read many of your sporting accounts, with great pleasure: but I suppose you, like the rest of the press, have lashed me severely.
>
> Egan: No, upon my word, I have not written a single line at present about you to the public.

The interview ended with Thurtell requesting Egan to ask his solicitor to visit him. At the second interview.

> Thurtell read to me several detached parts of his defence, with strong emphasis, observing such a passage was 'beautiful', another was 'fine', and a third 'very good' . . . [He] then read the whole of his defence to me with great animation: but when he came to the passages which spoke of the piety of his mother and the universal good character of his father, his tongue faltered, and he put up his hand to wipe his eyes. Indeed, he was very much affected; and I partook of his sorrow, knowing him under circumstances of a very different description. . . .
>
> Thurtell: I would not attempt to impose on you in the slightest degree. I did not *commit* the murder. I declare solemnly to my God (*laying hold of my hand and pointing to the sky*). I did not *commit* it. I repeat to you (*with great animation*) by the Great God Almighty, before whom perhaps I shall appear in a short time, I did not *commit* it.

Nevertheless, Egan uses Thurtell's career and end as a warning against a dissipated life and indiscriminate mixing with riff-raff: 'I wish it most clearly to be understood, that I am not dazzled by his talents; I am not to be misled by his fortitude; neither am I to be deceived by that contempt for death which he displayed on the scaffold. .... I likewise most perfectly join in the verdict given by the jury, and the sentence of the learned judge.' But, he adds, 'I hope I shall not be despised when I acknowledge that Christian charity teaches me to pity his misfortune; to drop a tear over his errors and crimes, and to conclude with the words of the learned judge, "May God in his infinite mercy grant him the favour of his indulgence."'

The most extraordinary scenes, as Egan reports, attended Thurtell's execution on 9 January. The gallows was the first of its kind erected in Hertford, and some 15,000 people crowded into the small town to see its first victim die. The roads from London, Cambridge, St Albans and elsewhere were covered with vehicles of every description moving towards the place.

> In fact, all the rabble who are wont to frequent scenes of this description seemed to have congregated in Hertford upon this occasion. In many instances, where persons could not afford to pay for a conveyance to the spot, they walked from considerable distances, and submitted to no ordinary fatigue and inconvenience, in order to be present at the execution.

The roof of a barn on which men and boy spectators were crowded collapsed, injuring two boys seriously; the rest were saved by piles of straw.

According to Egan, standing with notebook and pencil at the foot of the gallows, Thurtell met his end with fortitude, saying to his gaoler, '"I admit that justice has been done—I am perfectly satisfied." He was in an instant launched into eternity. His sufferings were but momentary, for, with the exception of a few convulsive movements of his legs and hands, he seemed to be deprived of all sensation.' Egan gives a detailed and gruesome description of the appearance of the dead man's face and body after the cap was removed from his head. Just before the drop, he says, 'I received his last *nod*, or token of remembrance in this world', although one takes leave to doubt this.

The effect of Thurtell's fate upon contemporary writers testifies more to the power of the Press and the skill of Egan's reporting than it does to any special quality in Thurtell's personality. Hazlitt drew him, not unattractively, as Tom Turtle, in 'The Fight', but then Hazlitt knew very little about pugilism and was certainly ignorant of the mixture of courage, honour, and devotion with avarice, cunning and crime that characterized its various devotees. George Borrow took time off from his amateur philology, gipsy-fancying and Catholic-baiting to describe his encounter with Thurtell in *Lavengro*:

In the whole appearance of the man there was a blending of the bluff and the sharp. You might have supposed him a bruiser; his dress was that of one in all its minutiae; something was wanting, however, in his manner—the quietness of the professional man; he rather looked like one performing the part —well—very well—but still performing a part.

Borrow met Thurtell in 1820 at Westwick House on the North Walsham Road, where the former had gone to convey money from his employers to a Mr Petre. While Borrow waited, he witnessed an interview between Petre and Thurtell, who wanted to find a field for a fight between Ned Painter and Tom Oliver. Petre could not help him, since he was a magistrate, and Thurtell was forced to look elsewhere for a site. Later, Borrow was to see the contest, which he describes, at the same time recording the prophecy of his friend the gipsy, Petulengro, who, observing a strange cloud, foretold a bloody fortune for 'the sporting gentleman of my acquaintance'. Borrow was among the crowd when Thurtell was hanged.

Charles Lamb, who was not present, imagined what had happened. In a letter to Bernard Barton on the morning of the execution, he wrote:

'Tis 12 o'clock, and Thurtell is just now coming out upon the New Drop—Jack Ketch alertly tucking up his greasy sleeves to do the last office of mortality . . . It is just 15 minutes after 12. Thurtell is by this time a good way on his journey, baiting at Scorpion perhaps, Ketch is bargaining for his cast coat and waistcoat, the Jew demurs at first at three half crowns but on consideration that he may get somewhat by showing 'em in the town, finally closes.

Even Sir Walter Scott turned aside while on a journey to Scotland to inspect the green swamp into which Weare's body had been thrown; later he criticized John Bull for being 'so maudlin as to weep for the pitiless assassin, Thurtell'. A supposed, but apocryphal, reference by a witness during the trial that Thurtell must have been a gentleman 'because he kept a gig', was the source of Carlyle's terms, Gigmania and Gigmanity, his contemptuous words for social appearances of respectability.

It was from Egan that many such writers, including De Quincey and Lytton, learnt the full story of the Weare murder. That Egan, while deploring the deed and not glamorizing the murderer, somewhat enjoyed the special place his acquaintance with Thurtell gave him is shown

by the fact that he was more than once to quote in his various publica-
tions the report from the *London Magazine*: 'I know it for a fact that
Thurtell said, about seven hours only before his execution, "It is,
perhaps, wrong in my situation, but I own I should like to read Pierce
Egan's account of the great fight yesterday" (meaning that between
Spring and Langan). He had just inquired how it terminated.'

There is no doubt that Thurtell would have revelled in his posthumous celebrity. He was vain, boastful and had 'a sullen, low love of fame'.
'But what a piece of work this affair has made, ain't it? ... Do I
appear dejected?' he remarked just before his execution. The excitement
his crime stirred up and the publicity accorded it, which exceeded that
given to many great historical events, are curious aspects of an age in
which a morbid love of thrills and excitement and a certain taste for
cruelty existed side by side with genuine moral indignation and a pru-
dential sense of morals to be drawn.

The Thurtell affair had an odd sequel seven years later, involving
Egan and Bulwer Lytton. The account of the episode given by Bulwer's
grandson, riddled with condescension though it is, affords us one of
the rare glimpses of 'Fancy's Child' as seen by his contemporaries. The
Earl of Lytton writes:

> The book [*Eugene Aram*] brought Bulwer a curious compliment
> from another author of a very different type. Pierce Egan, author
> of *Life in London* and *Tom and Jerry* appears to have regarded the
> author of *Pelham* and *Paul Clifford* with the sort of mild
> approbation that a retired prize-fighter would bestow upon a
> promising young student of 'the noble science' and called upon him
> one day shortly after the publication of *Eugene Aram*. After a long,
> mysterious, and magniloquent exordium, in the purest dialect
> of the Seven Dials, he stated that he had called for the purpose
> of bestowing upon him a curiosity of the greatest interest and
> value—a unique treasure, of which, said the author of *Tom and
> Jerry*, the author of *Eugene Aram* was of all literary men the
> only one worthy to become the possessor. He then produced a
> silk bag, opened it, drew from it, and unfolded with great pride
> and admiration a repulsive object which was, he declared—the
> genuine caul of THURTELL the murderer!'[8]

Unhappily, Bulwer's grandson does not record the novelist's reaction
to this strange offering, nor whether or not he accepted it.

Early 1824 saw Egan involved, not only in the Thurtell trial and
reporting such events as the Spring-Langan bout, but with two other

projects of a demanding kind—a new book in parts and the establishing
of a newspaper. The first work, *The Life of an Actor*, is as complete a
testimony to his devotion to the theatre as *Boxiana* is to his interest in
pugilism. It was the first collaboration between Egan and the young
artist, Theodore Lane, whose seemingly abortive visit to him in 1822
has already been recorded; it was issued in monthly parts, illustrated
with hand-coloured aquatints, at 3*s*. each, beginning January 1824.
The complete volume, also with Lane's illustrations, hand-coloured,
appeared [in January 1825. It was Lane's first considerable work;
later he was to declare that it had been an important stepping-stone
for him towards recognition as an artist and illustrator. Certainly his
plates for Egan's book are exceptionally clever, not as individual,
perhaps, as the work of the Cruikshanks, but imaginative, full
of gay humour, quaint characters and realistic detail and skilfully
composed.

The Life of an Actor is fulsomely dedicated to Edmund Kean, who
was virtually adored by Egan and who is constantly referred to in his
writings as the greatest actor of his day—possibly, Egan infers, of all
time. The flamboyant romantic style of Kean, as well as his raffish
character and his delight in tavern carousing, made him the novelist's
obvious choice for his ideal man of the theatre. In this dedication Egan
apologizes for the episodic character of the book:

> The Work before you, Sir, has been produced at moments as
> it were *snatched*, a few at a time, from the small portion of
> leisure hours, which ought to have been devoted to relaxation
> and rest; indeed, after the drudgery and fatigue necessarily
> attendant upon a Weekly Journal was over; therefore the plates
> must plead as an apology for the insufficiency of the present
> Work. Peregrine Proteus was written principally to introduce
> the Artist to the attention of the Public.

Despite this modest disclaimer, despite, too, the fact that the novel
itself is still in its way picaresque in form, like its predecessors, in that
it wanders widely and encompasses many different scenes, it has more
of a plot, story, or at least progression than *Life in London*, and shows,
if tentatively, Egan's growing awareness of the need for more carefully
integrating his material.

The expected moral imperative is there, too. Egan begins at once by
disposing of the false glamour that surrounds the theatre. The life of an
actor, he warns, 'is far from proving a bed of roses'. The actor is, more
often than not, the 'plaything of circumstances'. Such remarks, he

avers, are intended 'to operate as a pause upon the feelings of those hot-headed, stage-struck youths'.

His hero, Peregrine Proteus, gets his first taste of the theatre from his teacher, an ex-actor, Mr Scenic Emphasis. Then, like Egan himself, he is apprenticed to a printer, Mr Quarto, from whose employees and books he receives further education. In Quarto's office, too, he makes friends with Horatio Quill, an aspiring dramatist. Together the two young men engage in amateur dramatics and Peregrine gradually becomes obsessed with the idea of a theatrical career. In various places haunted by actors, 'The House of Call', The Harp and William Oxberry's Craven's Head Tavern, he encounters seasoned professionals, several of whom warn him of the hazards of a life on the boards.

Eventually Peregrine is hired by Mr Plausible Screw, a theatre-manager and actor, to join his very mixed company. The young man is at once plunged into the squalor, disorder and frenzy of a third-rate touring band and is greatly disillusioned to discover that the provincial barns in which they play are very different from the elegant auditoriums of his imagination. However, he is a hit as Romeo, captivating the ladies of the company, who quarrel over him.

He returns home more determined than ever to succeed in the theatre; he studies leading parts and rehearses madly. His next engagement comes from Mr Up-to-Everybody, who finds a place for him at Brilliant Shore. He impresses his audiences, among them Sir Harry Gayboy, a lover of the drama, and makes an even deeper impression on Sir Harry's mistress, 'Fair Eliza'. Through his association with Sir Harry, Peregrine becomes intimate with Eliza. When the two, after a hectic love-affair, are discovered together by Sir Harry, Eliza leaves with the young actor, who is more than a little perturbed by the lady's importunity. She proves to be a very extravagant luxury, and Peregrine is soon heavily in debt and tired of what has become an incubus.

Eventually Eliza leaves him. Peregrine, upset by the whole affair, loses his reputation as an actor. His 'benefit' plays to almost empty houses, and he quits Brilliant Shore for London. Here he is tracked down by bailiffs and sent to a debtors' prison (as, indeed, are so many of Egan's characters). Among his assorted companions in misery there is Bob Thimble, a former tailor's assistant, whose rapid-fire conversation marks him as one of Mr Jingle's immediate ancestors. Horatio Quill visits Peregrine and helps him to find a way out of the prison, which he quits, like Mr Dorrit, to a generous chorus of leave-taking. Unlike the Father of the Marshalsea, however, Peregrine is in dire poverty and is forced to pawn his cloak. He is in sore straits until he meets a Mr

Teazer, who offers him a job with Richardson's travelling company at Bartholomew Fair.

Peregrine enjoys his time with Richardson. Egan takes the opportunity to praise the high quality of Richardson's mounting of his plays, the props, *décor* and scenery, and to insert Richardson's own story of his career and his many struggles over the years. Writing and acting for Richardson give Peregrine valuable experience. His engagement concludes with a 'bespeak' performance, as for Nicholas Nickleby in like circumstances. After wandering in search of another job, Proteus reflects on the problems of an actor's life—the uncertainties of engagements, the fickleness of the public, the long hours and tiring days, rehearsing one play by day and performing another by night, the miserable pay and the wretched conditions in the theatres themselves. But he has a stroke of luck, getting in with Mr Bring-em-Forward's company, a good one, playing major Shakespeare, and in a short time establishes himself as a favourite in the North of England.

Peregrine is now able to live and dress as a gentleman. He dines with the well-to-do Mr Mildmay and is smitten with his daughter, Marian. The relationship blossoms, but Mildmay disapproves and warns the actor off. The two elope and Mildmay is furious until Marian has a baby, upon which the old man welcomes Proteus into the fold. When Mildmay dies not much later and leaves his money to Peregrine, the young man decides to use it by launching out as an actor-manager. He gets a good opening in London, and takes over a major theatre. He remembers his friend, Quill, whose career he wishes to promote. Together, Peregrine as actor and manager, Quill as playwright for Peregrine's house and others, the two men rise high in their profession. Now a thoroughly experienced man of the theatre, Proteus is able to give Horatio sound advice on writing for actors, rather than for readers. Finally Peregrine crowns a distinguished career by appearing before the King as Prince Hal in *Henry IV*.

This bare outline of the plot of *The Life of an Actor* gives no idea of the astonishing amount of information about the contemporary stage, especially the metropolitan minor theatres, and travelling companies in the provinces that Egan packs into his book, either as part of the narrative or as lengthy footnotes. There are details of the careers of such personalities as William Oxberry, George F. Cooke, 'Muster' Richardson, Kean, Walbourn, Wrench and other actors, while certain well-known managers and hangers-on of the theatre appear under thin disguises. We also learn much about conditions of employment, the physical state of the main theatres in London and smaller centres, the various categories and types of actors, their vacillating social status, the wealth and position of the successful and the degradation and poverty of the unsuccessful. Egan takes us behind the scenes as no previous novelist had ever done, showing the methods of rehearsal—or lack of it —the scenic designers, the wardrobe women, musicians and other functionaries, the many auxiliary jobs an actor was expected to undertake in the theatre (and still is in provincial repertory), the hasty cobbling-up of scripts for new plays, the barbarous adaptations of Shakespeare and the classics, the back-scenes rivalries and jealousies in situations where 'temperament' ruled, the aspiring young actors with ideals yet untarnished and the tired old pros going mechanically through familiar motions and cutting corners wherever possible. From his descriptions of plays we can get some idea of the ludicrously poor standard of a great amount of contemporary theatre—the sloppy presentation of poorly prepared pieces, themselves run up by hacks virtually overnight, actors playing several disparate roles or ridiculously miscast, whole armies represented by a little man with a wooden spear, ageing females playing young girls, and so on. It is, in fact, the world of Mr Wopsle's Hamlet.

The book has a strong smell of grease-paint and oil-lamps about it, and, for all its disillusioned presentation of the more squalid aspects of theatre, it is suffused with a warm enthusiasm for everything that pertains to the stage. Egan's nose for the seedy and his joy in low life, as well as his inside knowledge of the popular theatres of his day, make *The Life of an Actor* a great deal more informative about the real conditions of the acting profession as experienced by the vast majority of Regency Thespians, as well as much more lively, than the pompous, self-congratulatory memoirs of actors and managers that proliferated during this age and the following one.

As a novel, the book hardly asks to be taken seriously; its plot is limp and commonplace and many of the incidents appear to be taken from observation rather than invented. The characters, too, including Peregrine Proteus himself, tend to be stereotypes. But there are a host of minor characters, which look back to Smollett and Fielding and forward to Dickens—among them, Horatio Quill, who has something of the bounce and likeableness of Herbert Pocket, Comical Dick, who falls from public favour and ends up in the workhouse, Bob Thimble, chatterer, trickster and pimp, and Mr Plausible Screw, who has more than a touch of Mr Vincent Crummles in him.

With Lane's illustrations, as careful in their theatrical detail as Egan's prose and Tom Greenwood's 'poetical descriptions', *The Life of an Actor* had its own decent success, although, of course, it made nothing like the impact of *Life in London*. It was reprinted several times in Egan's lifetime, and the last edition appeared as late as 1892 in a very handsome volume. It was, too, plundered by contemporary dramatists. Tom Farrell, who had written a version of *Life in London*, was first in the field with *Peregrine Proteus*, 'most truly depicting the "Ups and Downs" of an Actor', which opened at the Royalty Theatre in June 1824, long before the serial numbers had been completed. Egan's friend, Richard Brinsley Peake, also ran up a version which was produced at the Adelphi Theatre as *The Life of an Actor*, beginning on 13 December 1824, with Wrench, the most celebrated Corinthian Tom, as Peregrine.

And Charles Dickens, it appears, read the novel with profit before embarking upon *Nicholas Nickleby*.

❧ VII ❧

The Ring in Decline

Although Egan had for some years been earning his living in various ways by writing, publishing and selling books and by miscellaneous journalism, he relied a good deal for a steady income upon his permanent employment by the *Weekly Dispatch*. It was, therefore, a rude blow to him when he returned home one evening in January 1824 to find the following note awaiting him from the the printer of the newspaper:

> Dear Sir—I am most unpleasantly situated, as I have received orders not to insert one line of your own communications this week. I wish you would come down and put all to rights.
>
> Your humble servant,
> E. Young.
>
> **I received this order early this morning, but I did not like to say so to you. It has since been repeated.

Whatever Egan did when he 'came down', it failed. From that day nothing of his was to appear in the *Weekly Dispatch* again. Why the proprietors or the editor should have placed a boycott on Egan after his lengthy connection with the paper and the great contribution he had made towards increasing its circulation is obscure. John Camden Hotten affirmed: 'It appears that the success which had befallen Tom and Jerry made the conductors of the *Dispatch* [*sic*] very jealous, and they forthwith resolved upon excluding Mr Egan's contributions from their paper.'[1] If this is true, the conductors had waited an unconscionable time after the *Life in London* furore was at its height before taking action. Hotten's statement, which has been taken as gospel by other writers, seems a pure guess. In the event, Egan himself, although he had ample opportunity, advances no such reason; indeed, he appears baffled by the newspaper's action. Had he been neglecting his work for the *Dispatch*? This is hardly likely, in view of the large number of sporting reports and accounts of trials from his pen which the paper had so recently printed. The most probable cause is some personal quarrel, what today is euphemized as 'a clash of personalities', between Egan, with his Cockney perkiness, his unflagging self-assurance and, I have no doubt, his insensitivity and one or other of those responsible for the *Dispatch*.

In any case, the connection was severed. At once, with characteristic resilience, Egan determined to begin his own paper and capitalize on his own name, instead of letting others profit by it. On 13 January 1822, very soon after the completion of *Life in London*, a William Macdonald had issued the first number of a Sunday paper called *Life in London*. It did not catch on at first, and Macdonald moved from printer to printer until, in March of the same year, the journal was taken over by Robert Bell of the *Weekly Dispatch*. Macdonald stayed on as editor but the newspaper was renamed *Bell's Life in London* from 3 March 1822.

Egan thus had a double cause for resentment, the exploitation of the title of his book by a newspaper and his dismissal by the same people who had done so. He determined to show them. Accordingly, moving to 113 The Strand, where he set up his 'Gallery for Sporting Prints, and all Works connected with the Sports of the Field, etc.', he launched from these premises on Sunday, 1 February 1824, his own Sunday newspaper, *Pierce Egan's Life in London and Sporting Guide*, price 8½d. He began the first number by reprinting Young's letter, as above, adding:

> N.B.—The printer acted according to his order; not a line of my communications was inserted. Pierce Egan is too GAME yet to be made a dummy of; therefore he is determined to have a shy for himself, and a new Sunday newspaper is the result.

He then delivered himself of an 'Address to the Sporting World':

> 'Gentlemen; as brevity is the soul of wit, it is my intention to be brief on the present occasion. Picture to yourselves, my numerous friends, as I cannot address you individually, Pierce Egan standing up with his hat in his hand, and the other

placed upon his heart, making his bow to you for past favours; and I hope you will believe him, that he does it with sincerity and gratitude. I trust I may say without egotism that for the last twelve years as a Reporter of Sporting Events (having dedicated my first volume of Boxiana, July 29 1812, to Captain Barclay), I have endeavoured to perform my duty, and act with the strictest impartiality to all parties. I have been tried by you, Gentlemen, from one end of the kingdom to the other, and I trust that I have not been found wanting. In my new capacity, as the Editor of 'Pierce Egan's Life in London and Sporting Guide' connected with the events of the Turf, the Chace and the Ring, I only solicit to be treated as I deserve. If I am viewed in the light of a rival, I publically declare I am an honourable one, and as I have often said upon other occasions in which I am not *interested*, I hope I may be permitted to repeat it in my own case —May the best man win. Respecting myself, I only request a *clear stage* and FAIR PLAY. That I may have an opportunity of supporting the principles of my king and the honour of my country; upholding the corner stones of the English nation— humanity of heart—generosity of disposition—firmness of mind— and courage of soul. To support these native characteristics of Britons has long been my aim, and I shall never lose sight of them but with my life. If I possessed the brilliant eloquence of a Canning, the powerful talents of a Brougham, and the profundity of my Lord Chancellor, I could not explain myself more to my own satisfaction, than—in a word—I trust I shall always be found at the

SCRATCH with HONOUR

Gentlemen,

I remain your much obliged and humble Servant,

Pierce Egan.

His newspaper was an efficient one, much the same size and of the same character as *Bell's Weekly Messenger*, *Bell's Life in London* and the *Weekly Dispatch*. It contained reports on sporting and theatrical events, a large number written by Egan himself, paragraphs of gossip, poems on sport and drama, obituaries of notabilities, letters from pugil- ists challenging each other to contests and from the Fancy commenting on recent fights, complaining of crosses and so forth, as well as copious extracts from Egan's already published books as fillers and advertise- ments for the same works and works in progress, such as *New Series of Boxiana* in parts ('Beware of Imposters. Foul Fighters are in the Field'). Egan acted both as editor and chief reporter, and appears to have written most of the paper single-handed, which was a decided feat for one so heavily involved in other activities.

Although it was up against firmly established competition, *Pierce Egan's Life in London* at first did well, the editor's name giving it a wide circulation among the amateurs and the general public. One of those who helped to spread it around was 'Young Dutch Sam'. Samuel Evans, whose father 'Dutch Sam' had been one of the giants of the ring a few years before. Sam Evans began as a printer, but came to work on Egan's paper as a runner, distributing it to the various public-houses where the Fancy gathered. It was Egan who later introduced the young man to Gentleman Jackson, and, as he himself says, 'Sam soon afterwards cut the newspaper concerned for the more heroic achievements of the ring',[2] rivalling his father as a noted boxer.

For the next four years Egan's Sunday newspaper was to be a familiar part of London sporting journalism. Naturally, it made a special feature of his boxing accounts, but it did not fail to report 'cruel and mysterious' murders and also such noteworthy criminal proceedings as the trial of Henry Fauntleroy for forgery, which Egan began to describe in his paper on 13 October 1824. This case almost equalled that of Thurtell in the amount of public interest it aroused and became one of the most remarkable *causes célèbres* of the day, as revealing of certain social mores of the time as the Weare case had been. Here on a high social level was a juicy scandal to match that of the earlier trial on the lower one. Egan, with his delight in contrast and in the knowledge that banker and gambler were brothers under the skin, was inevitably attracted to the Fauntleroy case and gave it of his reporting best. He had already written a brief account of the career of another contemporary forger, Henry Weston, in *Life in London*, Book V, but Weston's tens of thousands of pounds of defalcations paled into insignificance beside the massive thefts of Henry Fauntleroy, the very Emperor of Forgers.

Fauntleroy's career, as Egan tells it, throws a good deal of light on the free-and-easy social manners of the day, as well as on the readiness in that age—perhaps in any age—of people to treat a criminal with respect if his crimes are on a 'heroic' scale. Fauntleroy's father had been the managing partner of the Berners Street Bank. When he died in 1807 the remaining partners were quite willing to let his eldest son, Henry, aged twenty-three, who had worked in the bank since he was sixteen, take over control of the enterprise. He was offered and accepted a partnership. But although Henry was undoubtedly a very able banker, even as a young man, this was a bad time for banks: money was hard to come by during the Napoleonic Wars. The failure of a building firm in 1810 cost the bank some £60,000, and Henry, when he became Manager, found the business close to bankruptcy.

He had meantime made an unhappy marriage and had separated from his wife, taking in compensation many mistresses. While seemingly the very pattern of respectability, he was actually leading an extremely loose and dissipated sex life. This cost him a large amount of money, which he never seemed to lack, despite the shortage of funds at the bank.

When, in a particular crisis, the Bank of England refused to extend any more credit to the Berners Street Bank, Fauntleroy resorted to forgery. He forged the names of various stockholders authorizing transfer of stock to his own brokers, had the stock sold and transferred the money to the credit of his bank. As he alone controlled the bank's private ledger, he was able to conceal the appropriation of close on £400,000 of Government stock. Shareholders were credited with dividends to the tune of £16,000 a year.

On the proceeds from these pilferings Fauntleroy became one of the most profligate spenders of his day. He collected expensive paintings and expensive mistresses, he gave luxurious dinner parties and threw splendid balls; he raced around in elaborate carriages. Among his paramours was Mary Bertram, *alias* Mary Kent, the daughter of a Brighton bathing-woman, who was known as 'Mrs Bang' because she was 'bang-up', or, in more modern parlance, 'bang-on', the very acme of fashion. Bernard Blackmantle describes her in *The English Spy*: 'Every body knows *Bang*; that is, every body in the fashionable world. She must have been a delightful creature when she first *came out*, and has continued *longer in bloom* than any of the present *houris of the west*.'[3] It was said by some that she was the prototype of Egan's Corinthian Kate, but Kate is so generalized that this is most improbable. At any rate, Fauntleroy, attracted by Mrs Bang to Brighton, bought a large house there in 1821 and was often seen in the fashionable circles at the Royal watering resort. But the two soon tired of each other and, shortly after their separation, Fauntleroy seduced a schoolgirl, Maria Forbes, setting her up in a luxurious villa in South Lambeth.

In September 1824, after ten years of systematic embezzling, during which it seemingly never occurred to anyone to ask how the manager of a comparatively small banking concern could live in such an extravagant way, Fauntleroy was snared. A client of the bank whose stocks, worth £40,000, Fauntleroy had converted, died in that year, and the trustees, visiting the Bank of England, found that the stocks had been illegally transferred to the banker. After a public examination on 18 September, he was arrested and committed for trial at the Old Bailey on 21 October. The doughty James Harmer and his partner, John Forbes, appeared for Fauntleroy. The most sensational piece of evidence at the trial was the disclosure of a paper found in Fauntleroy's safe-deposit box, and dated 7 May 1816:

> In order to keep up the credit of our house, I have forged powers of attorney and have thereupon sold out all these sums without the knowledge of any of my partners. I have given credit in the accounts for the interest when it became due. The bank began first to refuse our acceptance and thereby destroy the credit of our house: they shall smart for it.

Then followed a list of some £170,000 of securities. Harmer made much of this document in Court, alleging that Fauntleroy's defalcations had been motivated by a desire for revenge against the Bank of England for refusing credit to the Berners Street Bank. Fauntleroy's own defence, which he read from a written statement, claimed that all he had done had been solely in the interests of the family concern.

Such pleas were without avail; he was sentenced to death after five hours' trial. The Press, which, in the beginning, had been almost uniformly hostile to the defendant, changed its tune to one of near-sympathy after Fauntleroy's conviction, except for *The Times*, which remained aggressively vengeful. The death sentence for forgery had been regarded as barbarous for some time by many members of the community. Harmer, appealing to such sentiment, waged a campaign for clemency through the columns of the *Weekly Dispatch*, and collected over 3,000 signatures on a petition for reprieve. Another more generally circulated petition collected over 13,000 signatures. Yet, although there was a widespread feeling that the punishment was unduly severe, the banker, who had been lodged in Newgate, was executed on 30 November before a crowd estimated at 100,000, some of which had paid £1 for a reserved seat at the show. Jemmy Catnach the same day issued a penny broadside, with a woodcut of the hanging, some verses and an account of Fauntleroy's trial and dying behaviour. *Pierce Egan's Account of the Trial of Mr Fauntleroy for Forging at the Sessions in the Old Bailey*, after appearing in his newspaper, came out as a small book towards the end of 1824 and was several times reprinted. He again uses the occasion to warn all and sundry, especially the young, against riotous living and to restate his favourite moral, 'Honesty is the best policy.'

In his shame and degradation, which stirred the pity of many, even including some of those who had enjoyed his lavish hospitality, Fauntleroy became the prototypal forger for his contemporaries. His embezzlements had cost the Bank of England over £360,000. He was the inspiration for more than one fictional character, among them Richard Crawford, the forging banker in Lytton's *The Disowned* and Philip Ramsey, another fraudulent banker, in G. W. M. Reynolds's *Mysteries of the Court of London.*

The year 1824 had been a hectic one for Egan, and it is not surprising that the following one saw somewhat less than usual from his pen. His boxing activities continued without respite, including stakeholding, umpiring, chairing meetings, arranging bouts and making such presentations as that of the silver cup to Josh Hudson, his good friend. Another boxer who was intimate with Egan was Ned Neale, 'The Streatham Youth', as he came to be called. One of Egan's idiosyncrasies which I have mentioned was his singling out for praise in *Boxiana* of any fighters of Irish origin or with Irish connections. For all his vaunted 'Englishness', he never quite forgot his Irish ancestry. Hence both he and V. G. Dowling, the able sporting editor of *Bell's Life in London*, who was also of Irish descent, would often give more than merited attention and praise to such fighters as Peter Corcoran and Andrew Gamble, and Egan claimed, inaccurately, an Irish origin for Jack Randall, 'The Nonpareil', and for Ned Neale, whose name both he and Dowling spelt 'O'Neal' until the boxer himself corrected them. Egan and Neale came to be on very good terms, and early in 1825 the journalist sponsored a visit by Neale to Ireland and accompanied him as his manager on a short exhibition tour, combining business and pleasure. Under Egan's tutelage, Neale paid his way by 'set-tos' against local champions in Dublin and elsewhere. These were well received by the Irish Press,[4] and Egan appears to have enjoyed this renewed contact with the land of his fathers.

The second edition of *Sporting Anecdotes* was published in the same year, a handsome volume, considerably enlarged from the 1820 version and with appropriate illustrations by Robert Cruikshank. Its success prompted a new publication in the same vein from Egan's hand, *Pierce Egan's Anecdotes, Original and Selected, of the Turf, the Chase, the Ring and the Stage.* In monthly numbers, it ran from June 1825 to the end of 1826, and the whole was issued as a volume in 1827, illustrated with thirteen coloured plates by Theodore Lane, whose work for *The Life of an Actor* had so delighted Egan. One of these plates—'The Ascot Races', showing King George IV and the Duke of York watching the meeting—is especially fine and, like some of the Cruikshanks's work, looks forward in its bustling detail to such Victorian genre pieces as those of Frith. The material in the *Anecdotes* is the mixture as before. Egan was prone, as many journalists are, to use the same material over and over again in different contexts, and there are a fair number of familiar pieces in this new collection. Indeed, Christopher North, in a friendly *Blackwood's* note on the earlier *Sporting Anecdotes*, had mildly remonstrated: 'many of the stories are old—venerable Pierce—with the rust of ancient magazines upon them'; the same could justly be said of some of the pieces in the *Anecdotes*. Nevertheless, Egan's encyclopaedic knowledge of sport and his catholic reading of sporting literature enabled him to keep the collection sprightly. He retails many good yarns about racing, boxing, sailing, rowing, shooting, wrestling, pedestrianism, fishing and so forth, includes the details of some outstanding chess games, and gives a valuable compendium of the contemporary rules for the major sports. Among the sporting anecdotes are interspersed pieces of theatrical news and gossip, obituaries and brief lives. It is altogether a typical piece of Egan book-making, and only the inimitable, slangy zest of certain sections marks it off from the similar compilations of the day.

Egan's association with Lane, which had been exceedingly fruitful and cordial, had a further issue in 1826. Remembering the success of 'Going to a Fight' and such attempts to imitate it as that of Alken, Egan persuaded the young artist to embark upon a similar panorama, this time dealing with the Ascot Races. In *Pierce Egan's Life in London* for 12 November 1826 appears an advertisement for 'A Trip to the Ascot Races, 17 feet long, Designed and Etched by Theodore Lane under the direction of Pierce Egan. With a Key by Pierce Egan.' In his memoir of Lane, Egan was later to single this work out as one of the artist's happiest and most popular compositions. Unfortunately, no copies of the work, so far as I am able to ascertain, have survived, nor has Egan's key. But from the latter's description of the panorama and extracts from the key which he published in the 25 March 1827 issue of *Pierce Egan's Life in London*, it appears to have been very close indeed in subject, mood and general effect to Robert Cruikshank's clever strip.

Sadly, Theodore Lane did not live to develop those talents of which he had given ample evidence in his work with Egan. On 21 May 1828, while waiting for his brother, a surgeon practising in Gray's Inn Lane, Theodore entered the Horse Bazaar close by and soon afterwards fell through a skylight in the roof of a portico which stood in the betting-room. The coroner's jury, which brought in a verdict of accidental death, severely censured the proprietors of the Bazaar for allowing the exposed skylight to stand unprotected. Lane was only twenty-eight at the time of his tragic death. Egan was deeply distressed by the untimely end of his protégé and collaborator; he was soon to pay him an affectionate printed tribute.

In these years certain extra-curricular activities varied Egan's editing, writing, reporting and boxing work. In July 1827 *Pierce Egan's Life in London* advertised 'Pierce Egan's Trip to the Nore, accompanied by his pal, Josh Hudson, to take place on 20 August on board the steam vessel, The Sovereign. . . . It is the avowed intention of Josh and Pierce to exert themselves to produce, throughout the company, all happiness. 7*s*. single; 10*s*. double.' The cruise went off splendidly, if we are to judge by the report in the issue of 2 September, headed 'Sporting a Toe in the Water'. A full ship set off from the Customs House and the Town Stairs. A salute of twelve guns accompanied its departure and a band on board played 'Rule, Britannia'. The party was delighted on their way to the Nore with the sight of warships in the Medway, which were heartily cheered. The cup presented to Josh Hudson was exhibited, filled with port and shared by the company. After the banquet, the Royal toasts and songs sung by various artists, there was dancing on the deck. The tired but happy crowd, some, doubtless, a little the worse for liquor, disembarked at 10 p.m. Egan lost no opportunity of turning an honest penny.

The Tom and Jerry craze was now in the past, but there was still a great deal of life in the characters. *Life in London* was re-published in monthly numbers in 1827, and dramatic versions of the book were still being played to good houses in London and the provinces. Moncrieff's play, for instance, was successfully revived in June and July 1826 at the Liverpool Amphitheatre (Cooke's Olympic Theatre) and scenes from Egan's *Tom and Jerry* were performed in February 1828 at the same theatre, while audiences in Edinburgh, Dublin and elsewhere seemed always available for similar revivals or even new versions. Egan himself, of course, profited little or not at all by such productions.

By the middle of 1826 it became apparent that *Pierce Egan's Life in London* was in trouble. For all his name and reputation, Egan had had to struggle against formidable competitors, most notably the *Weekly Dispatch*. Most of these had been much longer in the field than he, were part of a group or owned by proprietors of other papers and were well capitalized, as his was not. An additional difficulty was the iniquitous Stamp Duty, amounting to 4*d*. a copy, which kept the price of newspapers high. At 8½*d*., *Pierce Egan's Life in London* was among the dearer journals, competing with others at 7*d.* or 6½*d.* Although he claimed an average circulation of 4,500 and up to 7,000 for the issue containing the report of the Spring-Langan fight, it was clear that, after a good start, the circulation did not increase markedly, and towards the end even began to decline. Egan, it seems, could not afford to give the extensive coverage to general events that papers employing more staff were able to do.

The first signs of problems came in the issue of 10 June 1827, in which an announcement states that Egan has been asked to reduce the price, and that accordingly, from the following Sunday, the cost will be lowered to 7*d.* and the paper enlarged to four folio-sized pages, with much more matter in smaller type. On 24 June there is a typically-worded Egan exhortation to his readers, which includes a statement about 'numerous complaints having reached us of another Paper, under false colours, having been substituted for *Life in London*'.

In the 187th number, 26 August 1826, Egan makes a much more impassioned appeal for support. The issue is headed with a page-wide etching by Theodore Lane, showing a wide variety of types of people, from Corinthians to dustmen, pouring into Egan's premises at 113 The Strand. Outside the shop is a notice-board, 'Pierce Egan, For Life, Wit, Fun, Talent, &c., &c.,' and the whole is entitled 'The Great Interest Exhibited Throughout All Classes in the Sporting World to read Pierce Egan's description of a prize battle'. Beneath this are printed some contemporary encomiums on Egan's prowess as a reporter, including a somewhat ambiguous one from the *Monthly Critical Gazette:* 'The talents of Mr Egan as a writer on living manners have obtained him considerable celebrity among certain classes of the community.' Egan follows this with another 'Appeal to the Sporting World'. He complains of unfair competition by other papers, especially *Bell's Life in London,* and lists his own works in proof of his mana:

Those celebrated characters, Tom, Jerry, Logic, will back the Blunt Depot against a Feather, that the title of Life in London belongs to no one else but Pierce Egan. . . . Who ever heard of Mr Bell in the sporting world? . . . Fair play is a jewel, but when a man makes use of a title that does not belong to him, in point of equity, and finds fault with the real Simon Pure, it is highly necessary that an explanation should be made to the sporting world in general—Fight me fairly, I will not grumble; floor me if you can by superior talents, and I will not complain; but do not get the 'best of me' by *fibbing* to the public—i.e., making use of a title which only belongs to Pierce Egan.

However, all such appeals and even the production of a Saturday edition of his paper as well as the Sunday one did not save it. On 20 October 1827 a notice appears in the journal advertising the sale of the 'well-known, long-established and highly esteemed Sunday newspaper *Pierce Egan's Life in London and Sporting Guide*', and on 4 November 1827 *Bell's Life in London* announces that Egan's paper is 'this day incorporated into *Bell's*'. In November 1826 *Bell's Life in London* had a regular circulation of some 9,000; by December 1827, after the amalgamation, it rose to 20,000 and was to continue to rise. For all the undoubted selling value of Egan's name, Clement, the proprietor of *Bell's*, decided that the 'Bell' designation had the greater pull. The full title of *Bell's Life in London and Sporting Chronicle*, which was the sole Sunday paper to give a coverage of all sports, was kept until 1859, when it was shortened to *Bell's Life*. It was incorporated into *Sporting Life* in 1886.

This absorption of Egan's newspaper into one which had preceded his own by two years and was to outlive it by sixty-one years has given rise to curious misunderstandings in reference books, almost all of which state that *Bell's Life* grew out of *Pierce Egan's Life*.[5]

The failure of his newspaper and the financial loss he sustained in having to quit it for a song to a competitor did not keep 'Glorious Pierce' down for long. He bounced back early in 1828 with the long-awaited Volume I of the *New Series of Boxiana*, which had been coming out in parts since 1823. This was to be followed in 1829 by Volume II, the final *Boxiana* book. The *New Series* brings the history of the ring right up to date, and includes accounts of most of the important bouts staged from 1821 to the end of 1828. While some of the fights recorded in the earlier three books, those of Molyneaux, Mendoza and Cribb, for instance, have more intrinsic interest than any described in the *New Series*, the style and spirit of the later volumes make them, in my estimate, the best of the bunch. Egan is now writing almost wholly from his own experience and observation, not drawing, as he often had to before, from earlier writers and some contemporaries for parts of his material. His extensive reporting experience, if it still leaves him rather slapdash at times, allows him to describe fights in quick, brilliant shots like a well-cut film; his biographies of boxers are less prone to imagination and gossip and more completely factual; his eye for a crowd and for odd characters remains as keen as ever, and his style, still that inimitable mixture of rhetoric and slang, is more assured and fluent and less clogged with space-filling irrelevancies.

His description of the scene along the road before the battle between

Tom Hickman and Tom Oliver on 12 June 1821 offers a scene of variety and animation that would surely have appealed to Dickens:

> The road was covered with vehicles of every description, and the numerous barouches and four were filled with *swells* of the first quality, to witness the Gas again exhibit his extraordinary pugilistic powers. The *toddlers* were scanty indeed. But in addition to the *great folks* on the road anxious to participate in the sports of the Prize-Ring, the *Hero* of the Castle took the shine out of all of them, with his *stage* load of SOVEREIGNS, who had *condescended* to ride *outside* upon the occasion; and on Belcher passing the President of the Daffies, he sung out— 'Blow my Dickey, there never were such times as these, Jemmy; here, only look, I have got SIX SOVEREIGNS *inside*, with their *Crowns*.' 'That's not a *bad hit*,' replied Major Longbow, who was in company with the President. 'Tom's a *wonderful* man. I bet a hundred, *once*! Pon my soul, it's no lie.' The Greyhound, at Croydon, was the rallying point for the SWELLS and *Riddlesdown* was passed and left to the *Waggoners*, in consequence of the Ould One's larder being empty, and the accommodation rather *queer* at the last mill. The FANCY stood it once like *winking*; but, say they, 'It is a good *flat* that is never *down*; and we must not be had a second time.' This ought to be taken as a friendly hint by all the *Bonifaces*; so as not to have to *huff* upon future occasions; and also to avoid too strong a *figure* when the bill is produced. The fight was a good *turn* for this road; the lively groups all in rapid motion; the *blunt* dropped like waste paper, and no questions asked, and all parties pleasant and happy. The delicate *fair-ones* were seen *peeping* from behind their window-curtains, the tradesmen leaving the counters to have a '*york*' at their doors; the country girls grinning; the joskins staring; the *ould* folks hobbling out astonished; the *propriety people* stealing a *look*; with all their notions of respectability and decorum. Indeed, it might be asked how could they help it? Who does not love to see a 'bit of life', if they can't enjoy it? A *peep* costs nothing. The fun met with on the road going to a *mill* is a *prime* treat, and more good CHARACTERS are to be witnessed than at a masquerade. View the *swell* handle his ribands, and push his *tits* along with as much style and ease as he would *trifle* with a lady's necklace—the 'bit of blood' from his fleetness, thinking it no sin to hurl the dirt up in people's eyes—the *drags*, full of

merry coves—the puffers and blowers—the dinnets—the tandems
and the out-riggers—the wooden coachmen, complete *dummies*
as to getting out of the way—the Corinthian Fours—the
Bermondsey tumblers—the high and low life—the genteel,
middling, respectable and *tidy* sort of chaps—all eager in one
pursuit—with Bill Giles's pretty little *toy*, giving the *"go-by"* in
rare style, and the whole of which *set-out*, it is said, the
table-lifter could remove from the ground with the utmost ease—
forming altogether such a *rich* scene, the 'Blue Devils' are left
behind, and laughter is the order of the day.

He keeps his eye as firmly on the audience as he does on the par-
ticipants in a bout. In a fight between Hickman and Neat on 11 December 1821, he observed: 'Hickman was met right in the middle of his
head with one of the most tremendous right-handed blows ever witnessed, and he went down like a shot. . . . "How do you like it?" said
one of the *swells*, who was pretty *deep* in it, to another. "Why," replied
he, "that blow has cost me, I am afraid, fifty sovereigns."' He even
gives such marginal but interesting details as a report of the sermon
preached after the funeral of the unlucky Hickman and Rowe, who,
it will be remembered, died in a drag-cart accident while under the
influence of drink:

He [the preacher] also deprecated prize-fighting as
unchristian-like and unmanly; and likewise read a very
awful lesson to the Fancy in general, and the dreadful
punishment that awaited them, if they did not take warning from
the shocking deaths of Messrs Hickman and Rowe, and reform
from their evil ways. 'The above unfortunate men had not time
for repentance, but were killed like a moth, trod upon like a
grasshopper—or run over like a dog.'

But Egan also gleefully notes the ironical fact that the parson who
preached this sermon wore around his neck 'a *Belcher* handkerchief—
a designation of the *Fancy*!'

Amateurs of the ring suffered almost as much from the pious distaste of the Evangelicals for boxing as they did from the zeal of magistrates, and Egan loses few opportunities of getting in a dig at them,
having as little love for the canting hypocrite as Dickens did, and
incidentally in the process being as unfair as Dickens was to Evangelicals and Nonconformists as a whole. He quotes, for instance, a

section from an alleged sermon by 'one of the lower order of ranting preachers':

> I dare say you'd all pay to see a boxing match between *Turner* and RANDALL, and yet you don't like to pay to see a pitched battle between me and Beelzebub. Oh! my friends, many a hard knock, and many a cross-buttock have I given the *black-bruiser* for your sakes! Pull—do pull off these gay garments of Mammon! Strike the devil a straight blow, and *darken* his *spiritual day-lights*! At him manfully, and I'll be your *bottle-holder*!—I ask nothing but the *money*, which I hope you'll not forget before you go.

The new volumes of *Boxiana* are explicit on the various hazards that could attend a match. England's unpredictable and temperamental climate often soaked the spectators to the skin. In December 1821, just after Abbot had fought Sampson at Moulsey Hurst, a pitiless, pelting storm broke, and

> a *character* of some note, belonging to one of the theatres, who was anxious to return to town to obey the Prompter's call, made hastily towards the river, singing out full of glee—
> A boat! a boat! haste to the ferry!
> A little punt soon appeared in sight, answering the call, when the *chaunter*, as lively as a grig, jumped into it; but he was followed by eight rough *coves*, (who had been shivering and shaking with wet and cold on the beach), in spite of the remonstrances of the waterman as to the danger of going to the bottom. They replied, 'they were determined not to give a chance away; that their *blunt* was as good as any *swell's*', and insisted on being put across the Thames without delay. There was no alternative; so off they went with a stiff'ning breeze. Hampton would soon have been out of sight, the puntsman's *ladle* being no match against General Wind, had they not, luckily for their friends and acquaintance, come bump up against a small ridge of land, and upset within three feet of the water's edge. After a splashing scramble for the shore, amidst hope and fears for their safety, they at length reached *dry land*. [Meanwhile] hundreds were seen scampering to get under the waggons to avoid the hail-stones, and *flooring* each other only to obtain an inch of shelter; lots looked like drowning rats, their

clothes sticking to their bodies as if they had been pasted on; while
a few of the *Corinthians*, in post-chaises, were laughing at the
ludicrous scenes, and blessing their happy stars for the comfort
and advantages derived from their possession of the blunt.

Another hazard was the not infrequent collapse of one of the hastily
erected grand-stands. On 7 January 1824 at Worcester, when Spring
fought Langan, 'the right wing belonging to the stand gave way, and
fifteen hundred persons, at least, were all thrown one upon another.
. . . It was affecting beyond every thing to behold a Noble Lord
frantic with agony, as he had the moment before placed his brother on
the scaffold as a place of safety.' Fortunately, on this occasion, nobody
was killed; only a few broken arms and legs, sprains and bruises were
sustained.

At this same contest, during which the two pugilists fought seventy-
eight rounds in two hours, twenty-nine minutes, the pressure of the
crowd broke the ring and the following scene ensued in the seventy-
second round:

> Spring had no room to get away . . . and Colonel Berkeley, the
> Referee, said, 'I am so disgusted with the treatment I have
> experienced, that I will give up the watch—Here is no
> ring. It is impossible to stand still half a second without being
> assailed with a cut from a whip or a blow from a stick; and no
> good done either.' In no fight whatever was there such a scene
> of confusion in the space allotted for the men to fight. The
> battle was now little more than pulling and hauling; and, in
> closing, both down. During the time Spring was on Painter's
> knee, Sampson, Oliver, and Israel Belasco were giving advice.
> 'Hallo!' said Josh, 'do you call this fair play? How many
> seconds is Spring to have?', and, snatching a whip out of a
> by-stander's hand, with the strength of a lion, endeavoured,
> regardless of any person before him, to whip out the ring,
> followed by Oliver. Not a single person in the mob but received
> numerous blows, and was in great danger of having his nob cut
> to pieces. 'Only give us a chance', cried Josh, 'and we can't
> lose it.' . . . The constables and their long poles were all mixed
> in the mob struggling for breath; the fighting men hoarse with
> calling out 'Clear the ring' and dead beat from the exertions
> they had made. Nothing less than a company of the Horse
> Guards could have made out a ring at this period, so closely
> jammed together were all the spectators.

Egan is always ready with a colourful phrase or a literary allusion to describe a boxer or his friends. Ned Brown, 'The Sprig of Myrtle', 'had a blue bird's-eye tied loosely round his squeeze, and a collar so high that, to use the expression of a sporting man, it was big enough to make a white waistcoat; in fact, he was a *swell* milling *cove* in duo-decimo!' 'The superiority of Langan was so great in point of his scientific movements over the brave and hardy sailors that he disposed of five or six after the manner of an auctioneer *knocking down* a lot of sundries.' 'The Chatham Caulker', in peeling, gets rid of the 'swell, white upper-tog . . . which, by the bye, seemed to fit him like a Purser's shirt upon a handspike'. 'Sampson came up *piping* like a fifer, but as desperate as a man-of-war's man, determined to do mischief.' 'Jem, on the contrary, was as fresh as a daisy, and capable of dancing a horn-pipe on the *upper crust* of a twopenny loaf.' 'John Bull came up to the scratch as jolly as if he had been *blowed out* with prime roast beef and plum-pudding . . . while on the contrary, the Caulker came up tottering, and as *weak* as *soup-maigre*.' 'Moore, with as much ardour as the love-sick Romeo scaling the garden-walls to converse with his Juliet, and equally high in chivalric notions as Don Quixotte [*sic*] in search of his *Del Tobosa*, went to work with Joey.'

We find in the new *Boxiana*, too, several Cockney exchanges which take us forward into the world of Sam Weller and his father. Consider this one, for instance:

A very lusty man, who was completely fatigued with the heat of the sun, asked one of the proprietors of the waggons the price of admission. 'Vy,' replied the *Cove*, 've charge, as how, three shillings; but such a heavy one as you, and who takes up as much room as two people, ve can't take less than *five bob*, and that's werry reasonable, I'm sure, governor.' The *fat One*, who loved his *blunt*, stood haggling for some abatement of price, but the *drag Cove*, who was a *downey one*, gave the office to his pal, to *bonnet* a little for him. 'Here they come,' said he, 'my eye, if it an't dangerous to be safe any *veres* now.' 'Who's coming?' said the *fat One*, agitated. 'Vy, only the *Conveyancers*! But you can't stand here any longer, Sir, you deprive me of customers.' 'Well, my good fellow, help me up, and I will give you five shillings.' 'No Sir, I can't take that now, the men are just ready to mount the stage; you shall get up for eight!' After a heavy sigh, and counting his money several times, he handed over the *rag* to the *drag Cove*, which the latter carefully deposited in his

clie. 'But, Sir,' said he, with a grin on his face, 'you must give me
2 *bob* to help you up; you know you did not agree for that 'ere,
and I cannot strain myself for nothing.' The *fat One*, with tears
in his eyes, paid his '2 bob', and was literally dragged up amidst
the roars of laughter of his brother spectators on the waggon.

These are some of the special pleasures of Volume I of the *New Series*,
apart, of course, from the splendid reports of the bouts themselves.

Volume II, dedicated, with Egan's usual habit of 'going to the top', to
the Duke of Wellington, as the 'prime example of True Courage',
continues in a similar vein. Pierce's friend, Josh Hudson, 'as big and as
full of turtle soup as an alderman, and possessing the rotundity of
abdomen belonging to a Falstaff', receives generous attention. There is
a lament for Josh's defeat by Tom Cannon on 23 June 1824:

> The John Bull Fighter defeated by an *out-side* boxer in
> TWENTY MINUTES AND A HALF. Tell it not in the WEST. Tell it
> not in the EAST! Members of the *Partiality Club*, shut up your
> *listeners*! and TOM OWEN, pull out your *fogle*, your *peepers* must
> be deluged with tears, at the above adverse turn of circumstance
> against your darling boy, who was within one grasp of the
> CHAMPIONSHIP. How are the mighty fallen! How will the *yokels*
> triumph! and how will the *cockneys* get rid of their grief?

Egan records, too, the sense of comradeship and general mutual respect
among the boxers, as well as their simple sentiment. For instance
Jack Scroggins, at a benefit at the Tennis Court in April 1826 for the
family of Ned Turner, who had died the day before, said, 'Gentlemen,
Ned was always a gentlemanly sort of man—he is now gone to his long
home, and I pray God will forgive him, as well as everybody else. Let
us all live while we can, and when we can't live no longer, why, I
suppose we must die; and I don't see why a fighting man shouldn't
see eternity, as well as anybody else.' He is also anxious to show that,
outside the ring, most of the pugilists had a strong sense of chivalry
and were often able to use the manly art of self-defence to protect
their wives or other women from predatory rogues. Thus, when Peter
Crawley's pregnant wife was accosted by a fellow named Sullivan, who
affected to take her for a prostitute, Peter

> immediately planted such a tremendous blow on one of his
> *ogles*, as to produce the *claret* in torrents, leaving also a serious
> cut over it, and *Sullivan* likewise measuring his length on the
> pavement. The fellow, as soon as he recovered the use of his

pins, started off like a race-horse, leaving his hat behind him. CRAWLEY, as a token of victory, publicly hung out the hat at his own shop-door, but *Mr Sullivan* never had the courage to claim his *topper*.

Even when the business of the ring seemed to conflict with family obligations, the boxers, he implies, managed to reconcile the two. Such, at least, was the case with a certain Harry Jones,

> who set such little value on his opponent, that he led to the altar *Miss Evans*, his present wife, on the day appointed for the battle. Scarcely had HARRY JONES sworn eternal fidelity, constancy, and all the other *etceteras* connected with the marriage ceremony when suddenly recollecting himself of his other *match* with *Jem Aldridge*, he bolted out of the church, *sans ceremonie*, leaving his friends and his bride in the greatest suspense at his strange conduct, merely observing to the *gent* who gave the lady away— 'Take care of my wife, for I shall soon return to make her happy.' Off JONES went to the destined spot . . . entered the ring almost out of breath, shook hands with *Aldridge*, punished him in all directions, and also *polished* the poor *typo* off in the course of twelve minutes. After receiving the congratulations of his friends, and the shouts attendant upon victory, he returned to his 'better half', comparatively none the worse for his battle, spent the evening of his party in fun, merriment, and happiness, and completed his *match* with *Mrs Jones*—thus *winning* two matches in one day.

And there are, of course, innumerable accounts of heroic mills between boxers in prime twig in which the claret runs in torrents, heads are put in chancery, nobs receive teazers, ogles are blackened, conks are flattened, torsos are fibbed, wisty-castors exchanged, mugs pulverized, tripe-shops smashed, tinglers land on lugs, experiments are made on pudding-bags, taps fall on the magazine, facers fly like lightning, muggers bounce on the upper-works, staggerers are planted on bodies, liberties are taken with pimples, peepers are plunged into blackness, mauleys are damaged, ivories pirouette like opera-dancers, until one or the other ends up floored for good, whereupon blunt changes hands among the Fancy, and the victor is saluted with lashings of heavy wet varied by occasional flashes of lightning.

Throughout these two books Egan continues to preach the ENGLISH-NESS of pugilism, its cultivation of manly courage, its superiority to the ways of decadent foreigners. No, he protests against the attempts of preachers and magistrates, 'to put an end to the sports of Englishmen in a land of liberty' would be to undermine the very qualities which make England great:

> Our ancestors were distinguished by their love of TRUE COURAGE; our own times have been raised indeed in the pages of history by the TRUE COURAGE displayed under *Duncan, Vincent, Howe, Nelson, Sir Ralph Abercrombie, Sir John Moore,* and the *Duke of Wellington*; and our hope is to carry it still further, that every succeeding generation in happy old England, to the end of time, will prove themselves real lovers and supporters of TRUE COURAGE.

Yet, despite such rhetorical flights, despite his still enthusiastic reports of contests, despite the evidence he produces to show the wide extent of public interest in pugilism, there are increasing signs that, from about 1824 onwards, something of the old glory and glamour has departed from the sport and that all is not as it used to be in the palmy days of the Prince Regent. True, the boxers still are made to speak with the dignified utterance of the 'straight' characters in Scott's novels, as Neale to Sampson, 'You behaved unmanly to me in my own house, Sampson, while I was in a bad state of health, and I will never forgive you, till you and I have decided our fight in the ring.' True, Egan is still able to print a report of a meeting which says: 'Who was in the chair? PIERCE EGAN himself!!! though no Greek, still the Xenophon of the Fancy.' But there is a growing consciousness throughout his last volume that pugilism is fast on the decline. What is often implied in the New Series, becomes explicit at the end of the second volume:

> All things, it is said, must have an end, and *Prize Milling* has already, if not quite, arrived at this CLIMAX. The truth must be told—DISGUISE would be culpable. The thing altogether has *degenerated*, and the highest patrons of the P.R. have retired in disgust. . . . It is decidedly the fault of some of the boxers: as it is clear that if they did not *listen* to the offers of designing men, nothing WRONG would take place! Let any unbiased spectator look around the RING at the present moment: let him report progress of the exact description of personages who are to be met with upon the ground, and he will find that, at several of the late fights, the *swells* have been *missing*, and will be *missing*, till something like RENOVATION takes place in the Prize Ring. Why?

Because *judgement* is out of the question. It is *laughable* now-a-days to calculate about the *talents* of fighting men as was formerly the case, when *Jem Belcher* and *Tom Cribb* took the lead. The *secret*, and the *secret* only is the knowledge required, to learn from some *knowing friend* 'How to bet your money!' We again repeat that *Prize Fighting* has been at the LOWEST EBB for some time past.

Later Egan reports a speech made by V. G. Dowling, of *Bell's Life*, which further reinforces his own sense of disquiet. Dowling was speaking at the Tennis Court on Friday 20 May 1828, following allegations that Ned Neale had accepted a bribe to lose his fight with Ned Baldwin two nights before. Denying that Neale had sold the bout, Dowling nevertheless went on to say, as Egan reports it:

The time was, when men of first distinction in the country, from national prejudice, were the liberal supporters of the Prize Ring. He believed he might with safety rank among those individuals his present Majesty; and he himself had seen the Heir Presumptive to the Throne among the anxious spectators of a fight. This, he need hardly say, is no longer the case. It was equally familiar to his auditors, that, from among those respectable persons, a club entitled 'The Pugilistic Club' had been formed, which on occasions supported those men who acted with honour and integrity in the *milling* circles, in a manner calculated to excite their gratitude and respect. The club had ceased to exist. .... And last, though not least, he might mention that Mr Jackson, the gentleman who had so long acted as the 'Commander-in-Chief' of the pugilistic school, whose hand and whose purse had always been open to men who, like himself, had conducted themselves with integrity, had withdrawn himself altogether from their association. For such defection it was natural to look for a cause: and this, he was sorry to be obliged to confess, was to be found in the misconduct of some members of the Prize Ring themselves—and of those who, by temptation, had led them to abandon every principle of honesty, and render pugilism rather a source of fraudulent speculation, than that of fair and manly competition. (Hear! Hear!)

The great Regency age of boxing was at an end; it had lasted from the founding of the Pugilistic Club in 1814 to the retirement of Jackson into private life in 1824. As Dowling points out, the dissolving of the

Pugilistic Club and the removal of the steadying influence of Jackson were factors in the deterioration of pugilism; they were both, in fact, partly causes and partly effects of a steady lowering of standards. But other things helped accelerate the decline. The withdrawal of royal patronage, and of aristocratic patronage outside of the Pugilistic Club as well, made it increasingly hard for boxers and their promoters to defy the law. As the 1820s advanced and the Napoleonic Wars retreated in memory, there was a growing reaction against the looseness of Regency living, a long-overdue reform in social manners and a revival of propriety. The influence of Wesley and of the Evangelical Movement was starting to make itself felt in many areas of society—in the increasing self-discipline on the part of many among the middle and working classes and in the tendency to confuse respectability with grace and worldly success with God's favour. The corrupt Georgian style and its raffishness, the indolence of the Corinthians, the ostentatious vulgarity of the too quickly rich, the hectic plumage and affectations of the dandy—these were fast being outmoded following the revival of Pietism and a new tone of decorum in various upper-class sectors. By the mid-1820s the gay outfits of the Regency bucks were already beginning to look old-fashioned; staid broadcloth was replacing them. A new temper of moral seriousness, associated with a more responsible sense of national purpose and destiny, was invading society. The characteristic attitudes of Victorianism were already shaped before the young Queen ascended the throne in 1837 and, by her personal example and with the aid of her gifted husband, gave them sanction.

In such a developing climate, bare-knuckle pugilism was becoming increasingly anachronistic. At the same time the general state of the sport was alienating, not only the noblemen and such moral pillars as Jackson, but men like Egan, who made much of their living from the sport. Swindlers, ruffians, crooked gamblers, thugs, bullies and pick-pockets, who had always lurked on the fringes of pugilism, greatly swelled in numbers, until, to some observers, it seemed as if the crowds at bouts consisted exclusively of the sweepings of the London slums and prisons. Crosses and suspected crosses multiplied, and decision after decision came under a cloud of suspicion. Decent boxers and impartial referees often went in fear of assault; indeed, they were sometimes not only threatened, but beaten senseless for not falling in with the wishes of the gamblers. Few boxers were, in such an atmosphere, coming forward with the skill and stamina of the old ones.

The dissolving of the Pugilistic Club removed a body of respectable and well-to-do supporters which had acted as a disciplinary and supervisory committee. To attempt to retrieve the situation, the Fair Play Club was formed at a public meeting in the Castle Tavern, Holborn, at that time managed by Tom Spring, on 25 September 1828, with much the same objects as the earlier Club, but, lacking finance and aristocratic backing, it soon lapsed, and in any case could have done little to halt the advanced decline of the sport. The formation of the Fair Play Club is the last event Egan records in what was to be the final volume of *Boxiana*. After that pugilism sank into further degeneration, losing the bulk of its popular support, until, to save it from total obliteration, the Marquess of Queensberry introduced his celebrated rules in 1860. But Egan was not to live to see this day and the advent of a new era of boxing. He had outlived his importance as a boxing reporter by 1828, and the often dispirited tone of his final pages of scraps of boxing gossip shows that he recognized this fact. Yet in many ways, as we shall see, Egan shared in the new moral sensibility that was developing, and, while he lamented the decline of his favourite sport, did not lament the changes in social attitudes that accompanied it.

❧ VIII ❧

The Return of Tom and Jerry

This consciousness of new values is shown most markedly in *Finish to Life in London*, which began in numbers in 1827 and was published in a volume in 1828, with thirty-five coloured illustrations, other pieces and a frontispiece, all by Robert Cruikshank. The full title of the work is *The Finish to the Adventures of Tom, Jerry and Logic in their pursuits through Life In and Out of London*, and Egan begins his narrative by picking up immediately where *Life in London* ends. But before this he fills a lengthy chapter with thanks to his supporters, self-justifications, attacks on the pirates, plagiarists and imitators who had made money out of his inventions, a list of the various derivatives from the earlier book, a great deal of self-advertisement, including quotations from various reviews of his works, and a cheerful resolve to win further admirers with his sequel:

> The cheery smile of FAME will now inspire us with more
> confidence than ever towards the completion of the Work before
> us, flattering ourselves that we have kept our promise with the
> Public in the most rigid point of view, namely:—that we have
> made the GRAVE to smile, the GAY to feel delight; the COMICAL
> laugh heartily, and the PATHETIC have occasion for a *wipe*. The
> MODEST have not had occasion to turn aside with disgust, nor the
> MORALIST to shut the book offended.

It is impossible not to like the cheeky, boastful, assured 'scribbler', as he calls himself, for his Cockney resilience and his bouncy self-confidence. Even the cocky certainty of his superiority to the various imitators of *Life in London*, his alternation of appalling doggerel quotations with lines from Shakespeare and Pope, his name-dropping, his 'hints for Reformation' of the pirates, his snook-cocking at the snobbery of Sadler's Wells and Covent Garden and his reprinting of newspaper tributes to his prowess are part and parcel of his extraordinarily vital and never-discouraged personality.

Finish to Life in London is the best piece of fiction Egan ever produced. Digressions and elaborate footnotes still impede the flow, but there is more plot, the language is less of an Irish stew and the set pieces have more detail and completeness than anything in his other books. He had clearly learned something from his earlier experience with *Life in London* and *Life of an Actor*, and especially from his association with the theatre, for there is now more dialogue and while it is usually stylized it quite often approaches naturalness. More than this, perhaps, there is a genuine imaginative colouring to the narrative, notably in the way the characters are presented. Of course, by comparison with his contemporaries, Jane Austen, Scott and even Galt, Egan is unsophisticated, old-fashioned and sub-literary, yet there is much in the book to give pleasure, and in it we find ourselves several steps closer to popular Victorian fiction.

On his way home to Somerset, after leaving his friends at Piccadilly, Jerry finds himself accompanied by an Old Maid who is always complaining. Bill Put-'em-along, the gentlemanly coachman, says to her, 'You may depend upon it . . . there is not the slightest danger in the world. My coach is built upon new principles! It is one of the *Patent Safety* Coaches, The roof is strong enough to carry St Paul's Cathedral from one end of the globe to the other, if you could but get that venerable pile upon the coach, as luggage.' This is in response to a new passenger taking his place on the roof at Speenhamland. The fresh arrival is Sir John Blubber, a very fat knight, who makes friends with Jerry as they move towards Pickwick. Sir John, a jovial bachelor, proves to be a wealthy, retired citizen, who had once been Sheriff of London and in his retirement is determined to enjoy 'those advantages which health and a long purse can procure'. A self-made man, who had risen from being a workhouse orphan by his business skill and industry, he had a benevolent heart and was always ready to help the poor and unfortunate.

His purse was never closed against the real object of unavoidable misfortune and distress; indeed, it was the opinion of the fat

knight that it was much better to be duped at times, than to let a
deserving man or woman, in need of charity, be 'sent empty
away' as a token of revenge on the plausible wretch and sanctified
hypocrite. ... To sum up the character of Sir John Blubber: he
was a most facetious, jolly, good-natured soul; one of that class of
persons deemed independent, and his property enabled him to
'care for nobody'; if family pride was the predominant failing,
yet he was most anxious to respect the feelings of every
individual, and to treat no person with contempt, more especially
those characters whose circumstances reduced them to the
appellation of being called—POOR.

Here, surely, is the crude original of Dickens's Mr Pickwick. If the
coincidence of the name of the obscure little Somerset town appearing
for the first time in fiction in conjunction with the appearance of the
fat knight were not enough, the character of Sir John is amply suggestive of the benevolent Pickwick.

Jerry is given a warm homecoming at Hawthorn Hall, one full of
Dickensian exuberance and family feeling. As he recuperates from his
strenuous life in London, he renews his acquaintance with Miss Mary
Rosebud; his town-won sophistication deserts him when he becomes
smitten anew with her innocent charms. But Mr Rosebud, one of
Jerry's hunting companions, tells the young man, 'You are a bit of a
rattler, a *gay* sort of chap, and rather a general lover among the girls,'
and insists that the young couple wait a while before marriage, putting
Jerry on trial, as it were. With this warning, Jerry begins his courtship.

Sir John Blubber, at Jerry's invitation, arrives at Hawthorn Hall on
a visit. 'The uncommonly large gentleman' gives them an entertaining
anecdotal evening to the 'gaily circling glass'. Then Bob Logic writes to
say that he has left the Fleet, 'and given up my commission on that
tack; and once more, to all intents and purposes, become a *landsman*',
and that he and Corinthian Tom are on their way to the Hall. On the
way down there is a ludicrous incident, during which Logic mistakes
a sleep-walker who intrudes into his room at a Bath hotel for a ghost.
The next morning he receives a letter of apology from the somnambul-
ist, the lanky Phil Splinter. All goes as merrily at Hawthorn Hall as at
Dingley Dell:

Hawthorn Hall, by the accumulation of visitors, was one
continued scene of gaiety, hospitality and friendship. Rustic
sports in the morning; holly dances during the day; musical

parties and balls in the evening, were given to prove that our heroes were not deficient in *gallantry* to the neighbouring fair ones.

Jerry, Logic and Sir John go on a 'flying shoot', but Logic, as inept a sportsman as Mr Winkle was to prove to be, falls through the ice and discharges his gun through the window of a farmer's cottage. That same evening all assemble in the Hall for a cosy domestic evening. Cruikshank's happy plate and Egan's text make this occasion into a snug Victorian family set-piece. After a hunt, in which Logic most reluctantly joins, Tom and Bob return to London and Sir John goes home. Logic leaves with

> When again shall we three meet
> Among the *Swells* in Regent Street?
> Come soon, my boy—come with glee.
> For lots of *fun*—another *Spree*!

On a visit to Bath, Jerry encounters Lady Wanton in the pumproom, but, on reminding her of her promise made at the London masquerade, is rebuffed. Soon afterwards he is called to London about some property left him by a maiden aunt. He finds Bob broke again, in dingy lodgings, and the two collect Corinthian Tom and decide to see those parts of London they had not visited before. With Sir John Blubber, who is also in the city, they explore the 'great Bore', the London conduit, and are soaked by an unexpected influx of water. They also go to Bartholomew Fair, to witness a performance at 'Muster' Richardson's theatre, where Jerry is smitten by a slavey, Jane Merrythought. He conducts her home and finds that her mistress is none other than Lady Wanton.

During the company's visit to a dance-hall at Bartholomew Fair, Egan reproduces the speech of the spieler:

I manages it myself, and you may believe me, *Marm*, there will be no *raw*; for anybody that is *obstropolis*, they are sure to be pulled up for it. I have a *trap* [Peace Officer] in the room, to make it all right. If I was to know you, *Marm*, as well as I knows my own vife, you may depend upon it, I should never *split*. I knows better, my lady, that's vat I do!—I should not be supported by any *genteel* folks, if I was to chaff out of doors about my visitors. Vy, Lord bless you, last Bartelmy Fair, Squire ——'s vife had like to have been cotched jigging a bit with her footman; but, howsomdever, as soon as I got the *office*,

I made it right—by the female voman bolting out of the *back
slums*; and the slavey made his *lucky* as vell as he could.

A trip to the Harp in Great Russell Street, where Blubber is initiated
into the Order of Buffaloes and a visit to a fête given by the Duchess of
Do-Good are followed by an evening in the Finish. This was the
tavern used by the market people who frequented Covent Garden
early in the morning. It was a favourite spot for slumming by those
going home from a masquerade or after the breaking up of a large party.
Because of this, it attracted the genuine unfortunates and the cadgers,
who hoped, by a tale of woe, to charm some money from the pockets of
the more generous swells. Saucy Nell catches the attention of Tom,
Jerry, Bob and Blubber and her story is told—the familiar one of a
young country girl seduced by a Lord, becoming a courtesan, but, after
an illness, delicately undescribed, sinking down to prostitution. Unlike
so many of the sisterhood, however, as depicted in Georgian and Victorian fiction, Saucy Nell is a gay soul, passionately fond of dancing,

> Nell's a Vestris in attitudes—a Stephens in her song
> And for a 'gay and merry life', be it short or long.

In the Cruikshank plate, she is dancing spiritedly to the delight of Sir
John.

By way of contrast, Sir John takes his friends the next day to the Dock
Yards at Chatham. While there, they see a company of convicts on their
way to the hulks, and Corinthian Tom is astonished to glimpse among
them Splendid Jem, 'at one period of his life one of the gayest members
belonging to the fashionable world'. Tom tells Jerry about Jem's
raffish life and how he was brought to ruin by the extravagant Diamond
Nancy, 'a coquette of the highest quality—and a mistress of finesse',
and concludes: 'The awful lesson which Splendid Jem's career affords
to many thoughtless young men upon the town, ought to be turned to a
good account.' In a long footnote, Egan describes the situation of the
convicts in the Dock Yard and indicates that there were, at the time,
serious attempts to rehabilitate them by work, education and religion.

When Logic goes to visit old friends in the Fleet, Tom and Jerry take
the opportunity to play a game of rackets there with Sir John, who is
floored by a false step, much to the amusement of the spectators, including old Mordecai the Jew. Sir John, who has lost money to Mordecai, tells the others of the Jew's sharp practices as a moneylender,
marriage-broker and sharp.

The friends next appear at the Ascot Races. The fact that the King,
when Prince of Wales, was much attached to horse-racing comes in for

special mention; Egan's description of the scene, in fact, reads like a society gossip page. Tom tells Jerry of the Epsom Races and emphasizes the contrast between the two meetings. Ascot is the 'rallying point for all the nobility and gentry, for miles round Windsor, to pay homage to their beloved Monarch'. Epsom Races are 'more a sort of holiday for the *Cockneys*—it is a day of feasting, drinking, and chit-chat,' says Tom.

> Every vehicle has its basket of *grub*, hamper of wine, *heavy wet*, and cigars; and *enjoyment* is principally the order and outline of the vast assemblage of persons; and 'here the horses come, and there they go', is the most they experience for the expenses of the day. . . . Deny them not their pleasures; let them say their *say*; *blow up* the great folks, if it suits their whim; and *grumble* at anything they do not like, and contentment is the result.

The swindlers, thimble-rig men, trainers and backers are described; Jerry is somewhat surprised to find in the gaming rooms under the Betting Stand two magistrates and a divine busy playing Une Deux Cinque. Shortly afterwards he again glimpses Lady Wanton and passes a note to her by means of Jane, who is accompanying her mistress.

The next expedition is under the direction of the Fat Knight, who takes Tom, Jerry, Logic and Splinter to a fancy-dress ball near Rag Fair, conducted by 'The Sage of the East'. Here the company enjoy another low-life gathering, with characters like Jack Mainmast the sailor, Billingsgate Nan, Merry Peg and Inquisitive Fan. Back at Sir John's snuggery, they all proceed to get drunk and set out on their separate ways to enjoy 'a bit of life'. When Jerry wakes the next morning he finds himself 'in a filthy hotel in the vicinity of the Theatres, and destitute of everything in the way of wearing apparel except his *shirt*'. An old beldam tells him he has been robbed of his purse and that he won't get his clothes back until he pays for the night's lodging. He writes a note to Logic, who comes to the rescue, and, seeing Jerry draped in a blanket, exclaims:

> Be thou a spirit, or a young *Swell* prigged;
> Be thy intentions wicked or charitable;
> Bring with thee *lush* from Sir John's or *Jacky* from Tom's
> Thou com'st in such a questionable shape,
> That I will speak with thee.
> I will call thee *Spooney! Flat!* O Jerry
> Let me not burst with laughter. But tell why——

Rescued from his embarrassing predicament, Jerry next accompanies his friends and Splinter, who is in debt, to Old Screw, a moneylender. Screw refuses to discuss terms in the presence of the others. Logic, an old hand, warns Splinter against moneylenders, and hands him a remarkable document he has composed, which sets out the fraudulent tricks, the exorbitant rates of interest and numerous social and other devices used by moneylenders to catch their clients and then bleed them. So heartfelt is this denunciation that one wonders if Egan himself may not have at one time fallen into the clutches of an Old Screw.

For some time now Tom has been neglecting Corinthian Kate. She is unfaithful to him, and Tom, informed by a malicious serving-maid, surprises Kate with her military 'gallant' and casts her off. One of his ways of trying to erase her from his mind is to accompany the others to the Half-Moon Tap, kept by Egan's boxer friend, Josh Hudson. Here they meet the John Bull Fighter, admire the famous presentation cup and drink champagne from it, and exchange reminiscences of Molyneaux, Sam Robinson and other Negro pugilists.

With the help of Jane, Jerry's intrigue with Lady Wanton progresses. But just at a crucial moment the Baronet arrives and Jerry is forced to leave hastily through an upper storey window, 'mortified beyond description'. We then follow the melancholy career of Kate. Like so many other courtesans whose fate Egan describes, she sinks lower and lower in the scale, with more and more humble lovers; she takes to drink and finally is cast out on the street without a protector or money. The four friends, meantime, ignorant of her plight, follow the social round, playing forfeits at the home of a banker, Sir Gregory Chance, visiting the 'Cock and Hen Club', a mixed gathering of pickpockets, con-men and tricksters, looking in at Regent's Park Zoo, where a kangaroo escapes, flooring Sir John, whose fate it is always to get in the way of moving objects, and taking their place amidst the medieval-attired members of the Toxophilite Society (Logic opts out of drawing a bow, on account of his green specs). But on their way home one night, the trio stumble across Corinthian Kate under the Piazza of Covent Garden. She is drunk, diseased and starving, one of London's most notorious prostitutes. Tom is stricken to the heart to find her in such a state. Logic and Jerry see that she is cared for, and later, with Tom's aid, make arrangements for her rehabilitation, but she cannot bring herself to face Tom, and, with a touching note left for him, she disappears again. Logic sombrely reflects upon the misery endured by the many prostitutes of London:

The Theatres, and other public places of amusement are *filled*
and *thinned*—*filled* and *thinned* again, in rapid succession, with
those unhappy girls who *dazzle* and become the 'playthings of an
hour', until dissipation, distress, and disease, compel a hasty exit,
and they are then heard of no more. Such are the direful effects
and terrible end of Vice and Infamy in the metropolis.

Tom is plunged into deep sorrow at Kate's disappearance and Sir John
does his best to drive away 'the blue devils' by finding new diversions.
They are respectable enough—visits to the House of Lords and the
House of Commons, a rowing match in which Sir John falls overboard
and is rescued by Logic, a pigeon-shooting in which Tom, with a
patent gun like a walking-stick, outshoots the fat knight. Meantime,
Kate has been enticed back into the 'game' by a procuress. In the
extremity of her misery, she drinks poison and dies. Her fate would
have remained hidden from the friends but a night-constable having
Ragged Bet, 'a low, impudent, brazen-faced prostitute' before him
on a charge of theft, recognizes her as a companion of Kate's.
Knowing of the trio's interest in her, he tells Logic and Jerry of her
tragic end; they keep it a secret from Tom, out of respect for his
feelings.

Splinter is the next of the band to get into trouble. Old Screw has
him shut up in 'Banco Regis' for debt. His friends call on him in the
'college' and we get a full description of the various ways in which the
incarcerated debtors pass away the time, including the 'Cameza Stakes',
in which the female prisoners race around the courtyard. The visit
ends with dinner in Splinter's rooms at Blubber's expense. The Fleet
of *Pickwick Papers* and the Marshalsea of *Little Dorrit* are just around
the corner.

The sprees of the quartet are now drawing to an end. Jerry, mindful
of his last experience while drunk, is at first cautious during a final
visit to Sir John's snuggery. But alas for his resolutions; egged on by
Logic and by a song from Sir John, 'A good fellow means a good
drinker', he becomes drunk again. He

> *staggered* over *Tower Hill* reasonably well; *reeled* down *Cornhill*
> and *Cheapside,* so as to have escaped notice; zig-zagged by that
> noble piece of antiquity, *St. Paul's Cathedral,* better than could
> have been expected, and was getting over the ground *tidily,*
> although his steps were of an in-and-out description, towards
> *Temple Bar,* when the progress of our hero was arrested by the
> advances of a dashing Cyprian.

*HE DEA*H OF CORIN*HIAN *OM

One favour bestow—'tis the last I shall crave
Give a rattling *hulloo* thrice over my grave
And unless at that warning I life up my head
My boys you may fairly conclude I am dead

6 Death of Corinthian Tom by Robert Cruikshank

7 Pilgrims at Gravesend by Pierce Egan, Jnr.

Under her influence, Jerry is decoyed into a well-known hotel 'dedicated to gaiety and pleasure'.

During the night the hotel catches fire. Jerry, awakened by the prostitute, escapes with only his trousers, carries the girl down the stairs and manages to quit the blazing building. 'In the fervour of the moment, and with a sincerity of heart that would have done honour to the piety of an aged Archbishop, he "thanked God for his preservation!"' All his other clothes, his pocket-book, his notes, letters and valuables are lost. He is lent garments by a friendly landlord, who, with the class-consciousness of the time, recognizes that Jerry is a gentleman. From the tart, Ellen Prettyflower, who comes from Bath, he hears the now-predictable tale of early seduction by a Captain of Light Dragoons and the descent into prostitution to stave off destitution. Shaken by their narrow escape from death, they both swear amendment. 'I am not what I was,' says Jerry. 'Indeed, I shall be a different fellow altogether in future.' He conducts Ellen to the Penitentiary, where she will begin a new life, and returns, chastened, to Corinthian House, to dispel the rumours that he has been burnt to death. His mood is sombre. 'The whole of the sprees, rambles, larks, rows, fights, &c. were as *shadows*, when contrasted with the *brothel on fire*; indeed, his *mirth* was absolutely changed to *melancholy*.'

Tom tries to divert Jerry's mind, but news comes from Bob Logic that he is very ill. Tom and Jerry hasten to the bedside of the Oxonian, who is, indeed, on his last legs, although still full of puns and jests. They read his will, in which he distributes his few possessions to the cousins. He says, 'You must perceive that the *comical* part of my career is at an end, and you are well aware that I was always a merry fellow; but, as Mercutio says, I shall be found a *grave* man to-morrow.' After Logic's death, brought on by excessive indulgence, and his funeral, Tom has a large monument erected over his grave, punningly praising his qualities as a man of the world.

Logic's passing puts an end to any further sprees, and Jerry returns home to Somerset, taking Tom with him. He loses no time in visiting Rosebud Cottage, accepts Mary's reproaches, and in time becomes accepted by her. Tom is to give the bride away. But before the wedding the men set out on a foxhunt. Tom is thrown by his horse, his neck is dislocated and he dies. It is some time before Jerry recovers from the double loss. He tells Mr Jollyboy, the curate:

Appearances . . . might be against both of their characters with the fastidious part of society; yet hypocrisy, cant, humbug, or dissimulation, never disgraced their conduct; a love of honour shone conspicuously throughout their actions, and, by an acknowledgment of their own errors, displayed a noble generosity towards the faults of others.

At length he is married to Mary by Mr Jollyboy; the celebrations are truly rural, with the whole village invited, dancing on the green and general jollification. Jerry then settles into the life of a country gentleman and squire, his well-regulated life profiting from the lessons he had learnt during his 'day and night scenes' in London. We leave him ' "all happiness" ' with an amiable handsome wife, a fine estate, a capital stud of horses, and a crack pack of hounds, to promote LIFE IN THE COUNTRY'.

Finish has many of the qualities with which *Life in London* has made us familiar; there are still the generous ladlings of cant and slang, the continual facetiousness, the lengthy footnotes of gossip, social information and glosses, the irrelevances and the loose narrative. But there are significant differences from the earlier book. Fewer scenes of 'low life' are to be found, and these show more restraint than do the earlier accounts of Tom and Jerry's slumming. The original trio is expanded into a 'club' by the addition of Sir John Blubber and Splinter. Although the whole thing is still fairly primitive in form, it does move towards a climax and has a rounded conclusion. The country, while fairly featureless by comparison with the town, figures more prominently, and some attempt is made to convey a rural atmosphere. Above all, perhaps, sport is more prominent than it had been in *Life in London*. Pugilism makes its appearance in the visit to Josh Hudson's tavern; but it is possibly Egan's sense that boxing is declining in popularity that accounts for the attention given in *Finish* to hunting, horse-racing, athletics, archery, pigeon-shooting, and other sports.

Again there is his acceptance of social diversity and of the divisions in society with each class pursuing its own pleasures; again there is the contempt for the fops and dandies, the warnings against tricksters, moneylenders, procuresses and con-men. Egan's attitude towards vice is still a little equivocal; on the one hand he rejoices in the existence of low life; on the other, he condemns profligacy and dissipation with something of the solemnity of the Evangelical preachers he had scant time for. But in *Finish* the tone is darker, or steadily becomes so, with the successive incarcerations of the characters in debtors' prisons, Logic paying for his reckless living with an early death, the tragic fate of Corinthian Kate, and Tom's mortal hunting accident.

It has been suggested by, for instance, J. W. Ebsworth in his *D.N.B.* article that the climax to the sprees and follies of the ebullient trio reflects Egan's response to the changed climate of manners and the passing of the days of Regency tolerance. But to say this is to ignore the wealth of moral comment in *Life in London* and the general 'cautionary' tone of that book. These injunctions may have been overlooked by the book's early readers, who were more taken with the low life and the larks, but they do undoubtedly occupy a significant part of the text, even if the final effect is ambiguous. More than this, it is plain that, back in 1821, Egan had planned a serious chastening of his characters, although he had not at that time intended to kill Tom and Kate. It had always been his intention to draw a clear line between 'fun' and dissipation and to show the consequences of the unremitting pursuit of wholly self-indulgent pleasure. Nobody who worked as long and as hard as Egan did could think otherwise.

The draft outline for the play which he sent Harris of Covent Garden in 1821 concludes:

[Scene] 23—Effects of Life.
    Chaffing Crib—Darky over—Jerry's symptoms of uneasiness— Cracked Heads—debilitated—out of wind—can't come to time; and the Constitution fast on the decline; Logic lumbered; and Tom *done up*—portraying that LIFE IN LONDON without the check-string is a rapid trot towards Death! Jerry sees his folly— acknowledges his error—Hawthorn Hall in perspective—Jerry united to Mary Rosebud—Tom and Corinthian Kate made happy.[1]

It is of some interest, too, that in this early outline the whole of Act 1 is devoted to Somerset activities, including fox-hunting, a dance on the green and so on.

Finish to Life in London, old-fashioned as it was, had its comparative success; several editions of the volume were called for, and it was reissued by Virtue in 1830 in twelve parts at 3*s.* each, simultaneously with parts of *Life in London*. It was reprinted as late as 1887.

The year 1829 saw Egan's second and last venture as a newspaper proprietor. On 4 January appeared the first number of a new Sunday paper (actually published at 3 p.m. on Saturday) called *Pierce Egan's Weekly Courier to the Sporting, Theatrical, Literary and Fashionable World*, price 7*d.* A woodcut of a phoenix heads the front page. The editor begins with a 'few words' in expected style to his 'numerous friends and acquaintances in the United Kingdom':

Having been left to grope his way in the dark for the past 12 months, owing to circumstances over which he had no control, he has, within the last few days, struck a light and found himself at his old Residency, 113 Strand. Being now awakened from his trance, he is determined to have another shy; and he hopes to hit the John Bull's eye like winking, although an old friend with a new face.

Then thus it is:—being now wide awake, he trusts, that after nearly 20 years before the Fancy and the Public in general as a Sporting Writer, no promises are necessary to be made as to Superiority, Excellence and such like Gammon respecting the 'best Accounts'. Pierce will be found at his Post, and endeavour to hit his Customers hard, or rather to tackle them, as to Fun, Frolic and Humour, in every shape, either in Town or Country. —For further particulars, as to 'bits of good truth', enquire of Tom, Jerry, and Logic.

After a hit at *Bell's Life* from crowing over the failure of *Pierce Egan's Life in London,* he concludes with his usual plea for 'a clear stage and fair play' and

> The Title's changed, but not the Man;
> To be original his only plan:
> Quality, not quantity, his aim,
> The steady, sterling road to Fame:
> To seize the helm, his flag unfurl'd,
> And bid defiance to all the world:
> For fun, frolic, spree, and 'The Fight'
> With all the scenes of Day and Night.

Alas for Egan's optimism! The paper was to last for only a few months. It ranged more widely than his previous newspaper. Boxing, hunting, horse-racing and other sports naturally occupied much space, as well as pugilistic challenges and answers to sporting inquiries, but there was also a good deal of police news and theatrical information, market reports, parliamentary proceedings, comments on O'Connell and the problems of Ireland and general news. It was efficiently produced and set out and competently edited. Yet, for all Egan's confidence in the appeal of his name and his hope of attracting the support of his old subscribers, the paper never really caught on. It limped along, with a steadily falling circulation, until its seventeenth number, when it expired quietly on 26 April 1829. There was no auction this time;

Egan had already sold his newspaper equity and goodwill. He could not do it again.

The failure of the *Weekly Courier* seems to have in no way dampened his spirits, for later in the same year he ventured a second time into matrimony. His first wife, Catherine, had died a year or two previously, leaving him with several children. On 19 October at St George's Church, Hanover Square, Pierce took a second wife, Mary Sarah Paul. She was twenty-nine; he was in his middle fifties. Mary was to give him a second family.

He retained the premises at 113 Strand, the 'Life in London Office', as publishing and bookselling quarters. But now, with the diminution of public interest in pugilism and the passing of the *Life in London* vogue, Egan had to cast around for other ways to supplement his income and provide for a wife and family and a new family as well. Marian, his first child by Mary, was born in 1830. What better avenue for his talents he thought, than the popular theatre? He had done well out of his own dramatization of his book; others had made fortunes out of *Life in London.* He had long been interested in the stage, and he had played Bob Logic more than once with resounding success. Hence he determined that his new career would be that of a playwright, not a hack adapter of other men's novels, like Moncrieff, but a genuine original.

Thus began the half-comic, half-pathetic assault of the chronicler of the ring upon theatrical fame, which was to engage his energies for the next eight years and bring him little reward and even less kudos. From this period date most of the few letters from him that have survived, which provides some indication of the volume of correspondence he engaged in with theatre managers, impresarios and actors in his deter-mined endeavour to scale the slippery Thespian heights. These letters, with their mixture of cheerful confidence, self-salesmanship, unflagging facetiousness, execrable puns, slang and verbosity give us a pretty fair picture of the middle-aged Pierce Egan, the prototype of his own Bob Logic.

From 20 Waterloo Road, Lambeth, where he was living at the time, he wrote on 12 June 1830 to R. W. Elliston, who had in 1828 become lessee of the Surrey Theatre, trying to sell him a play:

Dear Sir,

I feel highly flattered by your note and it has encouraged me to proceed with nothing else but the idea—that the piece in question will turn out successful—at all events, I hope so. To be candid with you, Sir, I have written it under the impression that it would be better got up at your establishment than at any other Theatre. My reasons are the two Heroes that I have had in my 'mind's eye' are Mr T. P. *Cooke* and Miss *Vincent*—it may be boldness on my part, perhaps, a little too bold (when I am addressing one of the most brilliant dramatic Heroes in the circle of Talent), but nevertheless, in my humble opinion, he could not have a *stronger* part (a complete portrait of a British Sailor) or be placed in more favourable, interesting situations before an audience. The character is truly original; in fact, I have not been able to *borrow* a line anywhere. So much the better. Miss *Vincent* is the other hero (not a heroine) also a small part for Mrs *Egerton*, scarcely worthy of her attention, I admit, but her acting would add strength to it. Likewise, a short part for Mr Osbaldeston, but affording an opportunity for a display of the passions connected with an agonized heart in a bad husband, and an abandoned Parent. Vale, an original Comic Song, with some dialogue exactly in his line, and I am mistaken if it does not alter the faces of his friends *aloft*! A small, rather funny taste for Mrs Vale, but not a bad comic bit neither. An original song for Miss Vincent. The first act concludes with an original Glee and Chorus—from which I anticipate, if it is taken up in a spirited harmonious manner by the Composer, will become a favourite. I hope you will excuse the above remarks—they are *rather out of precedent*, I am afraid; but I am sure you will, when you recollect we are both at MUM Point. I have now a fair copy at your service. In order that I might not excite any undue influence on your mind, I have not seen Mr T. P. Cooke since his arrival; nor indeed, for the last Four Months; therefore, he is quite a stranger to what I have written to you on this subject.

The Bill for the Public, as far as the first Act goes, I shall also have ready—it is my intention that it should be Original, strong, and catching! nay more, a sort of *hold fast*!

I return you my sincere thanks for your kind offer, as to hints towards the improvement of the Piece—I have lived long enough to know the importance of—'The King's name is a Tower of Strength'. But it is a *sine qua non* with me—that the *Title* must remain—and I flatter myself it will meet with your approbation.

As the first Act (in my humble opinion) will create a strong feeling in the minds of the audience to become acquainted with the future destination of the Hero—I am quite aware that the

Second and Third Acts will not only require serious
consideration—but also that sort of Taste—which Artists term
'*good-keeping*'. To place here and there some good touches
of *light* and *shade*, in order to work up, and ultimately produce a
good oil painting.

  I think it will be much better to keep my name a secret for
the present, as I am rather afraid, that even yourself, although
I have received from you several unflattering testimonials of my
abilities, and I am well assured that you are a lover and supporter
of genius—I again repeat, *that I am afraid you are not wholly
exempt from a sort of prejudice—a kind of thinking that the author
of Life in London and the dramatist of Tom and Jerry cannot
write anything else but vulgar flash and low slang.* I have felt this
impression against me in more instances than one—I know that
I have to move from my shoulders *almost a mountain*, but 'True
Hope ne'er tires'. However, in this instance, I fearlessly
challenge criticism. I have used no sophistry—no dwelling upon
worn-out, wretched, half-witted, far-fetched puns to extort
applause from the unwary—but I have left unsophisticated
NATURE to tell her own Tale. How far I have succeeded is another
matter, but I do not tremble for the result.

  Whether, Sir, you will condescend to give me a call at my
little crib to permit me to read it to you; or that I should attend
upon you in Private—the Commodore will have the kindness
to give the signal. But in honouring me with a visit, you will kill
two birds with one stone—I have got a complete set of Theatrical
Chairs—quite *unique*: also a splendid screen, likewise *unique*,
and made for the late Lord Byron and once valued at 200 guineas
by his Lordship.[2] The Screen not only contains some valuable
original drawings by the late Rowlandson, but in other respects
will be found highly interesting to a gentleman like yourself, fond
of everything which exhibits Talent. I am sorry to say I have no
Wine—therefore it must be an *intellectual* meeting—and although
I have nothing to treat the *Duke of tranza* with, befitting his
dignity of station in life,— if I am not destitute of *animal spirits*,
I am sure that will suffice. Only give the word—*cue*, if you like
it better—I shall be at your home after 5—or at your mansion—
or tomorrow morning, and it shall be punctually attended to.

I remain, my dear sir,

Yours truly,

Pierce Egan.[3]

No further correspondence between Egan and Elliston seems to have survived, but a biography of the latter by an intimate of the comedian supplies at least part of what happened:

> The notorious Pierce Egan having introduced himself, by letter, to the Surrey manager at the early part of the season, transmitted to him proposals, in various shapes, for furnishing the theatre with dramatic pieces. The variety of his epistolary style was even more remarkable than that of his proposals. Sometimes he wrote with the air of a dashing blade—at others in the burlesque heroic—and occasionally in the terms of a jolly tar. This Protean diction was, doubtless, employed to have its due effect with the manager, who might naturally, after so many examples of versatile humour, be duly sensible of the available quality of Pierce Egan's fancy and intellectual resources. But whether, like an over-eager witness in our courts of law, the author of 'Life in London' proved too much; or whether, from a positive want of perception on the part of the manager, of his correspondent's dramatic qualities, is not sufficiently clear; but true it is, Elliston lent no favourable attention to his applications; and when at last Egan forwarded to the manager a direct specimen of his quality in the shape of a 'Comic Sketch', all doubt was at an end by Elliston, under his own sign manual, requesting that all further correspondence might be stayed; for the manager was perfectly persuaded that his friend Egan was not precisely an author who, like Sophocles, would have been acquitted at court by merely reading one of his own plays. But Egan, no doubt, felt all the pangs of a slighted poet, exclaiming
>
> > That the vast universal fool, the town,
> > Should cry up Labeo's stuff, and cry me down!
>
> . . . But beyond all question, 'Tom and Jerry' enjoyed most extraordinary success; no one can rob Mr Egan of that.[4]

Elliston's rebuff was only one of the many disappointments the aspiring dramatist was to endure. He importuned other managers, with little more luck, although he seems to have persuaded the famous comedian, Charles Mathews, whose 'monopolylogues' had some influence on Dickens's methods of characterization, to include a sketch of two of his in his popular 'At Homes'. These performances at the Adelphi Theatre, with Mathews's associate, Yates, drew material from many writers of the day, including Thomas Hood. Egan and Mathews en-

joyed some intimacy; they exchanged friendly letters, and Egan pays
the actor a lengthy tribute in his *Epsom Races* of 1835. In 1831 Egan
issued *Matthews's Comic Annual or the Snuff-Box and the Leetel Bird,
An original humorous poem by Pierce Egan. With eight original designs
by Robert Cruikshank.* (Egan, it will be noted, always spells Mathews's
name with an extra 't'.) This is dedicated to Mrs Mathews, lest, Egan
says disingenuously, he should be thought to be trying to influence her
husband to offer him a position, with the regret that 'I cannot upon this
occasion round my periods with the smoothness of a Moore; say what I
mean after the elegant diction of a Canning; and display that animating,
interesting mode which characterizes the writings of a Walter Scott.'
He goes on to praise the many talents of Mathews and refers to his
especial skill in reading Egan's poem.

The poem itself, apparently a rhymed version of a sketch or anecdote
featured in one of Mathews's 'At Homes' or 'Comic Annuals', as some
of his shows were called, is a trivial piece in Egan's typical 'crambo'
doggerel style about a Frenchman invited to a fashionable banquet
who pockets a cooked snipe to take home to his sick wife, and hence is
falsely accused of stealing a valuable snuff-box. All ends well, however:

> The Box was found—the Snipe was ate,
> The whole were friends, and Madam's *palate*
> The *Long*-ing gratified!
> Monsieur toasted Old England's King!
> Mine host in praise of France did sing—
> Thus—*Peace* was ratified!

A similar but more interesting book of the same year is *The Show
Folks.* This, too, is a crambo piece, relating the fortunes of a young
man, like Peregrine Proteus, who is bitten by the theatre-bug, makes
his way up from the bottom, is engaged by 'Muster' Richardson, and,
after the usual tribulations, rises to the position of prosperous actor-
manager. The book, which is embellished by nine designs on wood by
'the late Theodore Lane', was published by Egan to raise funds for
Lane's widow and to 'rescue his name from oblivion'. It is dedicated
to Sir Martin Archer Shee, President of the Royal Academy. The
interest of the poem is slight; even Egan took small pride in his powers
of versification. What gives the little book a particular value is his
'biographical sketch' of Lane, which is both detailed and affectionate,
showing a very close rapport with the young artist, cut off at an important stage of his artistic development. Egan is unusually and commend-
ably modest in introducing it. 'The only thing to be regretted [about the

book]', he says, 'is that the task has not fallen into other hands; at all events, to some person intimately connected with the Fine Arts, whose name might have given it an importance, which it does not, cannot now possess.' He pays a deserved tribute to Lane's gifts and perseverance, recalls their first meeting and how he had got up *The Life of an Actor* chiefly to bring Lane's talents to public notice, and concludes with a list of the artist's main works.

The footnotes to *The Show Folks* have equal interest and more than the poem itself. There are passages on Richardson's Variety Theatre, Bill Oxberry and his career, theatrical terms and convivial gatherings of theatrical people. One note calls for reproduction, since it sets forth fairly clearly the kind of activity that passed for 'fun' in those days among the wags of the town. If the practical joke framework is removed, it looks rather like the 'Amateur Night' entertainment still to be found in some English provincial theatres:

'The Kean's Head, 7 Russell Court, near Drury Lane: The
above tavern afforded considerable amusement to its visitors. A
few wags, fond of a bit of fun, frequented the coffee-room every
evening, and, in concert together, represented themselves as
managers from the country, in want of performers and waiting in
turn to engage young men for different '*lines of business*' to
complete their companies. This had the desired effect, and
numerous ludicrous scenes were the result, which defy anything
like communication; and enthusiastic, stage-struck, inexperienced
youths afforded these *pretended* managers sport and roars of
laughter, night after night. The plan generally adopted was, that
one of the party kept on the look out to pick up a simple youth,
and having got one on tow, he was formally introduced to the
assumed proprietor of a country theatre. The latter person,
with a face of gravity, then inquired whether he wished to engage
for the *light* or *heavy* business of the stage, or if singing was
his forte; or, perhaps, he could undertake the general line, and
assist in melo-dramas, spectacles, &c., &c. The manager, then,
with a polite request, wished to have a 'taste' of the young
man's quality, before he finally settled his engagement and fixed
his salary. And several young aspiring heroes, anxious to obtain
an engagement, have been prevailed upon to mount the table
and to give recitations from Romeo, Hamlet, Octavian, &c.
amidst the shouts of *pretended* applause from country actors,
wags of all sorts and men of the world, who nightly resorted to

the O.P. and P.S. [the actors' nickname for the tavern] to pick
up anecdotes and spent a pleasant hour. When the managers
thought they had had enough of this burlesque, 'The exit—the
exit' would be whispered one to another, and while the hero on
the table was spouting out some impassioned speech from
Shakespeare, his back would be rudely assailed with the contents
of their jugs; and upon the unfortunate wight hastily looking
around for the authors of such an assault, his front, from another
part of the company, would be attacked in the same manner.
Redress was out of the question, and the more passion and rage
exhibited by the youth, produced the more laughter; when he
was informed it was the way to teach him how to make his
'*exit* in a rage'; and that no person would deny him the title of
being a *wet* actor.

Egan's third publication of 1831 struck a grimmer note. This was
*Pierce Egan's Account of the Trial of Bishop, Williams and May for
Murder*, which was to be the last of his Newgate Calendar-style reports.
Although this particular case did not arouse anything like the public
excitement that attached to the trials of Thurtell and Fauntleroy, it
did cause something of a sensation because of the youth of the victim,
its grisly details and its revelation of the methods of the 'resurrection
men', or body-snatchers, whose activities had been widely publicized
by the trial of Burke and Hare in Scotland in 1828.

In October 1831 William Hill, porter at the dissecting room of King's
College, was offered the body of a boy, fourteen years old, for 12 guineas
by two men, John Bishop and James May. He knocked them down to
9 guineas, and they went away, returning with the corpse in a hamper.
Hill and a demonstrator in anatomy were suspicious, as the body was
fresh. They notified the police and the two men were arrested when they
came back for their money. A third man, Thomas Head (*alias* Williams)
was also arrested on Bishop's confession. The dead boy was identified
as Charles Ferrair, otherwise known as 'Carlo Ferrari', and the case was
publicized as the 'Murder of the Italian Boy'. He was an orphan who
had often been seen in the London streets with a little cage containing
two white mice slung around his neck. The cage was later found in the
possession of Bishop's children.

According to Bishop, he and Williams had enticed the boy to Nova
Scotia Gardens, where both men lived, on the promise of work. They
waited until Williams's family were in bed, then drugged the boy with
laudanum in his drink. His unconscious body was taken to the rear of

Bishop's house, where there was a well, a rope was tied round his feet and he was lowered head first down the well and left to drown there. While waiting for this to happen, the murderers buried Ferrair's clothes in the garden and walked around Shoreditch. On their return they put the corpse in a box and enlisted the aid of May, a 'legitimate' body-snatcher, to dispose of it. May was ignorant, so he claimed, that the boy had not died of natural causes.

The boy's teeth were crudely knocked out and sold to a dentist, then May and Bishop hawked the body about to several anatomical establishments, including Guy's Hospital, before arriving at King's College. In his statement Bishop also confessed to at least two other murders by the same method, that of a woman and a boy named Cunningham. The well in Bishop's garden, believed to have been the scene of even more murders, became a centre of morbid curiosity, and features in one of the illustrations to Egan's book. The case provoked a great deal of newspaper comment on the work of resurrection men and their habit of 'arranging' for the supply of fresh bodies for dissection.

The trial of the three men took place at the Old Bailey on 1 December. All were sentenced to death, but the confessions of Bishop and Williams exculpated May, who was reprieved. He had a fit on hearing the news. Bishop and Williams were executed on 5 December before a crowd of some 30,000 people, much the same number as used to attend a boxing match. The removal of one of the three chairs on the scaffold was greeted with roars of disapproval; as the men were hanged there were groans, execrations and hisses from the mob. Because of the pressure of spectators in their anxiety to obtain a clear view of the entertainment, numerous accidents, some of them serious, were reported to have been caused.

As usual with his trial reports, Egan gives a straightforward account of the proceedings, together with some assessment of the characters of the accused, not omitting his moral injunctions and his expressions of horror at the sordid and brutal nature of the crime. Perhaps because of the comparatively limited interest in the case—after all, no sporting swell or any member of 'high society' was involved—the pamphlet, which is nowadays excessively rare, seems to have done less well with the public than any of his previous crime reports. There is no evidence of another edition, although at least one other report by another hand appeared at about the same time.

While he had set his heart on succeeding as a playwright, Egan did not neglect other avenues. Another sporting anthology from his hand appeared in 1832 in twenty-five weekly parts at 3*d*. each. This was *Pierce Egan's Book of Sports and Mirror of Life, embracing The Turf,* *the Chase, the Ring, and the Stage*, which was published in book form in 1832 and reprinted in 1836.⁵ It is Egan's best anthology and was certainly one of his most popular ones. It was reissued several times during the nineteenth century, was frequently pillaged by other compilers, and was read with profit by novelists like Surtees. With his customary skilful economy, he found such gatherings a useful way of reusing uncollected material from the pages of his two newspapers and of drawing attention to his books by printing extracts from them. He also had no hesitation in borrowing from his friends and contemporaries (he prints poems by Thomas Hood, for instance) and in soliciting contributions from his acquaintances.

Nevertheless, the *Book of Sports* is largely Egan's own work, and, as a whole, it gives a fine idea of the state of various sports in the 1820s and 1830s. Boxing, of course, angling, archery, rackets, wrestling, cock-fighting, horse-racing, boating, pedestrianism, athletics and cricket, 'the most manly of games', receive attention. There is an excellent article on 'Old English Rustic Sports', some account of the pubs kept by pugilists, a description of the various Friendly Societies of the time, among them the Oddfellows, the Noble Druids, the Bucks Lodge, the Loyal Britons, the Knights of the Cauliflower, the Old Codgers, the Eccentrics, the Philanthropics, an account by a French gentleman of a fox-chase, various horse-racing statistics, a history of the Cock-pit, a listing of the rules of cricket and a notable section on aquatic sports. Passages from *Finish to Life in London* are reprinted and Egan identifies his coachman, Bill Put-'em-along, as Harry Stevenson, a very popular and educated coachman of the day. He also prints the cricket-match section from Miss Mitford's *Our Village*. There are, in addition to the more substantial articles, several entertaining sporting anecdotes and light verses. One of the latter, 'From W. L. R. to his friend Pierce Egan', was contributed by the journalist and dramatist William Lemen Rede, a drinking companion of 'Fancy's Child', then in Scotland; in the course of wishing him well in this new serial publication, it at the same time gives some indication of the kind of experience they had shared:

> Success to thee, Egan, tho' I am afar:
> My wishes are with you, wherever you are:
> Your name wakens visions of many a scene,
> That I long ago number'd with things that *have* been;
> Of moments, most dear to my mind, to my heart,
> When night saw us meet, and the dawn saw us part.

Alas, ev'ry day is to me an apprizer,
That, tho' growing older, I'm not growing wiser:
Now far from the spot where I rambled with thee,
I sigh for the frolic, the fun, and the *spree*,
For the friendship that gave to existence its zest,
And the joke that ne'er carried a sting with its jest.

I can't but remember (tho' far apart now)
That we've met at a *mill*—that we've shar'd in a row;
That over the bowl we've forgotten our woes,
Drank success to our *friends*, and reform to our *foes*;
At many a scene of delight we have met,
That tho' *sweet* to *remember*, 'twere *wise* to *forget*. . . .

Even in this largely cheerful book there is a note of melancholy in the way Egan deals with pugilism. When Tom Belcher retired he writes: 'The times had changed for the worse—the *blunt* had got rather taper; and numerous patrons of the P.R. were growing too old to give it their usually animated support, and the young swells were not rich enough in the "cash account" to prop up the "decline".'

❦ IX ❦

Life in Ireland

For the next five years Egan, having seen the writing on the wall only too plainly, was virtually to abandon sporting writing for the theatre. He was clearly at this time at a low financial ebb, and, now almost sixty, would doubtless have been delighted to have found a permanent niche somewhere. But, although he bombarded managers with proposals, outlines and scripts for plays, burlettas, pantomimes and 'comic operas', almost all of them proved to be as unexcited at the prospect of presenting an Egan stage masterpiece as Elliston had been. One factor in his lack of success was undoubtedly that to which he referred in his letter to Elliston—his being labelled as a 'slang writer' and a portrayer of low life, and the difficulty managers found in considering him in any other role. Some were more sympathetic than Elliston, however, to the man, if not to his work.

For instance, Alfred Bunn, at the time lessee of the Theatre Royal, Drury Lane, reproduces a letter from Egan, written about 1833, in which he begs, in humorous fashion, for the chance of offering a play.[1] As the missive is written in the manner of a picture-letter puzzle, still to be found in children's magazines, with various picture-puns and drawings in place of key words, it is not easy to follow, but Egan's drift is that he is prepared to offer a pantomime or a comedy, that he is getting a little desperate with frequent rejections and that he is willing to defer any payment until the piece is established as a success—'should winning be the result, why then the sweetener would be acceptable, either at the *Blunt* Magazine, or the Treasury, not being "partikler to a shade" d'ye see, *where* it comes from'.

Bunn comments that 'From previous engagements, I was unable to avail myself of Egan's offer', and he adds: 'Poor Pierce! I really wish him all the luck his varied talent deserves. They say that Fortune knocks at every man's door once in his life-time; but if she ever did at Egan's, I am very much afraid he was not at home.'

Egan was finding it much harder to break into the theatre than he had thought. He did not so much mind being rejected as being rejected with ridicule. And something of personal bitterness, a note rarely to be found in his writings, creeps into one of his footnotes to *Epsom Races* of 1835. He does not make a direct personal reference, but to me at least the inference is plain when, after a long disquisition on the trials of authorship, he comments:

> The individual when only attempting to write a PLAY, ought at
> least to be cherished, thanked for his attempts to amuse and
> please the Million, instead of being laughed at, and hunted down,
> because he has not proved successful. . . . The Author tries again,
> with little better success; and like the poor Gentleman, who is
> ashamed to make his wants known, starves in private, and
> becomes reduced actually to the very worst class of POVERTY—a
> proud beggar—or rather a man too proud to beg.

Nevertheless, he persisted in his love-affair with the theatre, travelling around the country to supervise the staging of his *Tom and Jerry*, which was still a favourite piece in the provinces. One of the cities which gave it the warmest welcome was Liverpool. *Tom and Jerry* ran there for several weeks at the Amphitheatre early in 1833, and on 5 February, the night of his benefit, Egan appeared in his favourite part of Bob Logic. Audiences used to seeing women in their fifties and even older as Juliet and Miranda and aged Thespians as Romeo and Hamlet would presumably have found no incongruity in a man of nearly sixty appearing as the energetic young Oxonian.

The advertisement for Egan's benefit night gives some idea of what audiences expected for their money in those days.[2] The performance began at 6.30, with half-time and half-prices at 8.30. The first piece was a 'Grand Chivalric Oriental Spectacle', *The Knights of the Cross*, an historical melodrama that featured, among other delectable scenes, one representing the destruction of the Spanish Armada. This was followed by Miss Tunstill singing 'Lo, hear the gentle lark', 'Wapping Old Stairs' and 'Cease your Funning', Mr Warrall doing the Highland fling, Mr Paul singing a new comic song, 'I want money', Mr Batty in

8 Tom Cribb by George Sharples

9 Theodore Lane—'Curtain Up'

10 Dusty Bob by
George Cruikshank

his character of the English Fox-Hunter, and Mr Hamilton, Jnr., exhibiting his celebrated 'Sections of the Broad Sword', with other novelties:

> The whole to conclude with the Comic, Operatic, Didactic [*sic*], Flashistic, Terpischoric, Analytic, Extravaganza Burletta of Fun, Fashion, Frolic, Humour . . . in 3 acts, the never-tiring *Tom and Jerry* in which Bob Logic (for this night only) will be humbly attempted by Pierce Egan. And in the representation of Cribb's Parlour, Jem Ward, the Champion of England, Matt Robinson, &c. will exhibit the Art of Self-Defence.

After all this, doubtless, the gorged audiences would stagger off to complete the night's entertainment in one of the many taverns in the vicinity of the theatre.

It must have been the failure of Egan to interest managers in his new pieces while the *Life in London* derivatives still held the boards that finally decided him to rework his old, tried formula. If *Life in London*, why not Life in Liverpool, Life in Dublin, Life in Brighton, and so on? And so it was. On the basis of *Tom and Jerry*, he devised a kind of all-purpose formula play or extravaganza, which could serve in plot and main characters for any town, but be made topical by inserting local scenes, local references and typical minor characters. At last his dramatic efforts were crowned with some success—in the financial if not in the literary sense.

In 1834 his own play, *Life in Dublin or Tom, Jerry and Logic on their Travels*, was presented, beginning on 18 February, at the Theatre Royal, Dublin, the city with which he had strong ancestral links and which had given a warm reception to Moncrieff's and his own versions of *Life in London*.[3] The play was one fruit of his acquaintance with John William Calcraft (whose real name was Cole), the lessee of the Theatre Royal. Calcraft was a remarkable, dedicated man of the theatre; it is surprising that nobody so far has seen fit to chronicle his interesting career or to record his many years of effort to maintain good drama in the largely indifferent Irish capital and to make the Theatre Royal the home of a genuinely national Irish theatre. Like so many managers—like, indeed, Egan's own Peregrine Proteus—Calcraft had been an actor before he took over the management of theatres and continued to combine both roles. In the 1820s he had been manager of the Theatre Royal, Edinburgh, and had acted there on many occasions, playing, for instance, Corinthian Tom in the successful Edinburgh season of *Life in London* in 1822. He had later distinguished himself in Shakespeare in the provinces and was to play Iago to Charles Kean's Othello,

Macduff to his Macbeth and Mercutio to his Romeo. When he became lessee of the Theatre Royal in Dublin in 1830 he went to great lengths to make it succeed. He even took time off from his job of managing and acting to write a book vigorously defending the theatre and the theatrical profession against the narrow bigotry of certain Wesleyan clerics, who regarded the stage as a trap-door to Hell.[4] After seventeen years of struggle in Dublin, Calcraft finally went bankrupt and was forced to give up the Theatre Royal. He later became Charles Kean's secretary and manager and wrote a very good biography of the actor.[5] But in 1834 Calcraft was still at the beginning of his Dublin venture. The Royal Theatre in Hawkins Street had been built in 1821, and was to survive as the only important theatre in Dublin until destroyed by fire in 1880. The rival theatre, the Adelphi in Abbey Street, had only a limited licence; this, and Calcraft's constant pressure against the Adelphi, kept it closed for long periods, opening only occasionally for variety and concerts.

Considerable rivalry existed between the Theatre Royal and the Adelphi, but the Royal always managed to maintain the ascendency. In his endeavour to keep his theatre open all the time, Calcraft presented an amazing variety of attractions, from Kean and Macready in Shakespeare, Otway and Massinger to French equestrians, monologists, ventriloquists, gymnastic displays and musical variety. Continually on the look-out for novelties and remembering the success of *Tom and Jerry* in the theatres of a decade before, Calcraft agreed to stage *Life in Dublin*. And he had no cause to regret it. The Dublin public took to it, as delighted to see local scenes and topical characters portrayed as London audiences had been. The play ran for several weeks, making a handsome profit for Calcraft, and Egan took a successful 'benefit', confirming him in his belief that, if only managers could be made to see it, they had a gold-mine in him.

Life in Dublin was never published, and the British Museum manuscript, for the Lord Chamberlain, is seemingly a draft, but it enables us to see something of Egan's new way with his original idea. It begins with Bob Logic reading a newspaper in London and speaking aloud:

Nothing stirring in town; we are all as quiet as Dummies
regularly told out; nothing on the wing and the sporting world
almost at a standstill and, last of all tho' not least in our dear
loves, the old Charlies, as it were, have become extinct and the
Rowdy here has lost its charms for anything like a lark and I,
the once gay Bob Logic, have almost been transformed into the

last man, or, rather, like Alexander the Great sitting down to
weep that no more sprees are in view. D—n it. I should be
laughed at as a perfect crying philosopher. (Looking at
newspaper.) Let us see if anything is stirring in this part of the
world—how the tight Irish Boys are carrying on the fun in
Dublin—Variety is charming, and Dublin is the place for a start.

When Tom and Jerry appear, Logic persuades them to go with him to
Dublin in search of new sprees. Then we meet Jemmy Green, a character lifted from Moncrieff's play, in Dublin with his Irish wife, who is a
river of malapropisms and who calls Jemmy 'a stupid, ignorant Cockney'.
The scene of the arrival of the trio in Dublin allows of a backcloth
showing a panorama from the Hill of Howth to the Customs House.
There is an encounter in Sackville Street with Irish carriers competing
in the fruitiest of stage Irish for the conveying of Logic; they are dis-
persed by Green on his arrival. Mrs Green is told by a servant that Mr
Green has been seen at the Customs House with three London gentlemen; two friends of Mrs Green, Kate Brilliant and Betty Tasteful, are
present. Egan indulges in one of his frequent pieces of self-advertisement, which also served to remind audiences of past pleasures: 'Tom
and Jerry, did you say?' exclaims Kate. 'What, those gay sort of fellows
that I saw in a play so full of fun and mirth. I should like to see those
merry fellows off the stage myself. I have heard great talk of them.'
Green is then upbraided for not telling Mrs Green of the trio's arrival.
The scene moves to Donnybrook Fair, where, after Green warns
Logic against shillelaghs, there is a brief boxing exhibition, and a jig,
and we hear the spiels of two boothmen. One of the menagerie caravans
breaks down and animals escape. Exit Green pursued by a lion.

In Act II the friends meet at Paddy Killarney's fruit-shop, a well-
known local male social centre, view the new railroad at Kingstown,
attend the Theatre Royal, where the stage in a much-applauded and
novel effect represents both the interior and the exterior of the theatre
in which the play is being staged, go hunting with the Kildare Club
(Green ending up in a ditch) and place bets at the Howth Races, where
the thimblerig-men say their piece and jockeys dance a hornpipe.

In Act III the four engage in a battle with Dublin Watchmen and are
carted off to the Watch-house; they discuss Irish fighters and Jerry
sings a song about the great Dan Donnelly, after which he and Green
have a bout with the 'mufflers' on. The extravaganza ends with all the
characters meeting at a Grand Masquerade Ball, some confusion over
the disguises and a final Gallopade and chorus:

> Fly not yet, ye jovial souls,
> Who love good wine and flowing bowls,
> To join the dance and lively song
> Mirth and good humour to prolong
> At the Grand Masquerade.

There are several other songs, some taken or adapted from Greenwood or Moncrieff, others Egan's own.

A plot would be hard to find. In its place is a series of loose episodes, each relating to a place or an activity of Dublin life, with Green as cicerone to the trio; there are back references to *Life in London* or *Boxiana* scattered throughout, several stock low characters, sporting scenes, two exhibitions of the 'art of self-defence', Irish stage patter, slapstick, speciality 'slots' for dancers and singers and such favourite Egan set-pieces as the thimblerig-man's spiel. It is almost wholly artless, but, considering its potential audience, a not unskilful reworking of the elements that had made *Life in London* a success.

The Dublin newspapers, if somewhat patronizing, commented particularly on the novelty of depicting actual Dublin scenes on the stage. As in London, the Dublin audiences were struck by the realism of the backcloths and of the settings and characters; like English theatre-goers, they were unaccustomed to seeing anything on the stage that related to their everyday life and environments. Others were less impressed. The great actor, William Charles Macready, who played many times at the Theatre Royal, was in Dublin during the second month of the play's run and recorded in his diary:

> 1834, March 5. . . . Went to see a piece which has been very attractive here, *Life in Dublin*—a piece neither calculated to raise the genius, nor mend the heart, and only fit for a minor theatre, but the indifference of the public to more intellectual amusements is some justification to a needy manager for any attempt he may make to sustain himself at the expense of taste.[6]

Like *Life in London*, *Life in Dublin* also went the rounds, being played in several British theatres, including the English Opera House, as late as 1842. Having hit upon his formula, Egan pushed ahead with yet another version, *Tom, Jerry and Logic's Grand Hop at Brighton*, which opened at the Theatre Royal, Brighton, on 4 November 1834. It is along the same lines as the London and Dublin plays, with, in place of scenes typical of those cities, such ones as the Elephant and Castle, on board the *Britannia*, the Oddfellows' Lodge, the Brighton Race-course, various sailors' haunts, the interior of the Brighton Theatre, and so on, the work again ending at a Masquerade. Corinthian Kate, Sue and Jane appear this time and play a slightly larger part, but otherwise it is all familiar stuff. The handwritten draft in the British Museum ends with a note scribbled by Egan to the Brighton Manager:

> I intend to take a very active part in getting up this scene [the Masquerade]—although the other scenes may be very funny— and please the audience—but the last scene must be the *Climax*— and I can get up the chandeliers to look dazzling and brilliant to magnificence—at a cheap rate—If this scene is well done—as so as I have it in my 'mind's eye', the piece will have a good run—as the People will come to see it again and again.

Again his optimism was misplaced. The local Press was cool to Tom, Jerry and Logic on its home ground. The *Brighton Guardian* praised the singing and dancing,

> for which no thanks are due to the playwright, who has introduced nothing of interest to a Brighton audience . . . a more insipid production never dragged its slow length along. The dialogue was, as the *Figaro* has said in another case, 'an avalanche of slang and rubbish', low and witless, full of hackneyed jokes and puns without point.

Its contemporary, the *Brighton Advertiser*, was a little kinder: 'To criticize a piece of this description is out of the question. It is all bustle and bother, without making the least pretence to plot, or dialogue, or any of the requisites of drama. Some of the scenery is, however, tolerably clever, and possesses interest on account of representing localities of the town.' Brighton audiences, being in large part members of fashionable society, were apparently rather more fastidious than London or Dublin ones, and, despite Egan's confidence that people would come to see his play again and again, it came off after a week's run.

He had better luck in Liverpool, however. Here the large Irish public, who were well acquainted with Egan as the author of *Boxiana*, gave a warm reception to his next variation on the formula, *Life in Liverpool*. The burletta, with the same 'plot' as before, but with Liverpool scenes in place of London, Dublin or Brighton ones, opened at the Liver Theatre on 5 January 1835 and ran for fifty profitable nights. The *Liverpool Chronicle*, like the Brighton papers, found the most impressive parts to be the individual 'turns' and the 'faithfully and skilfully executed' scenery, showing such local sights as Woolfield's

Bazaar, the Railway Station, St John's Market and St Nicholas Church. It adds, with the condescension Egan was by now accustomed to: 'Of the plot and the dialogue, the least said the better, being on a par with the other "lifes" by the same author.' Still, it recommended the piece as good, lively entertainment, and the Liverpudlians responded generously. Egan took his benefit on 25 March, and appeared that night in 'a New Character'.

From such activities he was deriving an income of sorts, but, as in the past, most of the revenue from his plays went into the pockets of the managers and lessees. The market for his sporting reports had run dry, and he could hardly saturate the bookshops with yet another anthology. So he turned to the most popular recreation of the 1830s, horse-racing, with a little volume which he called *Epsom Races* (1835). This is, alas, mainly a tired rehash of material which had already appeared in *Life in London*, *The Life of an Actor*, *A Picture of the Fancy* and *Ascot Races*. It appears not to have been a success, and to have had a comparatively small printing, since it is now the rarest of all Egan's publications, only one copy, that in the Huntingdon Library, California, being known. The book is subtitled 'A (Crambo) Sporting Poem, with copious notes, connected with the above great Sporting Feature, and including anecdotes of various public characters'. Published by Egan himself, and distributed by various booksellers, including Sherwood and Ackerman, it is a characteristic Pierce Egan product, an untidy mixture of doggerel and prose, with immense footnotes, wherein its main interest resides. In the eighty pages of the book there are eight pages of introduction, thirty-five pages of notes and merely seventy-three stanzas of his 'crambo' in the 'Don Juan' stanza. The whole is dedicated to John Gully, the only pugilist to become a Member of Parliament, whom Egan exhorts to defend the cause of British sports against their puritanical enemies. He hopes that 'whenever the *spirits of the people* are attempted to be frittered away, by any puritanical pretensions, you will, JOHN BULL like, appear at the *scratch* as a Representative for the Multitude, and "show fight", put in your *one*, *two* (words) like lightning, and *floor* all direct or side-wind attacks'.

The poem itself is a verse equivalent of the boxing and racing panoramas. It records the excitement and pleasures of the meet:

> I like a horse! nay more, I like the Races!
> Yes, have a Flare-up and enjoy the fun.
> But most of all, admire the pretty faces
> At splendid EPSOM, with its glorious *run*!

I like to see the Fours! the Swells! the Graces!
  And those 'would-be' wits, so inclined to *pun*:
The company lively, jolly, merry, gay,
Pleased with the ride, the races, and the play,

and goes on to describe the variety of conveyances and types of people,
high and low, streaming to the races:

Here's costard-Mongers, Dukes and Men of the Law,
  Actors, Ballad-Singers, and Jacks in the Green,
With Tramps—Fish Fags—Swindlers—and Men of Straw.

We catch glimpses of a Cockney family, the Slipslops, out for the day's
fun, we hear the coachmen's cries and the chaffing remarks of the
crowd; we see the side-shows, the thimblerig-men, the Cyprians on
the look-out for custom, the swells, the yokels, the sailors, Osbaldeston,
the Duke of Wellington, the comedians Mathews and Yates, and, of
course, the men of the ring. In one of the stanzas Egan, while noting
Jackson in the crowd, mourns the passing of the 'good old days':

Observe that fine Man, once the Prop of the Ring:
  When the days of the FANCY were in 'full flight'.
Boxiana—is silent! No Heroes to sing!
  Since *Belcher—Randall*, and *Ned Turner* did fight!
But they are all 'gone by', since Time's on the Wing
  And not more interest create—nor give delight.
But JACKSON for ever—shall still be my toast—
Of the P.R., its pride, success and its boast.

Three stanzas only are devoted to the Derby itself: what chiefly appeals
to Egan is the colour and the variety of the scene and the way in which
sporting events still bring together all classes of society in common
enjoyment. The stanzas have a certain jaunty vitality, even at times a
trace of wit. But what gives the little book its particular interest is its
social documentation; on a different artistic level from Frith's painting
'Derby Day', it nevertheless matches it in the amount it reveals about
the English at leisure on a great sporting occasion, and it also shows the
attitude of a fairly typical man of the people of his times towards such
an event. The scene, Egan has it, is 'Full of CHARACTERS, real subject
for the stage'; they range from 'the lowly peasant to the mighty king';
they include crooks and rogues and prostitutes, gipsies, ordinary
working men, Cockney labourers and their families, aristocrats, swells,
elegantly dressed women, but most of all the common people united
on a festive occasion. The English virtues are praised; as he says in one

of the notes, giving us assuredly a personal glimpse as well as a general statement;

> What can equal the pleasures of HOME; when the arm-chair
> presents itself to the view of the fatigued Traveller, the Old Coat,
> the Evening Slippers, a comfortable wash, getting rid of the
> dust, and welcomed home by friends or relations gives an
> additional zest to the Scene, that makes every man feel that
> 'there is nothing like home!' . . . where he can do as he likes, and
> no one to find fault with him. Domus amica, Domus optima.

Of course, the Press is praised as a great English institution: 'Greatest of luxuries—yes, a Newspaper!', the King is lauded in the final line and Egan's patriotism rises almost to the heights of McGonagall in lines like these:

> 'Tis beautiful! 'tis English! all, all around!
> The scene's quite enchanting to a British heart.
> . . . 'Tis interesting! wonderful! truly great!
> Yes, rich and happy England—most triumphant state!

A special feature of *Epsom Races* are the illustrations by Pierce Egan, Jnr. These consist of eight etchings in the manner of the Cruikshanks and Lane, showing such scenes as 'The Thimble-rig', 'A Pelting Shower', 'Starting from the Elephant and Castle', and 'The Running of the Derby'. If a little insipid and featureless by comparison with the work of Egan's other illustrators, these engravings have a distinct charm and attractive *naïveté*, and show the same concern for realistic details as Egan's text does. Pierce Egan, Jnr., was just at the beginning of his career in 1835. As a boy he had shown a talent for drawing, and his father ensured that he received some training as an artist. From 'Fancy's Child' he inherited a passion for the theatre, and while still a youth frequented plays, where he sketched the actors and scenery during the performances. Several such sketches were later used as frontispieces to the plays in Davidge's 'Acting Drama' series. Before the ambition to become a novelist seized him, he seemed destined to have a successful and profitable career as an illustrator. His father encouraged him and gave him early opportunities in such a work as *Epsom Races*, which may indeed have been written principally to allow the young man to show his skill. Pierce Egan, Jnr., was fond of his father and proud of him; there was clearly a close bond of understanding between them and they proved ideal collaborators in this case and later.

Although this book seems to have met with little response, for, after all, almost everything in it would have been familiar to Egan's readers, and tastes, anyhow, were rapidly changing, it did produce at least one dubiously flattering response by imitation. A prolific would-be poet, Charles Clark, used to issue from his private press at Great Totham, Essex, large numbers of squibs, broadsides, pamphlets and doggerel poems all written by himself. One of these called 'Epsom Races: a Poem, Comic, Punning and *Racy*!' uses a great deal of the material from Egan's poem of the same name, but is, in fact, a blatant imitation in form and style of Thomas Hood's 'The Epping Hunt'. Clark, indeed, signs the poem 'Thomas Hood, Esq., The Younger' (ignorant that there would indeed be such a writer) and says, impudently, that he has written it to supply Hood's unfulfilled promise of a sequel to 'The Epping Hunt'. Although the attempt to reproduce Hood's clever puns in the 360 four-line stanzas is a pretty feeble one, Clark seems to have been very proud of his effort and sent a copy of it to Egan, who replied in his usual friendly manner, but with a nice dash of caution:

> London, 4 Paget Place, Waterloo Road.
> August 30, 1836.
>
> My dear Sir,
>   Accidentally calling at Messrs Sherwoods in Paternoster Row, a few days ago, I received your polite present of 'Epsom Races', and also a copy for Mr Gully.
>   Permit me in the first place to thank you for the very handsome manner you have printed my name in the book; and also to remark that I had no right to expect such a flattering token from a Stranger and consider myself by no means entitled to such notice.
>   You ask me to place myself in the *Critic's Chair* on your Work! Impossible!!! Forbid it Oxford, Cambridge, Eton &c. No, no, Sir, the Flash Writer is more awake than to commit himself. But, nevertheless, I am very Glad to hear that *you* live in *Grub* Street; and are an *Eating* Scholar! I wish every Poet and Author could assert the same, as a 'bit of good truth'. Ha! ha! That 'would be a consummation devoutly to be wished'. Wishing you success and fame in all your literary exertions—
>
> I remain, my dear Sir,
> Yours very truly,
> Pierce Egan.
>
> P.S. Mr Gully is out of town, but I will send the Work to his residence.[7]

Epsom Races buttered no parsnips, and 1835 still found Egan in pursuit of elusive theatrical fame, always hoping to produce, somehow, some time, another *Tom and Jerry* to set the kingdom on fire. He importuned manager after manager in London to give him his chance, but was unable to break into the Metropolis again. Some returned his scripts or outlines with thanks and regrets; others sent them back unopened and unread; still others ignored letters and enclosures. Now and again the normally ebullient Egan was betrayed into something like exasperation by such treatment, as the following letter discloses. It was addressed to Benjamin Webster, the actor, author and theatre manager, at that time lessee of the Haymarket, and later to become the manager of the Adelphi:

Friday, Sept 2, 1836

My dear Sir,

Tempus fugit! Five Theatres will shortly open their doors! Have you read the comedy? There is no time to lose! Let me have your opinion—whether it is a *Go*, half a *Go*—or, *no Go* at all! You have had it long enough.

From yours truly,
Pierce Egan.
4 Paget Place,
Waterloo Road. [8]

Webster gave him no comfort, and Egan, now in his early sixties, was forced to turn to other avenues to try to earn a crust for himself and his expanding family. Calcraft, running the Theatre Royal, Dublin, with some success, needed an assistant to act as secretary, treasurer and business manager. Towards the end of 1836 or early in 1837, Egan sailed for Dublin to join his old friend, and took up residence with some of his family at 154 Brunswick Street.

Needless to say, it was not long before *Tom and Jerry* made a fresh appearance in the Theatre Royal repertoire; it was played in January, April and October 1837, and *Life in Dublin* was likewise revived in November and December of the same year. Both plays kept reappearing in the programmes of the Theatre Royal during Egan's stay in Dublin, and even afterwards; *Tom and Jerry* was still good for a revival in March and April 1842. Often, in a truncated version, Egan's piece preceded or followed more substantial fare, such as *Richelieu*, in which Calcraft played the title role, one of his favourites. It was still the case that the boxing scenes in *Tom and Jerry* excited lively interest among Irish audiences, and boxers were from time to time imported from

England to 'act' in the Tom Cribb scene. Sometimes the interpolations in the play took a more curious form, as the following advertisement for *Life in Dublin* on 8 January 1836 suggests: 'In Act II, in the Scene of the Theatre, M. Klischnig will appear, for the first and only time, in the character of a Frog, as performed by him with great success in Paris, and will execute several feats peculiar to himself.' The mind boggles at the ingenuity needed to integrate M. Klischnig's turn into even the tenuous structure of *Life in Dublin*—if, indeed, anybody worried about integrating it at all.

While the Egans were in Dublin one of Pierce's daughters became one of the leading *ingénues* of Calcraft's company and made a name for herself as a charming light comic actress. She had played before in the Theatre Royal, Margate, but had her Dublin début on 14 October 1837 in a short play called *The Rendezvous*. The *Dublin Morning Register*, praising her skill, said she looked no more than fifteen or sixteen years of age. She did not take long to establish herself. When Egan was about to take a benefit on 2 July 1838, the *Morning Register* said of him:

> In return for many a hearty laugh at his unforgettable
> quizicalities and for many a happy hour spent over the pleasant
> pages of *Boxiana*, we cannot do less that wish Mr Egan a bumper.
> But, putting his claims aside, we know of none of our comic
> actresses who have earned more of the play-going public than
> Miss Egan, or who is better entitled to expect a satisfactory
> benefit. Her sprightly and fascinating manners, and her natural and
> spirited performances, have placed her on the best of terms with
> the Dublin audience, and will ensure, more than anything we
> can say, a full and fashionable attendance.

Miss Egan continued to appear regularly at the Theatre Royal in such plays as *Turning the Tables*, *The Broken Sword*, *Rory O'More*, *The Haunted Inn* and *Her First Champagne* until 1841.

The advertisement for the Egans' benefit in 1838, unmistakably written by Pierce himself, indicates that, in the favourable Dublin circumstances, he was able, from time to time, to slip into the bill a new piece of his own which he had not been able to fob off somewhere else, and that, although he was now in his mid-sixties, he still played Bob Logic, at benefits, anyhow, that Dublin audiences, like London ones, expected quantity for money in the theatre, and that he had lost none of his slangy impudence or semantic stammering:

On Monday Evening, July 2, 1838, will be presented, under

the idea that Variety is charming—a little mirth in this melancholy
life is a good thing, and also that 'The right end of life is to live
and be jolly'—

Therefore 'The Play's the thing!'—Hem!—Shakespeare. Come
and join the merry throng, if you wish to have an out-and-out
Night's Entertainment, being for the Benefit of Pierce Egan,
Author of 'Life in Dublin', 'Life in Liverpool', 'Life in London',
'Tom and Jerry', 'Life of an Actor', 'Show Folks' &c., Miss
Egan and Mr Hudson.

The entertainment will commence with a Drama of peculiar
interest called 'The Youthful Queen.' . . .

Also the much-admired Overture to 'Life in Dublin' will
precede, in one act, Irish from top to toe, with a new song
written for the occasion, by the Author of 'Life in London',
'Paddy's Trip to the Coronation, and his return to his native
Isle to celebrate that most auspicious event at Donnybrook Fair'.

Followed by an original sketch, written expressly for this
Theatre by the Author of 'Life in Dublin', called 'I.O.U. or Irish
Dusts in Difficulties'. The whole to conclude—under the
patronage of all the choice spirits—trumps—wits—eccentrics—
odd fellows—intellectuals—old and young 'uns—lovers of broad
farce, &c. with

Tom and Jerry
Bob Logic (for this night only) by Pierce Egan.
Boxes 4s., Pit 2s., Middle Gallery 1s. 6d., Upper Gallery 1s.;
Half price at half past 9.

The play *The Youthful Queen* and the comic song both referred to the
major topical event of the day—the coronation of the young Queen
Victoria, which, coinciding with the Egan benefit, crowded any report
of the latter event out of the Irish papers.

Not many details of Egan's period with Calcraft survive. There is
only one anecdote on record, which may well be apocryphal, although
the separate events referred to in it did take place at the Theatre Royal
about the time Egan was employed there. The story comes from the
Recollections of the Rev. John Richardson and was reprinted by Hotten
in his introduction to *Life in London*. According to Richardson, the
then popular piece of *Monsieur Jacques* was being played with some
success in London at that time, in which a popular actor (actually
Morris Barnett, the author of the play) appeared. At the same time
another actor became known for his imitations of a monkey, called

'Jacko'. Calcraft engaged both Barnett, billed as 'Monsieur Jacques', and the monkey-impersonator, for separate occasions. However, a large audience turned up on one evening, expecting 'Jacko' and when instead Monsieur Jacques appeared, they expressed their disappointment and disapproval in a violent outburst which threatened to turn into a riot. According to the story, Egan came to the rescue. He rushed on the stage, took 'Monsieur Jacques' by the hand and, advancing to the footlights, managed to obtain a hearing. 'Ladies and gentlemen', he said, 'the manager is aware that you have paid your money and honoured the house with your attendance to witness the extraordinary performance of the man-monkey, Jacko. That gentleman is unavoidably absent from the theatre this evening, but he will be here tomorrow. In the meantime, here is a gentleman about to appear as "Monsieur Jacques". The mistake in the names might readily be made. "Jacques" and "Jacko" are two different individuals, both eminent in their respective lines. We cannot produce the monkey tonight. Ladies and gentlemen, allow me to introduce for your approval the best substitute we can find in his absence.'

His words had the desired effect; order was restored and Barnett went on with his performance to general approval. So, at least, the anecdote goes. In fact, it was M. Klischnig, whom we have already met as a frog, who was accustomed to perform as *Jacko or The Monkey of Brazil*, varying such dramatic masterpieces with *The Monkey and the Bridegroom* or *The Monkey Servant*. Much of the popularity of his impersonation came from the audience's memories of the celebrated fighting monkey, Jacco Maccacco, on whom Tom and Jerry sport their blunt in Chapter X of *Life in London*. Contrary to Richardson's account, Barnett's play, *Monsieur Jacques*, was, according to the Dublin Press, very coldly received. But at least the story enables us to get some idea of the kind of role Egan played in helping Calcraft in his theatre.

By 1842 the manager was getting into difficulties which were later to prove crippling and bring to an end his courageous venture in Hawkins Street. He appealed to the public for support in April of that year, pointing to the almost total desertion of the theatre during the season and the heavy losses he had sustained over several weeks. He begged the public not to let a National Theatre be extinguished. By this time Egan, either seeing the writing on the wall or being a victim of an economy drive at the Royal, was back in London at his old haunts. At a farewell function for him, his popularity with the company at large was demonstrated by the gift to him from 'the ladies and gentlemen of the Theatre Royal' of an inscribed silver snuff-box. He had made good friends in the company and kept in touch with them afterwards. In a verse-letter written in more than usually execrable 'crambo' to Mrs T. Hill at the Theatre Royal on 21 November 1842, Egan remembers individual members of Calcraft's band and wishes:

> Success, I must say, to Dublin's sweet city,
> Which gave such support to 'my humble ditty'.

He says too he is

> Sorry to hear of the *shocking bad houses*

and would have

> Better times, I hope, to free CAL. from alarms—
> To the *Autocrat*, tell him 'I present arms';
> Anxious, at all times, his cause to espouse—
> And, if I could; ev'ry night—give him a HOUSE.
> I wish him good luck, without any alloy!
> Box Sheets full, ev'ry night *capering* with JOY!

The whole tone of the letter shows that Egan left the Theatre Royal on excellent terms with all concerned with it and that he had had one of the pleasantest periods of his life there. On the outside of the letter he has written '*Pierce Egan* is not dead, and in answer to numerous enquirers on the subject—to account for his long silence, he has been employed on his Recollections of By-gone days on the Turf—the Ring—the Dramatic and Literary Worlds', yet another of his projects which was not to be fulfilled.[9]

The references in the letter, too, to poor houses at the Theatre indicate some of Calcraft's difficulties. The manager heroically struggled on until 1847. William Charles Macready, who had been one of the theatre's mainstays, recorded laconically in his diary for 3 May of that year: '. . . Letter from King, of the Dublin theatre, informing me that the theatre is smashed and Calcraft in the Marshalsea for debt.'[10]

Egan the Victorian

While in Dublin Egan had not let his pen be idle. Seeing that there was still a complete lack of response on the part of British managers to his plays, he decided, reluctantly, on another attempt to repeat the *Life in London* formula in fictional form. Accordingly, during 1836 *The Pilgrims of the Thames* began to appear in parts, and by the end of 1837 was completed as a book. This was to be his last work of fiction. When he began it William IV was still on the throne; at the end of Chapter IV Mr Makemoney says, 'The King, God bless him, still remains in health, with undisputed prerogative; and long may he continue to reign over a brave and free people.' By the time he had finished it Victoria was Queen. To whom else but her should he dedicate his finished work? The King, generals, noblemen and celebrated citizens had been so honoured before, and it was the least he could do to lay the tribute of his talent at the feet of the youthful monarch. Accordingly, the book had a dedication, by express permission dated, 1 January 1838 from 'Your Majesty's Very Humble and Most devoted Servant, Pierce Egan' to 'Her Most Excellent Majesty, Queen Victoria', and must have been one of the first books, if not the very first, so inscribed. Egan's wish is that

Literature, the Fine Arts, Sciences &c. may bloom healthily and brightly, under your Majesty's protection—who, while you foster the more elevated Rose, will not neglect the humble Violet—that your Majesty may long, very long, reign over a brave and free people, the Mistress of their Hearts, as you are of a Kingdom which is Mistress of the World, and that, in promoting the People's, you may secure your own, happiness.

Readers of Egan's previous fictions would have known just what to expect from *The Pilgrims of the Thames*. This time the central figure, in descent from Sir John Blubber, is Mr Peter Makemoney, 'a thorough-bred Cockney' who has made his way to the top by his industry, been an Alderman and served ably as City Sheriff. Wealthy both by his own efforts and through inheriting the fortune of his old employer, he decides to explore the Thames, of which, despite his long life in London, he finds he knows little. He asks his nephew, Jem Sprightly, to accompany him and Frank Flourish, a neatly dressed gay young dog, to make a third. For all the attractions of Italy, Germany and Switzerland, Makemoney declares, the banks of the Thames 'equal, in point of excellence and greatness, any known spot in the world'.

Together the trio make forays up and down the river, mainly by steamer—to Greenwich, to Richmond, to Windsor, Vauxhall, Gravesend and the supposed source of the Thames, near Cricklade in Gloucestershire. The full title of the book is *The Pilgrims of the Thames in Search of the National*, and the three men end their pilgrimage happily confident that, in their various encounters, they have come close to the 'National', the spirit of England—what makes the nation tick. Egan leaves open at the end the possibility of a sequel—which was never embarked upon—when he makes Makemoney say, 'I hope a time will arrive when we Jolly Pilgrims, sworn foes to melancholy, like giants refreshed, will be able to sally forth, with pen and pencil, in search of the National.'

On board the steamers and on the banks, the pilgrims acquire companions and make acquaintances, among them Charles Turf, who speaks the familiar Bob Logic sporting slang, Mr Bronze, a gentleman down on his luck whose flamboyant style anticipates Montague Tigg, Jack Scapegrace, the elegantly dressed con-man, 'The Duchess' and her 'Girls', who eat their way through Flourish's pocket-book, Nancy Grizzle, the pickpocket, Slender Billy, 'the safest *fence* in the kingdom', and a whole miscellany of more respectable comic types: the giddy Misses Brindle, Miss Azure, a would-be blue-stocking, Mr Pundit, a pedant, Tom Bouyant, an inveterate punster, Raleigh Walter, an incessant smoker, and Sam Smerke, a constant smiler. Like the characterization, the verbal humour and the knockabout fun are of a fairly elementary kind, and Egan finds it necessary to pad out the story with

a fanciful Gothic tale of the White Lady of Kew and a lengthy account
of the life of Charlotte Partridge, who goes to the bad, but comes out
finally on top. Many living characters are discussed or make their
appearance, Alderman Harmer, Police Officer Townshend, Edmund
Kean and 'Muster' Richardson among them.

The forty pages devoted to Richardson include a reproduction of his
barker's spiel, the text of his play-bills, a section from one of his
player's comic turns and a lengthy account, mostly in Richardson's
own words taken down by Egan during interviews with him, of the
eccentric showman's remarkable career. Among the anecdotes is the
story of how Edmund Kean made his first stage appearance (as Tom
Thumb) for Richardson and how, while he was with Richardson's
theatre, he was summoned to recite passages from various plays before
King George III. Richardson, too, gives Egan the opportunity for a
little more self-puffing, in what is also a rather charming scene:

> Muster Richardson often declared that the burletta of *Tom and
> Jerry*, at Bartholomew Fair, brought him the greatest houses,
> and the most money, he had ever received, during his career as
> show-man. The piece was concocted by Bob Keeley, rehearsed
> at Stepney Fair, and for which the comedian received five pounds
> for his trouble. The showman gave a dinner upon the occasion,
> at which the author of Life in London, in company with (those
> celebrated characters—Dusty Bob and Black Sal) Bill Walbourn
> and Saunders, dined off a prime baked shoulder of mutton and
> potatoes in his caravan, metamorphosed into a tidy parlour; and
> who enjoyed their meal with as much *gout* as if they had been
> seated in the most splendid domus in the world; a drop of *jacky*
> gave spirit to the affair, which was concluded over some red port
> that would not have disgraced the table of a king. Muster
> Richardson took pride to himself for the expensive and elegant
> dresses which he provided for the three heroes—Tom, Jerry, and
> Logic; and, in point of fact, they were never better dressed at
> any theatre either in town or country. On quitting the caravan,
> he filled a glass of wine, and said, Here, Muster ****** ****
> [which it does not take much ingenuity to interpret as Pierce
> Egan], here's your good health, and when your benefit takes
> place, I will take ten pounds worth of tickets, and so ought
> every manager in the kingdom.

Edmund Kean also receives a full tribute, and there is a lengthy description of the place and the environs of Woodland Cottage at Bute, where Kean used to retire to recuperate.

Some very pleasant little episodes enhance the book—a night stroll through the crowds at Vauxhall Gardens, kissing in the ring at Greenwich Fair, the gipsies fortune-telling at Richmond Park, the mothers and children enjoying the breeze on the steamer for Greenwich, the Yacht Club sailing match while quadrilles are danced on the deck of a steamer by Makemoney and his friends, the motley crowd having a sing-song in a tavern, the various pitch-men at the Hampton Races, and so forth. All in all, however, despite the presence of the odd Cyprian and crook, there is very much less of low life here than there is in *Life in London* and its sequel. Most of the characters are middle-class or family people or working-class Cockneys. The distance between Tom, Jerry and Logic and the very *bourgeois* Makemoney and his young friends is a measure of the change in manners and attitudes that had taken place in Egan's later years. He frequently puts into Makemoney's mouth statements of the contrast between the age of his own youth and that of the age now dawning. For instance, while passing Milbank the old gentleman observes to his fellow-pilgrims:

I have known this place for upwards of forty years, and, from the best information I have received on the subject, at the period I allude to, it was the favourite resort of a class of person, nick-named *Kiddies*—low-life sort of folks—both the young men and their girls. Their dress was also *peculiar* to themselves. The men wore their hair in close curls on the side of their heads, done upon leaden rollers; hats turned or looped up on the sides; and to their breeches eight, and sometimes, ten, small buttons were seen at their knees, with a profusion of strings, after the famed 'Sixteen-string Jack'; long quartered shoes, with very large buckles.

The language of those kiddies was low and illiterate—they never mixed with any other society but flash company, thieves, &c., and were altogether different from the present race of young men.

Milbank, on the Sunday and Monday afternoons, was crowded with this description of persons—idlers, apprentice-boys, journeymen, &c. It was a difficult matter to obtain a seat in the evening at any of the public-houses on the Bank. There was a numerous attendance of 'cutter-lads', so designated because they subscribed towards pleasure-boats, to row with four, six, or eight

persons—and their coxswain was dressed in a red jacket with
gold lace and white petticoat trousers. The above cutter lads
made quite a parade of their exertions up and down the River.

It was one continued scene of rude low-life and gaiety, which
lasted for several years; and the *ridiculous* and absurd idea of
being thought a 'deep one' and a '*knowing* character' was the only
great object in view with all these sort of people. The rooms at
night were turned into Free and Easy clubs—full of noise and
confusion, and obscured in smoke—and scarcely any thing heard
but the lowest of flash songs. . . .

But, I am happy to say, the scene has long since changed
altogether, and improvement is now the order of the day in
every point of view. Nothing of this kind is now to be witnessed
on Milbank, and the race of kiddies—thanks to the march of
intellect—have become extinct. Men's minds have undergone a
complete revolution; and every thing, low, blackguard, and
illiterate, is not only viewed as disgusting to the feelings of
sensible persons, but shunned in all directions.

The sentiment of these last words is repeated several times throughout
The Pilgrims of the Thames. For instance, in a sporting booth at Greenwich, the trio listen to 'The Slap-up Hounslow Highwayman', a 'prime
flash chaunt' which Egan glosses fully, mentioning the fact that Moore
and Byron used its slang and Lytton and Ainsworth also drew upon its
resources. When the chaunt is over, Turf observes; 'You rarely meet
with, now-a-days, slang songs, except at fairs and in booths of this
description; or at free and easy clubs; but when I was a much younger
man, they were very prevalent in companies. However, we are getting
more refined in our ideas every day, and every thing that is deemed low
and vulgar, is sinking fast into the shade.' Later, at Richmond, Turf
says: 'The spot on which you now stand has been distinguished for
several great sporting events—besides racing, coursing &c., most of the
principal prize battles have been contested at Moulsey Hurst. However,
that sort of amusement has had its day.'

For all its crudity and its old-fashioned character, *The Pilgrims of
the Thames* has more of the tone and flavour of a Victorian novel than
any earlier Egan work. Indeed, there is evidence that he had read and
appreciated Dickens's first novel, for some of the characterization
suggests an attempt at imitation, the first heading to Chapter X is 'The
Pilgrims turn Pic-nic-ians' and Makemoney's amiable and innocent
good nature is of the order of Mr Pickwick's. On the other hand, as

we have seen, Sir John Blubber is himself an early version of Pickwick, and while at first glance Frank Flourish's way of speaking may appear to derive from that of Mr Jingle, Egan had already used such a trick in several earlier characters.

Once more Egan displays what is his strongest feature—his pleasure in the life of the people, especially in their amusements, in the customs of the day, in the busy bustle of London scenes. And, while nobody could accuse him of having a coherent set of theories about literature, in various parts of *The Pilgrims* he comes as close to formulating a set of principles for fiction as he ever did. What it amounts to is a rejection of the Gothic trappings of popular romances and of melodrama and a plea for a depiction of real life. The book begins, in fact, with an assertion that he will have nothing to do

with *Romance* in any shape whatever. No! our castles are not of the 'Otranto' build; nor do we deal in matters like the 'Mysteries of Udolpho', it not being our intention to speak in—*parables*!

Corridors and subterraneous passages, likewise, are not necessary to illustrate our characters, as it will be seen they do not depend upon stage effect—abrupt entrances! awful exits! trapdoors! or blue fire; and ghosts and grinning spectres are much too frightful to be introduced for the *amusement* of our readers! Therefore, nothing of the phantasmagoric kind will be attempted; reality being the decided object in view: and our heroes and heroines are to be met with every day in public walks of life! sometimes on board of steamers; at others *inside*, or on the *tops* of stage-coaches; and not unfrequently to be seen on the *outsides* of horses. They are flesh and blood to the very touch; and words are not put into their mouths like puppets! but they *speak* for themselves, either 'good, bad, or indifferent'.

In Chapter IX there is a still longer disquisition on the same theme. Here Egan defends the truth to life of the reporter as against the fanciful embroideries of the romantic writer, whom he again identifies with the Gothic one:

When the author only takes NATURE for his guide, he treads on sure ground—he cannot err. His prospects are delightful—his FACTS are strong and conspicuous, as to speak for themselves; his mind is also free—his subjects are not *distorted*; and the opportunity *also* presents itself, 'nothing to extenuate, or set down aught in malice.' ... The Author who has his *facts* to work

upon, which enables him not only to write with spirit, but for a
time his *inventive* faculties are set to rest, the good or bad man
is within his view, he hears the one *talk*, and he sees the other
act; and marks down both their conduct; and, perhaps, he may
be surrounded by characters of every description, either eminent
in society for their superior talents, or *notorious* for their improper
and suspicious demeanour: his tale is then likely to become
interesting, in a greater or lesser degree; *singularity* may attach
to his descriptions, but probability is not in danger of being
lost sight of.

Shakespeare he cites as an outstanding example of exact observation;
Hogarth and Smollett are also praised for honesty of reporting. He
pleads for realism in the rendering of people's speech:

> *Obscenity* ought to be avoided in all instances—it may be done
> without—it ought to be done without—and authors are highly
> culpable who resort to offensive terms of expression. . . . But,
> nevertheless, effective humour, and perfectly in unison with the
> character which is represented, ought never to be *marred*, or
> reduced in strength by anything like far-fetched *squeamishness*,
> or an attempt to be *cautious* over much. There are persons to
> be met with daily amongst the mass of mankind, who have no
> value for *etiquette*—who study no rules—have no choice of words
> —no check upon their conversation, or demeanour—that their
> sort of dialogue may be found fault with by the well-bred and
> intellectual part of society, is not to be doubted; but surely, the
> author who is called upon to communicate with his pen, in an
> artist-like manner, sentences that he has nothing to do with
> *personally*, may retort, in the phraseology of the Queen to
> Hamlet 'Those words are not mine'!

This may not be a very complete or sophisticated theory of fiction, but
it shows that Egan had more sense of what he was about than he has
ever been given credit for. He may have himself resorted to Gothic
interludes, he may have derived some of his characterization from
Smollett and other predecessors, but in the main he is a faithful realist,
and his aim is, within the limits of his personal knowledge of aspects of
English life, faithfully to present scenes, characters and speech as he
saw and heard them. To him originality consists not in fantastic
invention, but in being true to the realities of social life and human
character. It is not too far from Jane Austen's practice, despite the

vast artistic gulf between the two writers. In such statements Egan shows himself still much a man of the eighteenth century and one of those channels, albeit a minor one, whereby the central eighteenth-century concept of fiction passed to the great Victorians, who to Egan's obvious talent for reporting added prodigious gifts of imagination and of style.

The Pilgrims of the Thames marked a further collaboration between father and son. Pierce Egan the Younger provided twenty-four illustrations 'designed, etched and drawn on wood'. They form a fine showcase of the young man's abilities, and were his most ambitious work as an illustrator before he turned chiefly to writing fiction. Some of the engravings, such as "The Pilgrims at Hampton Races' and 'Chelsea Reach', have a good deal of the Cruikshank spirit and gift for humorous detail, although the treatment is gentler and the faces tend to insipidity. There are quite delightful touches of wit in more than one drawing; if it is not Mr Pickwick himself who is at the right of the picture observing Mr Makemoney riding a donkey in 'The Pilgrims at Gravesend', I'll eat my hat.

As a final comment on this last novel from 'Fancy's Child', it seems worth recording that Louis James, in his authoritative study of popular literature between 1830 and 1850, *Fiction for the Working Man*,[1] finds that the book has, in his words, 'a certain symbolism'. He goes on:

> The chief character, Peter Makemoney, is a retired tradesman personalizing the prosperity of England, which is one of the book's themes. The trio decide to tour the Thames, since it is linked with England's fame in commerce, history and literature. Their main adventures, however, serve to discover the English character with its rogues, philanthropists, actors, sportsmen, and other types.

This is fair enough; and reasonably well reflects Egan's intention, but the 'symbolism', if it exists at all, is of the most elementary kind, and Egan would have retorted that he was simply recording the plain facts. *The Pilgrims of the Thames* is in many ways closer to *Three Men in a Boat* than it is to *Huckleberry Finn*.

Part, at least, of the novel was written while Egan was employed at the Theatre Royal. During the closed season in Dublin both he and Calcraft were frequently in London, and it seems likely that the younger Egan, in addition to drawing the illustrations, helped supervise the issuing of the numbers when his father returned to Ireland. The book does not appear to have received much attention; it belonged to an older mode, for all Egan's attempts to be up to date, and the genius of Dickens had plunged all other writers of a similar type into deep shadow.

In 1842 Pierce, whose devotion to *The Beggar's Opera* shows in his many references to, and quotations from, it in his books, published a collection of flash chaunts, slang songs, highwaymen's ballads and picaresque ditties under the title of *Captain Macheath*. Some of these are parodies, such as 'Miss Dolly Trull':

> Of all the mots in this here jug,
>   There's none like Saucy Dolly;
> And but to view her dimber mug
>   Is e'er excuse for folly.
> She runs such precious cranky rigs
>   With pinching wedge and lockets,
> Yet she's the toast of all the prigs,
>   Through stealing hearts and pockets. . . .

Others show how thoroughly Egan had assimilated the form and style of the older anonymous Newgate songs, as in 'The Bould Yeoman':

> A Chaunt I'll tip to you about a High-pad pal so down,
> With his pops, and high-bred prad which brought to him renown. . . .

or 'Jack Flashman':

> Jack Flashman was a prig so bold,
> Who sighed for nothen but the gold,
> For sounding, frisking any clie,
> Jack was the lad, and never shy.
>   Fol de rol.

But such fugitive publications did little to provide the kind of livelihood he and his family needed. There was no help for it but an application to Robert Peel, known for his generosity and for having more than once, as in the case of Thomas Hood, provided a pension for literary men who had fallen on evil days. Accordingly, towards the end of 1842, Egan addressed the following letter to him:

To the Right Honble. Sir Robert Peel, Bart. M.P. and First Lord of the Treasury, &c., &c., &c.,

> 17 King St. Soho.
> December 5, 1842.

Right Honble Sir,
    It is with the greatest reluctance to my feelings, and only under

the greatest necessity, rest assured, that I have presumed to
claim your attention on the present subject; but your well-known
love of literature and patronage of it, under any circumstances,
whether successful or otherwise, is the true cause of this
application.

Having been struggling for several years past against
numerous vicissitudes and overwhelming misfortunes, in order to
overcome them, but in vain: I am ultimately reduced to the
painful necessity of soliciting your assistance in my behalf in
any manner you have the power to grant.

For the last 30 years of my life as the author of several
Popular Works, Dramas, &c., having not only afforded, I trust,
considerable amusement to the Public, it has been averred, that
my pen in some degree had exposed the bad and inefficient
system of the Old Watchmen and led in some measure to the
introduction of the New Police. As the Proprietor of Two
Newspapers, I have expended some thousands of pounds in the
purchase of Stamps. I have also brought up a very large
family; and I am now upwards of 65 years of age. I have made
this statement, Sir, as short as I possibly could, well knowing the
immense value of your time; but what I have stated are facts. In
hopes, that I shall have the good fortune to hear that I have some
claim on your consideration,

I have the honour to remain,

Your very humble and obedient servant,

Right Honble Sir,

Pierce Egan.

*** A list of several works of mine will be found on the other
side.*²

Whether or not it was because Egan, unlike most applicants to Peel for
hand-outs or pensions, neglected to include testimonials from influential friends, or because his reputation as a flash writer put him out of
court as a 'literary' case, or because, while needy, he was still in good
health, we cannot tell, but his plea fell on deaf ears. The original of the
letter has on the reverse a laconic pencilled note by Peel, indicating to
his secretary the nature of the reply: 'that I regret it is not in my power
to accede to the request that has been proposed'.

Apart from the useful list of his works which he added to the letter,
the application gives an interesting insight into the ageing Egan's

* This list is reproduced and discussed in the bibliography.

character. It is dignified, by no means abject, and, for such a normally verbose writer, surprisingly compact. It also has a touch of Cockney cheek about it, for the claim that *Life in London*, with its larks on the Charlies, was ever seriously intended to expose, or had the effect of exposing, 'the bad and inefficient system of the Old Watchmen' is as impudent as Lionel Bart's making Fagin the comic hero of *Oliver*! We can only guess at the 'numerous vicissitudes and overwhelming misfortunes'; no doubt among them were the losses he sustained over the failure of his two newspapers, the lack of returns for plays written with such high hopes, the end of his employment by Calcraft and, possibly, over-indulgence on the Turf.

At any rate, such a rejection must have hit Egan hard, since it surely cost such an independent-minded man much agony of mind to compose such an appeal. He still from time to time obtained a limited income from his plays (*Life in Dublin*, for instance, was produced on 5 December, the same day as that on which he wrote to Peel, at the English Opera House), but this came chiefly in the form of unpredictable 'benefits'. Meantime, others were, in the absence of copyright, profiting still from the 'Tom and Jerry' mania of twenty years before. C. A. Somerset's play *The Nautical Tom and Jerry or The Life of a True British Sailor* had a successful run at the Liverpool Theatre in 1843. Although the piece owes little to Egan's original and Tom Trueblue and Jerry O'Flannigan are not the main characters, title, incidents and dialogue are clearly intended to capitalize on memories of Egan's own works.

Very well; if his theatrical ambitions had failed to bring him fame, if pugilism could not longer yield a living to 'the Xenpohon of the Ring' and if the Treasury could not spare him a crumb, he would himself try to exploit nostalgia for what were now 'the good old days'. Thus, on the threshold of seventy, Egan embarked on a new career, that of travelling lecturer. His subject, needless to say, was 'The Art of Self-defence' and his matter a retrospective look at the Golden Age of the sport, anecdotes of the giants of the past, a defence of boxing as a manly science, a history of the Ring, and a lament for the decline from its high standards of conduct and courage. He toured widely with this lecture, to Dublin, Edinburgh, Liverpool, Bristol and elsewhere, and also gave it in London at least once, on Wednesday, 26 January 1844 at the Garrick's Head Tavern, opposite Covent Garden Theatre.

The lecture, with typical Egan additions of notes and appendices, lists of taverns kept by ex-pugs, services of plate, and 'prime chaunts', was published as a small booklet in 1845, with a dedication to Lord

Panmure, as *Every Gentleman's Manual: A Lecture on the Art of Self-Defence*. Pierce Egan, Jnr., supplied a frontispiece, 'a spirited etching of John Jackson, Esq. illustrating the advantage of a knowledge of the Art of Self-Defence to the late Lord Byron'.

This was to be Egan's final publication. At various times he projected several others, which appear never to have seen the light of day. In the *New Monthly Magazine*, 1832, there is an announcement for 'Recollections of the late Robert William Elliston', by Egan; and in the same magazine for June 1836 a note that Egan was preparing two works for publication, *The Pilgrims of the Thames* and a new novel, *Eliza Bloomfield*, 'wholly founded on fact'. Of these only *The Pilgrims* seemingly reached completion. Hence *Every Gentleman's Manual* has a special interest, both because it contains rare moments of self-revelation and because it sums up his attitude towards pugilism after an acquaintance with the sport hardly to be paralleled for over thirty years. The dedication reminded the noble Lord, if he needed any reminding, that

> This great country (Old England) which stands so high in its
> character all over the world, is in all its institutions founded on
> the basis of fair play, from the high-born duke to the humble
> peasant. Tyranny is unknown in it; and the liberty of the subject
> so extensively and independently enjoyed by every individual,
> proves it to be one of its greatest bulwarks.

He defends boxing both because it is healthy and because it infuses 'a noble Spirit into the Mind of Man, to act nobly on all occasions, to curb the passions—and to put a stop to the *assassin-like conduct of introducing the knife!*' Duelling, on the contrary, is 'scientific murder'. He recalls the distinguished patrons of the sport in the past, including King George IV, King William IV ('I have often seen him at Moulsey Hurst to witness several bouts'), Byron, the Duke of Wellington and the elder Kean. He remembers Tom Cribb and the high standing the sport had in his day, Gentleman Jackson and the prestige he brought to pugilism, the distinguished members of the Pugilistic Club, Thurtell the murderer and his fear of punishment that made him decline Tom Belcher's challenge, Lifeguardsman Shaw, the boxer, and his courage at Waterloo, the Duke of Cumberland and his fury when Broughton lost against Slack. He praises the use of the dumb-bells and an hour's daily exercise with the gloves as a means of keeping fit and asserts that he owes his own good health in his old age to these exercises. He defends the pugilists of the past against the charge that they were brutal by pointing out how frequently they looked after each other in trouble and gave their services for charity; he describes the bout between Johnson and Perrins to show 'the advantage of science over weight and strength'; he gives a brief history of the rise of pugilism in England and of its fall.

Towards the end of his lecture, Egan once again deplores the sad changes that have come about in the sport: 'Since the days of Cribb, Molineaux, Spring, Neate, Cooper, Hickman, Jem Ward &c. the ring has not exhibited any *big* or great men, possessing anatomical beauty, with corresponding talents, so as to excite the attention of the public to come out and view their exertions.'

In other words, *Every Gentleman's Manual* is a distillation of the five volumes of *Boxiana*, seasoned now with nostaliga for the vanished Regency days, when British virtues and vices seemed simple ones, when boxing was the great national diversion, when Egan's star was at its zenith and when 'the lads of the Fancy at the Castle so strong' were a social force of consequence. It is fitting that Egan's last work should, like his first, be devoted to his major and enduring passion—pugilism. Doubtless because *Every Gentleman's Manual* was originally in lecture form, the style is smoother and less rushed than most of his earlier reporting. It is, too, an invaluable document for students of the history of boxing.

But its personal interest is also strong. There are several passages in which Egan, rarely for him, speaks of his life and interests. In the first he humbly proclaims his lack of formal education, but asserts that he has compensated for his scanty book-learning by experience of life:

I claim no attention as a scholar, for the truth is I am not University bred; and I tell you honestly that I am nothing else but a plain unlettered man, one who has read as he ran— treasuring up circumstances and events that crossed his path in the tablet of his memory—through rather a long but merry and diversified life, and I think I may say of myself that I am more of a laughing than a crying philosopher, or, in the words of the poet:—

With mirth and laughter let old wrinkles come,
And let my liver rather heat with wine
Than my heart cool with mortifying groans!

Therefore I take nothing from the musty, dusty shelves in the closet—neither have I made up my anecdotes by the fireside: No!

nothing like it—my observations have been obtained amidst the
frost and snow—the pitiless pelting showers!—over hedge and
ditch—good and bad roads—turf and turnpike; under which
circumstances I trust I shall be able to show you the real thing,
namely LIFE to the very echo!

In the second he talks of his health:

Respecting myself, after so long a period as 33 years, I do most
gratefully thank God Almighty for the possession of good health
and what is termed enjoyment of a green old age. It is true I
cannot get over the ground with the celerity of a greyhound;
ride in a steeplechase with Mr Osbaldiston; or jump over a
five-barred gate with Cy Davis, yet, thanks to the Mighty
Dispenser of Events—and I do flatter myself that all my old
patrons will be glad to hear it—I can handle my pen as well as
heretofore; my memory is as tenacious as ever, and my energies
and mind are equal to the task of producing something for the
amusement of the public.

Later he recalls the kind of prestige he once enjoyed and the influence
he wielded:

It has become one of the branches of education, necessary to
qualify a young man before he mixes with general society to
know how to 'take care of himself'; and few of our noblemen
and gentlemen in their youth but have taken lessons from some
of the professors of the art of Self-Defence, and I can assert
without the fear of contradiction that I furnished the present
Duke of Buccleuch with a pair of Boxing Gloves, and all the
volumes of 'Boxiana' during his study at Eton College.

And, finally, he talks, rather touchingly, of the joy and pleasure he has
taken in sport, his lack of regret for the years devoted to it and the
consolation his memory of the great days brings to him in his old age:

I have spent many days and evenings during my connection
with the sporting world, with great delight and satisfaction, and
in succeeding days I have reviewed them with equal pleasure and
felt perfectly satisfied that I have derived considerable information
from the various classes of society I have mixed with, teaching
me, after all, that

The proper study of mankind is man!

In truth, I have also to assert, for many years since, and sinking into the vale of tears, the recollection of them has not caused me the slightest regret; but, on the contrary, they have told me, with increased pleasure on my feelings, that otherwise I might have remained in my garret, *poking* out the ashes of my scanty grate, finding fault with the follies of society, or brooding over anticipated miseries of mankind.

With this swan-song, Egan retired at last from active life. In his last years he seems to have been little better off financially than when he made his rejected appeal to the First Lord of the Treasury, as the following letter to a Mr Brotherton, one of his creditors, shows:

July 3, 1845

My dear Sir,

My bad knee will not let me *run* away; and also prevents me from *running* after them that owe me money. A person promised me to send Five Pounds—only sent *Four*, which I send to you, as I am quite aware that Money is always acceptable—but in the course of a few days he will send, he said, the other £1 when you shall have it, and then you can send me the Receipt.

Owing to the Rail Road accident, I have not been able to get outside the House, since the 19th of May, going on for *nearly seven weeks*, which has been a great loss to me. But I intend to *sue* the Rail Road for remuneration, if they do not come to Terms—as it was entirely owing to the carelessness of their Servants.

I remain, my dear Sir,
Yours truly,
Pierce Egan.[3]

Having lived from the age of the coach to the age of the railway train, Egan was among the early victims, luckily not fatally, of the new iron horse.

The last personal impression we have of him is, fortunately, a fairly full one, an account by the journalist, G. A. Sala, of a meeting with Egan in his last year of life. The picture, if slightly inaccurate in some of its details, is a striking one, showing the old man still able to sparkle when the sports of the past were at issue and to display some of that fire and spirit that had made him so popular a chairman and entertainer in Regency gatherings. Sala was at the time associated with T. Littleton Holt, a Victorian journalist and editor: He recalls:

. . . Through him [Holt], I became acquainted with a man of

letters whom I looked upon, I should say with justice, as a
highly curious relic of the sporting days of the Regency. This was
Pierce Egan the Elder, the author of 'Life in London', of the
'Life of an Actor', of 'Boxiana', the editor of 'Jon Bee's Slang
Dictionary' [this is an error], and of a host of pugilistic and
horsey books and periodicals, once amazingly popular, but the
majority of which have long been completely forgotten. I never
had any appreciable success as the proprietor of any periodical
whatsoever; still I began in that line of business very early, and
in 1849 I was associated with Holt in the conduct of some little
periodical, of the name and purport I am at present wholly
oblivious. I know, however, that it was illustrated, and that the
illustrations were from my own pencil . . .

We had agreed that Pierce Egan should write a column of
sporting matter for us; and he made an appointment to meet us
in the coffee-room of a shady old-fashioned tavern somewhere
in Rupert Street, Haymarket. Pierce had long since faded into
the sere and yellow leaf, and was well-stricken in the vale of
years; in fact, he was 77 when I saw him [this is doubtful], and
the year of my meeting with him was the last in his life. 'A
little wearish old man, somewhat melancholy by nature, averse
to company in his latter days, and much given to solitariness.'
Such a one was Democritus, as Burton, in 'The Age of
Melancholy' described the philosopher of Abdera from the
word-picture left by Hippocrates. Pierce Egan, as I remember
him, had a rather quavery voice, and a shrinking, shuffling
manner, as though the poor old gentleman had found the burden
of his life a great misery to him and was yearning to shake it off.
I had drunk deep of his books from my earliest boyhood. I had
copied, in pen-and-ink, scores of the etchings made by George
and Robert Cruikshank for the illustrations of 'Life in London'
and I could not help asking myself, mentally, and with mournful
dismay, whether this withered patriarch could be the renowned
Pierce Egan, whose proficiency in slang had been praised in
Blackwood's Magazine, who had been the life and soul of several
sporting 'free-and-easies' and the referee at a hundred prize-fights.

Still, you will remember that which Burton says of the
occasional relaxation of Democritus: 'Howsoever it was, there
he lived at last in a garden in the suburbs, wholly betaking
himself to his studies and a private life, saving that sometimes
he would walk down to the haven, and laugh heartily at such

variety of ridiculous objects which there he saw.' So it was with
Pierce Egan the Elder. I forget whether he smoked; but Holt
and I managed to wreathe his old head with garlands of cerulean
vapour, not from cigars, if you please, but from good honest
'yards of clay', of the Broseley pattern; and then, after a few
glasses of rum punch, the cockles of Pierce's heart were warmed;
the old man became eloquent; he began to talk of Tom Spring,
and Tom Belcher, and Bob Gregson, and other famous gladiators
of the bygone; he told us of Jack Mitton and of Gully, the
pugilist, who retired from the prize ring to become eventually a
Member of Parliament. He descanted on the cock-fighting, the
bull-baiting, the badger-drawing, the ratting, and the dog-and-duck
fighting he had seen in the brave days of old; he had known Shaw
the Lifeguardsman, he had played billiards with Jack Thurtell, he
was the abstract and chronicle of the manners of an age which had
vanished, and which, it is most devoutly to be hoped, will never
repeat itself on this sublunary sphere again. It was not an
intellectual evening, and from the point of view of the higher
morality, not a very edifying one; still, altogether the night was
one of the most entertaining that I had ever passed.[4]

This was Pierce indeed in the sere and yellow. On 3 August 1849 he
died at his home at 9 Regent's Terrace, Thornhill Bridge, Islington.
The death certificate shows his age as seventy-four and the cause of
death as hemiplegia, with sixteen hours' congestion of the brain. The
death was registered by his daughter, Catherine, who was present when
he died. He was buried in the 'old part' of Highgate Cemetery, and,
according to an assiduous nineteenth-century collector of epitaphs,[5]
the words on his tombstone read: 'Sacred to the memory of Pierce
Egan. Author of several popular works, who died on the 3rd of August,
1849. Requiescat in pace.' The designation, we can be sure, would
have pleased him very much.

I have searched for hours, on several different occasions, in the Gothic
tangle of neglected graves, eroded tombstones, crumbling vaults,
split mausoleums, tangled creepers, overthrown urns, grave-cracking
saplings and shattering trees which constitute the old Highgate Cemetery,
to find Pierce Egan's last resting-place. It has eluded me. It seems
likely that he is one of those whose graves are certain to remain hidden,
perhaps for ever, in the riotous ruin of this neglected ossuary.

Although he had outlived his time, he was by no means forgotten at
his death. His old friend, Vincent Dowling, the editor of *Bell's Life*,

paid him a handsome tribute in the paper, recording the death of 'our companion "many times and oft" in the battle field'. 'Pierce was universally known and respected in the fancy circles', went on *Bell's*, 'and as the editor of "Boxiana", the class-book of the fistic art, he was an historian in his way as great as Plutarch.' After listing some of his other works, the obituary ends:

> Pierce was, with all his oddities, a right-minded fellow, and was respected by all to whom he was known. He has left a large family, most of whom are 'able to take care of themselves'. Of late he has lived 'on the quiet', and seldom disported in the gaseous atmosphere of jovial life; when he did, it was seen that the 'old light' retained somewhat of its pristine brilliancy.[6]

Egan's style, it will be seen, was infectious.

The *Gentleman's Magazine*, too, for November 1849 noted at some length the death of Egan, 'the veteran historian of the ring', listing many of his works and recalling the unusual success of *Life in London*, both as a book and on the stage.

The official English Census for 1851, two years after Egan's death, recorded as still living at 9 Regent's Terrace, Mary Egan, widow, annuitant, 51; Catherine Egan, stepdaughter, 41; Marian Taylor, daughter, actress, 24; Thomas Taylor, grandson, 8. It seems that more than one of Pierce's children took up the stage as a career.

At the time of his father's death, Pierce Egan the Younger had already become well known for his popular and sensational historical novels, such as *Paul Jones the Privateer, Robin Hood* and *Wat Tyler*, several illustrated by himself and usually coming out in weekly numbers before being issued in volume form. As history, these stories leave a good deal to be desired, and they tend to pile on the horrors in post-Gothic style, but they usually tell good, interesting tales with vigour and professional skill. When the *Illustrated London News* was founded in 1842, he contributed to it. He later edited *The Home Circle* for a couple of years, from 1849 to 1851. It was in this journal that one of his best-known works, *Quintyn Matsys, the Blacksmith of Antwerp*, first appeared. It was, however, when he transferred to the *London Journal* that his greatest period of popularity began. Egan moved away from historical melodrama to more domestic and sentimental fiction, still at times sensational, but with more attention to realistic detail, especially in the country scenes, in which he took great delight. Such serialized novels of his as *The Flower of the Flock* and *The Snake in the Grass* did a great deal to increase the circulation of the *London Journal*.

Indeed, so well-regarded were Egan's tales that when a new editor of the magazine tried to raise the taste of his readers by substituting novels by Walter Scott for Pierce Egan's, the circulation fell so sharply that the younger Egan had to be reinstated to save the day.

From 1859 to 1879 he, showing something of his father's industry, produced some twenty-five novels in serial form for the *London Journal*. Some of these were returns to his medieval style, but most were romantic tales, with a large seasoning of moralizing. He inherited from his father a love of contrast—in characters, scenes and situations—and he liked to offset scenes of rural integrity and poverty against scenes of urban decadence and ostentatious living, while his plots often turn on the reconciliation of classes or the vicissitudes caused by differences in rank and station. Among the most popular of his later books were *The Poor Girl* (1863), *The Scarlet Flower* (1862) and *Eve or The Angel of Innocence* (1867).

The younger Egan's work seldom rose above the level of manufactured fiction, designed for a wide, popular audience; he was, indeed, one of the Victorian age's most prolific producers of cheap romantic novels. But he was at times capable of better things; he could express powerful emotions short of melodrama and enhance his stories with genuine and unexpected poetic touches. *The Snake in the Grass*, which was reprinted in 1887, shows him at his best in this vein. Sensationalism and hectic feeling play a large part in all his novels, but what made him popular and well loved by his readers, apart from his story-telling ability, was his robust and unashamed morality, his love of innocence and his decent sentiments.

Pierce Egan the Younger bore a spotless reputation. Although he was a Freemason, being for a time Wine Steward of the St Andrew's Lodge and later Grand Master, he had no great love for conviviality. He was hard-working, and at times found the producing of incessant fiction for the *London Journal* and of other contributions to such papers as the *Weekly Times* a considerable physical strain. But his tireless writing brought him in a good income, on which he managed to keep his wife, formerly Charlotte Jones, and a large family in reasonable comfort.

He died at his home at Ravensbourne, Burnt Ash Hill, Lee, Kent, on 6 July 1880 at the age of sixty-eight. In his will he left to his eldest son, also named Pierce, his father's Theatre Royal presentation snuff-box, a set of eight mahogany chairs containing on their backs inlaid in ivory the names of the principal characters of *Life in London*, a portrait in oils by I. A. Slace of Pierce Egan the Elder and also crayon drawings of both Pierce and his first wife done by George Sharples.

The third Pierce Egan graduated M.A. of London University, was a teacher and published several works in an *Aids to the Classics* series, being cribs to books of Livy and Cicero. He, too, had a son, Pierce, as also, confusingly, did his brother, John Milton Egan, Pierce Egan the Younger's second son. I have been unable to trace a Pierce Egan in the present generation.

❦ XI ❦

The Man and His Heirs

Pierce Egan made his contemporary reputation not in literature, but on the remote fringes of it, although, as so often happens with practitioners of popular or sub-literary forms, he was to be a not insignificant influence on literature that came after him. His proper *milieu* is the world of journalism and the popular theatre; his concern was not with writing enduring works, but with recording the activities of those in the lower strata of society and revealing the unknown London and Londoners. He is an excellent reporter, not only of sports, in which he excels, but of people at their amusements, of crime and criminals, of Londoners individually and in the mass, and of any aspect of life and fashion that takes his particular attention.

As one who grew up in the eighteenth century and whose tastes were fashioned in it, he reflects the concerns and attitudes of that time. Sterne's special brand of sentimentality touches his work; he has something of the broad humanity of Fielding in treating of the various social classes; he has Smollett's delight in coarse characters and knockabout humour; he accepts the social hierarchy of his day and is as unaware as the bulk of his contemporaries of the increasing fragmentation of society and the concomitant problems of which the Victorians were to be keenly conscious. He stands in the line of Defoe, with his variety of reporting and his constant moral injunctions, giving us the details of a criminal's life in the avowed interests of an 'awful example'. He is, too, a man of Regency days in his toleration of eccentricity, although not of affectation and dandyism, in his insularity and xenophobia, in his complacency about the place of Britain in the world, in his conviction that social divisions of the day were natural and inevitable, in his lack of interest in social questions, in his celebration of sport, in his love of entertainment, 'fun' and 'sprees', in his admiration of the preposterous monarchs of the time. He is a typical popular writer of the day, also—a publisher's hack, a producer of pamphlets, guide-books, sporting compilations, panoramas, plays for minor theatres, slang dictionaries, a newspaper reporter and editor, a struggling 'scribbler' eager to earn a crust in any reasonably respectable way. Yet he is at the same time in many ways an innovator and in advance of his age.

For one thing, he is concerned with truth to life, as he conceives it, rather than with Romantic embellishments or rearrangements. He is a realist first and foremost, trying, within his limits, to put down on paper what he himself had observed, whether it be a protracted prize-fight, a drinking session in a slum pub, or the conditions of life in a debtors' prison, and to convey the special flavour of each by using the lingo and idiom appropriate to it, instead of the bland, all-purpose 'literary' style of most of his contemporaries. His notion of writing, rather than 'theory of literature', as he expresses it in *The Pilgrims of the Thames*, rests upon an assertion of truth to reality as against Gothic and Romantic subjectivity and fantasies. The result is that his books show the beginnings, crude enough, perhaps, of a new urban naturalism, with humble characters and low life being brought into fiction and the theatre as major rather than minor elements and without condescension, with hitherto ignored aspects of London life and the London scene being depicted from knowledge rather than from imagination and with the actual language of the people replacing literary stylizations.

In other ways, too, Pierce Egan was an innovator. In his most enduring work, *Boxiana*, he virtually created modern sporting journalism, bringing to it a wholly personal tone, colloquial, energetic, buttonholing, salted with humour and colourful imagery, and using the idiom and slang of the particular sport in a shared intimacy of experience; these characteristics are still part of the better sporting writing of today, if not in Great Britain so conspicuously as in other countries of the English-speaking Commonwealth. In his spectacularly successful accounts of the Thurtell trial, he pioneered the type of interview with people involved in major crimes which is still to be found in modern popular newspapers. His *Life of an Actor* was, so far as I can ascertain, the first book to be devoted entirely to the then much-despised profession of the strolling actor and the *milieu* of the minor theatres; his story of the humble beginnings, early struggles and final success of Peregrine

Proteus is almost the prototype of subsequent novels of the theatre; it also opened up the way for novels by Dickens, Charles Reade and others. His sporting compendiums, if not the first, were among the most successful of their kind, helped to establish the genre firmly in the nineteenth-century and were read with profit by 'Nimrod' and Surtees. In the theatre, his various 'Lifes' and the whole 'Tom and Jerry' craze, with their almost documentary renderings of London scenes and characters, marked a new departure on a stage almost overcrowded with exotic and romantic settings, improbable plots and mechanical farces, looking forward to later Victorian theatrical naturalism. London, and contemporary London at that, was revealed as the source of limitless material, of fascinating characters, of colour, fun and excitement. When *Life in London* and its derivatives are compared with the previous 'Warnings' literature, Egan's work is seen as a bold, imaginative leap. As a contemporary preface to Moncrieff's version of the book says: 'Who shall *now* say, "One half of the world don't know how t'other lives"?'

Did Egan assist in the glamorizing of criminals and crime which was to agitate the early Victorians and against which Thackeray protests at the end of *Catherine*? Such a charge may, to a degree, be justly levelled against Moncrieff's play. But Egan is always meticulous in showing the consequences of villainy. He seeks in no way to palliate the sordid crimes of Hayward, Bishop and Williams, nor does he give them a single dimension of the heroic. His acquaintance with Thurtell and the murderer's connection with the sporting world does lead him to praise Thurtell's fortitude at the execution, but he is quick to condemn the murder and to show that it was a consequence of Thurtell's dissipated life. He shares the widespread conviction that Fauntleroy's death for forgery and that of the unhappy Henry Weston for embezzlement were excessive sentences, but he in no way approves of or glamorizes their crimes, and his novels are full of stories of people like Splendid Jem, whose misdeeds lead inevitably to ruin, misery and retribution.

The people he does find most interesting are the petty crooks, the cadgers, the fair-ground swindlers, the fake cripples, the beggars, the touts and the cardsharps, as well as such honest but humble folk as costermongers, coal-heavers, dustmen, coach-drivers, flower-sellers—all, in their various ways, legitimate or illegitimate, trying to win a living from a tough and unresilient environment. He makes no apology for being attracted by low life, for finding there a special vitality and even gaiety, for admiring the way in which such people, deprived of the privileges of the comfortable, made the most of their leisure and were capable of rising above the burden of their lives. A good deal of Victorian criticism of Egan and of 'Tom-and-Jerryism' seems to have been based upon narrow notions of what constituted respectability and upon a confusion of Egan with his own characters, as if he were indeed either an idle Corinthian or a fair-ground trickster, instead of being an extremely hard-working journalist, an ideal family man and a consistent moralist.

Many of the characteristics of his writing were shared by such contemporaries as Theodore Hook, R. B. Peake, and Lemen Rede, but his tremendous popular success showed that he managed to achieve an originality and truth to aspects of life that eluded them. This was a decided attainment for a man who was almost wholly self-educated and who from time to time betrayed his lack of formal education in a syntactical confusion, a shapeless sentence or a solecism. But Egan scored by his colloquial energy and his vividness, his mastery of so much contemporary lingo, his direct personal knowledge of the environments he drew, his abounding love for London, his likeable self-confidence and Cockney impudence and the unfailingly robust sense of enjoyment he brought to everything he wrote.

For there can be no doubt that Egan enjoyed life immensely. He seems to have been quite free from political opinions of any serious kind—a vague 'liberalism' of the humanitarian rather than of the anti-monarchical type is almost all that can be deduced from his very occasional political comments; he ignores social evils; he has nothing to say about religion or economics or philosophy; he admires the British monarchy and he thinks Britain is the greatest nation in the world; he respects the English classics and he adores Shakespeare, but his own tastes in poetry are simple ones and are confined mainly to popular verses, street ballads and the like. He restricts himself largely to one area of community life—the amusements and the recreations of the people. He finds contentment and enjoyment in convivial circumstances, in sporting gatherings, in clubs like 'The Daffy', in an evening's sing-song, conversation and drinking. His writings show clearly the limitations of such an outlook, but at the same time, by expressing an unashamed delight in simple pleasures of the matey masculine kind, they add something to our experience of human nature and help us to understand that spirit which today can find its satisfaction in a football booze-up or in an evening in a crowded London pub or a quiet suburban one or in a club evening, where the ritual and the entertainment which may appear foolish, even childish, to outsiders, yet help to establish, if temporarily, a sense of identity and community and shared pleasures. Egan would surely have regarded weeks of evenings sitting blankly before television sets as the extreme of decadence and meaninglessness.

From his books and his letters we can construct his personality in broad outline. He was, of course, a gregarious soul, with a touch of exhibitionism. He vastly enjoyed singing his own songs at gatherings of the Fancy and the response with which they met; he valued his standing with the sporting world, especially with the pugilistic fraternity, and that prestige which made him play such a prominent role in the actual business of boxing, as well as in reporting it; he was proud to be the chairman at meetings crucial to the development of the sport. Almost equally, he enjoyed playing on the stage, and was delighted when his impersonations of Bob Logic and other characters won him Press acclaim. He was a tireless self-advertiser, needing, in the harsh struggle for existence in journalism, continually to remind his public of past successes and his record as a chronicler of the Fancy, particularly as the world of which he had made himself so integral a part receded. But he was essentially a modest man, making no great claims for himself as a writer, never pretending to be the equal of any of the eighteenth-century writers he respected. He knew his own limitations and also where his expertise lay. Charles Knight quotes him as saying of a certain fashionable novelist of the 1830s, 'Ah! He's very clever, but uncommon superficial in slang!'[1] He called himself a 'scribbler'; he is happy to be known as a 'popular author'.

He had a touch of Irish wit, more evident in the quickness with which he could turn an idea to good account than for any epigrammatic skill, but he had more than a dash of Cockney perkiness, being always ready with a quip or an outrageous pun, or to capitalize upon his acquaintance with the great. Did anyone ever dedicate his books with such confidence to so many eminent and exalted people? He was an indefatigable worker. Despite his full social life, his family cares, his deep involvement in pugilism, his frequent travels to various parts of Britain for reporting purposes, he produced an astonishingly large number of books and pamphlets as well as masses of uncollected journalism. Of course, to win a bare living, he, like his fellow-journalists, simply had to write incessantly, and it is easy to understand his irritation when others, exploiting his original ideas, made fortunes while he had to make do with a bare competence, and his disappointment when he could make no headway as a dramatist. But his sense of frustration never lasted long. It is one of his most likeable characteristics that nothing appears to have permanently dampened his spirits, and that he always bounced back, full of new certainties, bad puns and happy facetiousness.

His naïve philosophy of 'A clear stage and fair play' sustained him, allied as it was to that sound common sense in the face of life's vicissitudes which informs his novels, and a cheery adaptability that made him an Englishman in England and an Irishman in Ireland. His energy, love of life, freedom from neuroses and self-pity, as much as his manifest fairness of mind, his integrity and his reliability, won him more friends than his success made him enemies. Since he did not mix in literary circles, he knew none of the great writers of his day. The Cruikshanks, at least in early days, were among his intimates, but his closest friends were boxers like Josh Hudson, John Langan, Dutch Sam, the worthies of the Daffy Club and hacks, journalists and dramatic adapters like Rede and Peake. Editors, such as Dowling and Holt, and publishers, such as Charles Knight, one of Dickens's confidants, admired Egan's professional skill and were proud of his acquaintance.

He was, for almost all of his long life, a physically fit man. He was himself trained in the art of self-defence and, in addition to being a noted pedestrian, he exercised daily with the gloves or with dumb-bells. Only someone with a hardy constitution could have stood up to the rigours of pugilistic reporting over so many years and to constant travel in the miserable conditions of those times without some injury to his health; only such a one, too, could have sustained the many alcoholic evenings to which his accounts witness.

Egan seems not to have been prudent with money; perhaps he gambled, although there is no record of his ever having been inside the Fleet or any other debtors' prison, as so many of his contemporaries were for debts after gambling. His business acumen, too, is questionable, since, having lost heavily on one newspaper, he was rash enough to start another, only to have that also sink under him. The scraping and financial difficulties of his later years were most likely in large measure due both to the losses sustained by his two journals and to the falling off of public interest in those things about which he could best write. The fact that, in the last year of his life, he could seriously entertain the idea of writing a sporting column for the paper Sala and Holt were interested in suggests that he was on short commons at that time. Nevertheless, he did not leave his wife and family unprovided for, as his widow and children were still living at Regent's Terrace two years after his death and his wife was in possession of an annuity. His two wives are shadowy figures and very little is known about most of his family. But that his own home life was happy is shown by the passages already quoted in praise of the hearth and by the affection his son, Pierce, displayed for him and his continuing pride in his father's achievement and his name.

To a succeeding generation, anxious to dissociate itself from Regency looseness and to establish a norm of decorum and genteel behaviour, Egan, with his bruiser friends, his slang, his drinking, his Irish background, his cheeky journalism, his joy in low life, his association with minor theatres and slum taverns—just the things, ironically, that, had he been slightly more disreputable, would have made him a hero today —seemed to sum up all that was coarse and least desirable in his age. He *was* vulgar—no doubt about it, by any standards, but especially by Victorian standards. Yet it was a decent, robust vulgarity that he exhibited, the kind that sustains English comedy and popular entertainment to the present day and which is one of those blessed things that prevents literature from taking itself all too seriously or becoming too solemn, precious and esoteric. Most of the Victorians were reluctant to give Egan credit for even a minor achievement and preferred to ignore his existence; they failed to recognize that much that became familiar popular material in their times had in fact been transmitted to them from the eighteenth century through the medium of writings by Egan and others like him. Yet, although they are silent about his work, they had little hesitation in plundering it for their own.

In particular, Egan has a serious claim upon our attention as a precursor of Charles Dickens and as one of the possible direct early influences on the great novelist. The crucible of Dickens's imagination was so hot that it was able to melt down diverse elements from many different sources into a mass where the separate materials virtually defy identification. It is true, too, that he drew upon writers at all literary levels for inspiration and precedent and transformed all that he borrowed. At the same time, the sources of his early work are fairly clear. He began, like Egan, not as a literary gent, but as a popular entertainer. His models, the kind of writers he set out to rival, were not those David Copperfield read and which he would have us believe he devoted himself to as a child, Smollett, Fielding, Goldsmith, Cervantes, Lesage, Defoe, and other 'respectable' writers—although this is not to deny that he was influenced by these, too—but the mass entertainers of the age, Theodore Hook, Reynolds, the *Newgate Calendar*, Bulwer Lytton, Pierce Egan, the body of anonymous hackwriters of the age, and the producers of the staple melodramas and farces of the lesser theatres. For all the effect upon him of novelists like Goldsmith and Smollett, the roots of Dickens the novelist are deep in the soil of cheap popular writing.

Among such writers, Pierce Egan is in many ways the closest to Dickens—so close, indeed, that at times one might almost be persuaded that Egan is Dickens stripped of genius and heart and left only with energy and talent. Certainly contemporary readers took it for granted that the younger novelist owed a debt to the older one. For instance, the *Dublin Morning Register* of 30 June 1838, the year after that in which the volume of *Pickwick Papers* appeared, noted a forthcoming benefit for Egan in these terms: 'The popular writer of *Life in London* and *Life in Dublin*, the creator of Bob Logic and his immortal associates (the precursors of the "Pickwick Club") will take a benefit at the Theatre on Monday evening.' Without denying Dickens's originality, several contemporaries of both writers recognized that with Egan's work something new had appeared in English writing and that Dickens had, in part, developed this.

There is no doubt either that Dickens had read Egan's works—a copy of *Life in London* was on his shelves when he died. How indeed could he help but be aware of the books that had taken London by storm when he was a youth? (He was nine when *Life in London* appeared, thirteen when *Life of an Actor* was published, and sixteen when *Finish to Life in London* was completed.) Egan is not referred to by name in any of Dickens's early surviving letters, but in a note to Frederick Yates of the Adelphi Theatre dated 29 November 1838, in reference to the dramatization of *Nicholas Nickleby* currently playing at that theatre, Dickens asks, rather plaintively: 'Would you think me very unreasonable if I asked you not to compare Nicholas with Tom and Jerry?'[2] The editors of the Pilgrim edition of Dickens's letters comment on this reference that 'Egan's coarseness of language and glorification of "fast" Regency life would understandably have made Charles Dickens dislike such a comparison'. This is fair enough, but one takes leave to wonder whether in fact Dickens's distaste for comparisons between Egan's work and his own, justly conscious though he was of the quite different levels of achievement, and the lack of any direct allusions to Egan in his correspondence, may have been prompted equally by a not very happy awareness that he owed, in the beginning at least, rather more than he was prepared to admit to this 'disreputable' chronicler of London life.

The problem in assessing just how closely Egan affected Dickens is that of not claiming too much. 'Fancy's Child', like Dickens himself, shared in a popular tradition of writing; there were stock themes, plots and characters widely used by the producers of cheap fiction in the early nineteenth century; there were, doubtless, other novelists read by the omnivorous young Dickens who gave him ideas and hints that at first sight may appear to have been derived from Egan. And Dickens, of course, drew as much from his own detailed observation of London life as Egan himself did. Yet I believe that Dickens owed more to the creator of Tom and Jerry than to almost any other contemporary.

Despite the middle-class disdain Dickens has for vulgar types on Egan's level, the two men had a considerable amount in common. Both came from poor families—Dickens's admittedly shabby-genteel, Egan's Irish working-class, but both knew childhoods of poverty and drudgery; both had early experience of life in its grimmer and harsher aspects; both were, to a very large extent, self-educated, filling out the gaps of meagre schooling with hours of reading and self-improvement, and both at times showed the effects of this limited education in their works, Dickens in lapses of tact, taste and judgment, Egan in a *naïveté* about many areas of life and thought and in occasional grammatical uncertainties. Both taught themselves shorthand, reported parliamentary debates, were expert journalists and newspaper editors. They were both passionately attached to the theatre, and able actors in limited roles, Dickens in private theatricals, Egan in the minor theatres of England and Ireland. While Dickens made an international reputation as a reader—or, rather, performer—of his own works, Egan had his smaller fame, too, as a composer and singer of songs to many large gatherings of the Fancy. Their extroversion took similar forms. Both were absorbingly interested in crimes of violence, especially murders, and in prisons, which appear as frequently in Egan's fiction as in Dickens's. Egan reports the sensational murders of his day with a keen amateur interest in the personality of the criminals; Dickens explores the psychology of murderers in his novels and writes in his newspapers of crimes of violence.

The two men likewise had a special love for London and were endlessly fascinated by its quaintness, its oddities, its back streets, its history, its slums, its varied classes, its low life—Egan as a shrewdly observant reporter, Dickens as its great imaginative poet. Both, too, have a particular interest in crowds, in eccentrics, in seedy and shabby characters, and delight in rendering them. Like Dickens, Egan avows a moral purpose in his writing. At times he sounds like Defoe, seeking an excuse for the portrayal of vice, but the consistency of his attitude leaves little doubt as to his sincerity. The two men share a devotion to Shakespeare and a perfervid, if vague, patriotism, which includes a distrust and lack of understanding of foreigners, shading into a disdain. Both have a tolerance of the unusual personality, which was more typical of the Regency than of the Victorian period. George Cruikshank illustrated books for both of them and claimed the parentage of works by both. And, finally, the two writers possessed abnormal drive, energy and resilience, being notably and consistently productive.

All this only to indicate a closer resemblance between Egan and Dickens than may at first be apparent. Of course, the creative gulf between them is immense; in the light of Dickens's blazing genius, Egan's tiny taper cannot be glimpsed. The great novelist has imagination, inventiveness, humour, wit, poetic power, social indignation, pathos, verbal resourcefulness, art and constructive skill which Egan could never claim. In other ways, too, they differ. Egan was a great sporting writer. Dickens, like most of his class at the time, had no interest in sport, as the ineptitude of his very occasional references and the perfunctory nature of the sporting episodes in *Pickwick Papers* show. There are no 'Sporting Young Gentlemen' in 'Sketches of Young Gentlemen'. Dickens's world, while having in it much that carries over from the eighteenth century, is essentially a middle-class one; Egan, as we have seen, largely ignores the middle class in most of his work, and is concerned with duke and costermonger. He also accepts a hierarchical society and spares it condemnation; Dickens is alive with indignation at the abuse of privilege and at the injustice of class.

And yet, when we put their books side by side, it is surprising how alike the worlds of the two writers are. In Egan's novels the reader of Dickens enters into a universe many of whose features are more familiar to him than are those of the novels of Thackeray, George Eliot and Trollope.

Unlike most eighteenth-century songs, Egan's are wholly free from obscenities or broad bawdiness. His impromptus, club songs and ballads, written for performance before exclusively male gatherings of, to say the least, unrefined characters, would bring a blush to the cheek of no young person; they are simple, jolly, topical songs. Nor is there obscenity in his fiction. True, we have frequent mention of the Cyprians, a social phenomenon no honest reporter could ignore, and Jerry is found in a house of assignation when a fire breaks out. But there is no prurience in Egan at all. Dickens, too, has his prostitutes, although a less frankly-spoken age compels him to disguise their profession, and a change in attitudes caused him to delete the reference to Nancy's occupation after 1867 from the earlier version of his preface to *Oliver Twist*. The fallen woman is a familiar character in the fiction of both men, who treat seducers with equal scorn. Unlike Dickens, Egan was an expert in London slang and cant. His edition of Grose shows him to be thoroughly acquainted with current obscenities and bawdy. Yet he achieves realism in his novels in the use of low-class speech while suppressing obscene expressions. By comparison with eighteenth- and twentieth-century novelists, he is 'Victorian' in this respect.

The domestic warmth of many scenes in Dickens is rightly regarded as among his most characteristic strokes, and his family interiors are often looked upon as epitomizing the Victorian concept of family bliss. Yet it would be hard to find, even in Dickens, a more idealized picture of cosy domesticity than Egan gives us in *Finish to Life in London*, which I shall quote soon. When it is a matter of retribution for the profligate and married happiness for the virtuous in what seems typically Victorian terms, Egan yields nothing to Dickens, as both *Finish* and *Life of an Actor* show. If the gallant action of the poor coachman in returning part of her fare to an unfortunate woman at Bow Street reflects Egan's devotion to Sterne, its sense of compassion draws him close to Dickens.

Egan was the first writer to bring into fiction a faithful and friendly portrayal of the Cockney. As Julian Franklyn points out in *The Cockney*,[3] eighteenth-century criticism and fiction patronize the Cockney when they do not misrepresent him and his speech. Egan, he finds, shows him as he indeed was, and sometimes still is. We do not get a great deal of the Cockney dialect in Egan, although he has some delightful passages, but he is generous with the lively, colourful slang that peppers London popular speech. More than that, he portrays with relish and affection, and without a hint of condescension, not only the Cockney character, but the rich diversity of typical London types which the city had thrown up in the early nineteenth century—the costermongers and their wives, the coachmen, the small traders, such as the tailors and the shoemakers, the horse-dealers, the grog-shop proprietors, the publicans, the con-men, the gentlemen down on their luck, the watermen, the coal-heavers, the swells, the pickpockets, the fences, the card-sharps, the street musicians, the crossing-sweepers, the 'show-folk', the actors, the managers, the servants, the valets and the slaveys, the fake beggars, the lascars, the prostitutes, the bibulous old women and the hard-drinking young gentlemen, the idle young dandies, the sportsmen, the seduced young girls now kept mistresses, the carousers in wayside taverns, the bankrupts in debtors' prisons, the families of working-class people having a pleasant day out at Epsom or on the Thames, the gay crowds at Vauxhall. Here, brought into print for the first time, is the world of characters Dickens was to make his own and give immortality to. The debtors' prison, which Dickens, with the personal experience of his father's imprisonment in the Marshalsea always festering in him, was to make one of his major metaphors in *Great Expectations* and *Little Dorrit*, looms large in Egan's fiction, too.

Few writers up to Egan's time, if any, had known as much as he did about the theatre, both in London and in the provinces. He was the first to treat the theatrical profession as something other than glamorous and to give the intimate details of backstage life, to lay bare the struggles and bitter poverty that so often attended an actor's career, and to portray with affectionate amusement the more shabby and ludicrous side of third-rate companies' assault on the drama. Dickens's own plays are hardly better than Egan's own, and much less successful as popular entertainment, but he, too, had some knowledge of the workings of the theatre (would that Victorian poets had had a little of this before writing their verse plays!), acquired in his early unsuccessful attempts to become an actor, in his own amateur theatricals and during his pursuit of Ellen Ternan. He lacked, however, Egan's close knowledge of 'the profession'; nor indeed did he have anything of Egan's understanding of the problems of keeping theatres open and the drama alive in one of the most decadent of dramatic ages. He sees only the funny side of the Crummleses and of Mr Wopsle.

It is in particular details, however, that the firmest evidence can be found for direct debts by Dickens to the earlier writer. The most obvious one lies in the adoption of serial publication for *Pickwick Papers*. When, in 1836, Chapman and Hall cast around for somebody to write a text for sketches by the artist, Robert Seymour, dealing with the comic misadventures of the 'Nimrod Club', what they had in mind was a picture book issued in parts with just enough narrative to hold the illustrations together, and what they hoped to do was to cash in on the still active interest in sport and recapture the public that had made *Life in London* so profitable fifteen years before. William Combe's four versified burlesques of Dr Syntax with Rowlandson's illustrations, which had come out between 1812 and 1821, are often given the credit for first popularizing serial publication of this kind, but Egan's own *Boxiana*, with its plates of pugilists, had coincided in date with the first Combe work, *The Tour of Dr Syntax in Search of the Picturesque*, in 1812. In any case, while both *Syntax* and *Life in London* provided ample precedent for the 'Nimrod' project, the whole conception and nature of the Chapman and Hall enterprise are very much closer to Egan's than to Combe's. What happened when Dickens took on the assignment, reshaped the idea and, after Seymour's suicide, assumed complete control of the work and, with the able aid of 'Phiz', created *Pickwick Papers* is a matter of history. The fantastic popularity of the work repeated the success of *Life in London* in its own day and established the part-issuing of new fiction both by Dickens and other Victorian novelists as a regular practice up to the 1870s.

Even before *Pickwick Papers*, Dickens was working along Egan's line. It is remarkable how much in common *Sketches by Boz* has with the *Life in London* books. In the *Sketches* there are references to all manner of people, places and things already familiar to the reader of Egan—Jemmy Catnach of Seven Dials, Almack's and 'small assemblies in humble imitation of Almack's', Astley's Royal Amphitheatre, the Royal Coburg, the slums, including 'The Rookery', Belcher handkerchiefs, 'two notorious murderers, Bishop and Williams', the dances at Greenwich Fair, private theatres and their offerings, the entertainers at 'harmonic meetings', a trip to the Nore, costermongers, cab-drivers, young men's boxing-gloves, and slang, such as 'a knowing card' and 'a fast goer'. All of these, of course, would have been well-known to any close students of early nineteenth-century London, although it is curious how many aspects of London life already described by Egan the young Dickens elected to write about. More suggestive is Dickens's reproduction in 'Greenwich Fair' of the spiel of the thimblerig-man, who was such a favourite of Egan's and who appears at length in *Finish to Life in London* and *Epsom Races* and is frequently mentioned elsewhere, and also his description of Vauxhall Gardens in terms not vastly different from Egan's own, a description accompanied by a Cruikshank illustration which, like the Cruikshank Vauxhall plate in *Life in London*, makes a special feature of the orchestra. There are even such similar details in both Vauxhall accounts as Dickens's comment on the ham served in the Gardens, 'that the carvers were exercised in the mystic art of cutting a moderate-sized ham into slices thin enough to pave the whole of the grounds', and Egan's reference to 'ham-shavings', concerning which Logic bets Jerry 'that it was not *cut* off with a knife, but shaved off with a plane; and, if necessary, from its transparent quality ... it might answer the purpose of a *sky-light*!' Likewise, Dickens, in 'Gin-Shops', depicts much the same scene and characters as Egan does in *Life in London*, including the bloated women and their children and the contrasted servers and drinkers. Dickens gives much more detail, and his description is free from Eganesque slang, but the similarities are unmistakable and are underlined by the illustrations, that to *Sketches* by George Cruikshank, that to *Life* by Robert, both of which feature prominently a huge barrel of 'Old Tom'.

In book after book, Egan, as we have seen, makes much of 'Muster' Richardson's travelling theatre; and Richardson's is one of the main features of Dickens's piece on Bartholomew Fair. Egan is as aware of the limitations of Richardson's dramatic offerings as Dickens is; his quartet 'were more inclined to praise the liberality and industry of *Muster* Richardson and the exertions of the performers, than fastidiously to criticize and laugh at the pieces produced under so many disadvantages'. He has his fun, though, with an anecdote about 'the ghost being drunk' during one of the performances. Dickens, too, makes a great deal of the ghost in a Richardson play, but, of course, with his superior gift for humour, gets infinitely more out of his account of the presentation than Egan does.

In view of such resemblances, it is not surprising, remembering Bob Logic and his trade-mark, the green spectacles, to come across one young man similarly adorned in *Sketches by Boz*. This is Mr Edkins in 'The Steam Excursion', 'a pale young gentleman, in a green stock and spectacles of the same, a member of the Honourable Society of the Inner Temple', who is thereafter referred to as 'the young gentleman in the green spectacles'.

Of course there are many other influences to be detected in the *Sketches by Boz*, most notably, perhaps, the novels of Theodore Hook about Cockney picaros, but the *Boz* world and the Egan world resemble each other at so many points that one feels that it was Egan, above all others, who opened up the highway down which Dickens so triumphantly drove.

This conviction is strengthened when we turn to *Pickwick Papers*. Apart altogether from the fact that the number parts of *Life in London* were the main precedent for the form in which Dickens's book was issued, there is much in the latter that looks like direct borrowing from Egan. Nineteenth-century writers had little doubt that this was the case. An anonymous critic of *Pickwick Papers* quoted by John Camden Hotten in his *Charles Dickens*[4] called the novel '2 pounds of Smollett, 3 ounces of Sterne, a handful of Hook, a dash of the grammatical Pierce Egan—incidents at pleasure, served with an original *sauce piquante*'. But Dickens owed more to the older writer than this implies, and in this connection it is relevant to quote a letter from a friend, unnamed, which Hotten prints in his book:

> When I stated to you that Dickens took his idea of novel-writing from the works of Mr Pierce Egan, I had nothing but internal evidence to go upon. When he began to write, the most popular fiction were the descriptions of 'Life in London' connected with the names of Tom and Jerry. The grand object of Dickens, as a

novelist, has been to depict not so much human life as human life in London, and this he has done after a fashion which he learnt from the 'Life in London' of Mr Pierce Egan. If you remember that once famous book, you will call to mind that he takes his heroes—the everlasting Tom and Jerry—now to a fencing-saloon, now to a dancing-house, now to a chophouse, now to a spunging-house. The object is not to evolve the characters of Tom and Jerry, but to introduce them in new scene after new scene. And so you find with Dickens. He invents new characters, but he never invents them without at the same time inventing new situations and surroundings of London life. Other novelists would not object to invent new characters appearing in the same position of life as the characters in some preceding novel, and trusting for novelty to the newness of the surroundings and the situation. Dickens insists upon putting the new characters into a new and unexpected trade—doll-making, perhaps, or newsvending—and he has always in view some new phase of London life which he is far more anxious to exhibit than the characters without whom it is impossible to bring the phase into prominence. If you look to his writings, or if you talk to him, you will find that his first thought is to find out something new about London life—some new custom or trade or mode of living—and his second thought is to imagine the people engaged in that custom or trade or mode of living. Now this is Pierce Egan's style—and Dickens, with rare genius, and with large sympathies, has followed in grooves which the once celebrated Pierce laid down. Pierce Egan had no wit, and his conversations are not worth mentioning. Dickens riots in wit, and what Pierce would have shown in a description, Dickens makes out in a conversation. But the objects of the two men, to magnify London life and show it in all its phases, were the same.[5]

Whatever one may think of the view of Dickens's approach to character suggested by this comment, the general account of the resemblances between the work of Egan and Dickens is a shrewd and a just one and applies as much to *Pickwick Papers* as to any later work. But the resemblances in detail are more to *Finish to Life in London* than to *Life in London* itself. I have already drawn attention to the close similarity between Mr Pickwick and Sir John Blubber, self-made, respectable, charitable, 'a jolly, good-natured soul', with a penchant for getting into situations of physical discomfort from which he recovers with perpetual good-humour, and to the fact that Sir John joins Jerry's coach not far from the town of Pickwick, which Egan had already described in his *Walks Through Bath*. Other resemblances suggest that Dickens took more than Mr Pickwick's name from Egan's novel. The quartet of Tom, Jerry, Logic and Blubber, with the occasional addition of Splinter, is paralleled by the quartet of Tupman, Winkle, Snodgrass and Pickwick, with the occasional addition of Jingle. Tupman is the dashing ladies' man, as is Jerry, and equally frustrated; Winkle is as hopeless at sports as is Bob Logic. The episode in Chapter VII of *Pickwick Papers* when Winkle shoots Tupman reminds us of that in Chapter III of *Finish* when Logic, just as inept with a gun, shoots out old Catchpole's casement. Logic, incidentally, at that time goes through the ice as Mr Pickwick does, too, in a different episode. Mr Pickwick is transported in a wheel-barrow; Sir John, quite as ignominiously, in a basket on the head of a coster-woman; Mr Pickwick gets himself into the wrong bedroom in Chapter XXII; Bob Logic's sleep is interrupted by the appearance of an apparent ghost, actually Splinter, who has sleep-walked into the wrong room. In the same chapter Mr Pickwick meets a Mr Magnus, a man 'with an inquisitive nose and green spectacles'. Bob Logic finds himself in the Fleet in *Life in London* and gets out of it in *Finish* and Splinter enters 'Banco Regis' in *Finish*, just as Mr Pickwick, too, has his taste of the Fleet and finds Jingle there.

One of the most completely delineated characters in *Finish* is Bill Put-'em-along, a gentlemanly coachman with a taste for leg-pulling, a wry sense of humour and a friend in every inn-keeper. Here is a hint, and no more, for old Mr Weller. There is however, a large dash of Bob Logic in Bob Sawyer—both irresponsible students, both fond of the bottle, both keener on a 'lark' than on study, both slangy young dogs. At one stage in *Pickwick Papers* (Chaper L), as if to point the relationship, Bob Sawyer dons 'his professional green spectacles'.

Even the kind of domestic scene of merriment and contentment which Dickens made his own is foreshadowed in *Finish*. The mood of the party at Dingley Dell—benevolent clergyman and all—is anticipated in Chapter III of *Finish*, where, also in the country, the main characters relax in the evening. Egan depicts them all at their ease before a blazing fire:

> Bob, as usual, in order to make the company merry, is reading a laughable police account from a London newspaper to Jerry's mamma, who is so much *tickled* by the drollery of the circumstance, as to give way to loud laughter; and Tim Bumkin,

the waiting-man, is likewise so convulsed with the subject, as to
spill the wine over the garments of the Oxonian, apologizing
at the same time for his lack of attention to the company, in
consequence of the irresistible comic humour displayed by Mr
Logic. The father of Jerry, seated in the corner, enjoying his pipe,
is challenging Old Jollyboy, the Curate of the parish, and
schoolmaster to his son in his boyish days, to fill another horn of
his 'prime October'. The Curate was one of the most regular men
alive; and a great *stickler* for everything in its place. 'A sermon,'
he said, 'was *good*; all men ought to be *good*; eating and drinking
ought to be *good*, and hunting was *good*, i.e. *good exercise*; and to
take care of one's self was, most certainly, *good*.' ... Miss Rosebud has hold of Jerry's arm, who is pointing out to her his
friend Bob, stating that he is one of the funniest fellows in the
universe! ... The daughter of the Curate ... who is seated by
the side of the Corinthian, is complimenting Tom on the
excellence of his song. ... The 'uncommonly big Gentleman'
is told out with *fatigue*; and in order to 'come to time' when the
supper is announced, he is taking, on the sly, 'forty winks'.
The huntsman hanging up the horn; the little girl and her doll;
the child playing with the kitten; the greyhound at the feet of
Tom; the domestic happy couple contiguous to the fireside;
the stag's head and horns; guns; the brushes of Reynard &c.,
making the above interesting group complete.

The Cockney speech of Sam Weller and his father, too, finds precedent
in such passages as that quoted earlier from *Finish* which reproduces the
spiel of the dancing-room barker or in such lively pieces as Chaffing
Peter's appeal to the judge in *Life in London*:

Vell, my Lord, just as I caught hold of my ass, a squinty old
apple-woman came between me and my ass, and she tripped me
up, my Lord, so help me bob it is true; ven I, to save myself
from falling into a cellar, my Lord, I caught hold of a pair of
breeches that vas hanging upon a nail. But the *traps*, my Lord,
immediately took me into custody and said as how I stole 'em.
So help me bob, my Lod, I did not vant any breeches, I only
vanted my ass.

When Sam Weller sings his 'Romance', 'Dick Turpin vunce on Hounslow Heath', he is singing exactly the kind of slang chaunt which
features in every Egan novel.

Like the Pickwickians, Egan's quartet attend a masquerade ball; the Egan quartet go to an archery contest and a shooting party engages the Pickwickians. And just as Dickens works off some of his short stories in the course of the book, Egan, too, always has his irrelevant narratives related by some character in the main story. There is a direct reminiscence of Egan's world in the reaction of Dickens's magistrate to the news of the proposed duel: 'Do you happen to have heard, ma'am, that I rushed into a prize-ring on the fourth of May last, attended by only sixty special constables; and, at the hazard of falling a sacrifice to the angry passions of an infuriated multitude, prohibited a pugilistic contest between the Middlesex Dumpling and the Suffolk Bantam?' And, finally, the conversations of Sam Weller and his father are peppered with carefully selected slang words from Egan's copious stock: 'draw the blunt', 'lushy', 'out-and-outer', 'a screw loose somewhere', 'gift o' the gab', 'thorough-going pacer', 'horse chanter', and so on, not to mention 'slavey' and 'slums'.

Perhaps, too, the fact that *Pickwick Papers* is the most alcoholic novel that Dickens wrote may be in part as a result of Egan's influence. The quantity of brandy-and-water, rum punch, port and miscellaneous liquors consumed by Dickens's characters in this book makes it closer in spirit to *Life in London* than to the reformed George Cruikshank's later temperance tracts.

As Dickens gains confidence in his own powers and resources, there are fewer and fewer traces of Pierce Egan in his writings. But he did not free himself from this influence all at once. Both *Oliver Twist* and *Nicholas Nickleby* in different ways owe something to the author of *Life in London*. *Oliver Twist*, that strange, haunting, unequal book, is obviously closer to the Newgate novel proper than it is to anything Egan wrote. True there are references to Ikey Solomons, the original of Fagin, and his wife, also a fence, in Egan's newspapers and there are low-life tarts in both *Life in London* and *Finish*, sometimes, incidentally, called 'Nan', 'Nance' or 'Nancy'; but Sikes, Nancy, and Fagin and his gang are Dickens's own wonderful creations. One strange resemblance, however, seems to me worth noting. In *Finish*, Chapter VII, when Logic goes with his friends to visit old acquaintances still in the Fleet, they encounter Old Mordecai, a Jewish swindler, moneylender, marriage broker and con-man, against whom Logic warns the others in a lengthy passage. In Cruikshank's illustration Mordecai appears astonishingly like the Fagin drawn by George Cruikshank for *Oliver Twist*—flat shovel-hat, thin, straggly beard, dressing-gown and all. Could this, I wonder, be the real source of George's assertion that he had suggested the character of Fagin to Dickens?

In Chapter XXVI of *Oliver Twist* there is, too, a description of a 'sing-song' night in The Three Cripples, with the rogues and their women gathering to drink and carouse, which closely resembles similar scenes in *Life in London* at All-Max and in the 'Holy Land'.

Such similarities may, of course, be merely coincidental, merely indicating that both writers were carefully observant of these particular things in real life—although one takes leave to doubt if the young Dickens ever attended, as Egan undoubtedly did, convivial 'harmonic evenings' at gatherings of crooks and prostitutes. The main way in which Dickens seems to have used Egan in *Oliver Twist* is in taking over from his books most of the criminal cant he employs to such good effect. Egan's edition of Grose gives all the words Dickens puts in the mouth of the Artful Dodger and Bill Sikes; so too do the *Life in London* books. Every reader of Egan would have been quite familiar with 'blunt', 'out-and-outer', 'flash', 'green', 'fork out', 'lushed', 'prad' (horse), 'prig' (thief), 'fogle' (Sikes, it will be remembered, has 'a dirty Belcher handkerchief' around his neck), 'blown upon' (betray), 'castor', 'crib', 'file' (pickpocket), 'flat', 'heavy swell' and terms like these. And it is 'Daffy' that Mrs Mann gives to the orphans, obliging her, of course, to keep a bottle of gin in her home cupboard.

There is another direct reminiscence of Egan's special world in *Oliver Twist* also when, in Chapter XXXI, Mr Blathers speaks of Conkey Chickweed, who 'kept a public-house over Battleridge way, and he had a cellar, where a good many young lords went to see cock-fighting, and badger-drawing, and that; and a werry intellectual manner the sports was conducted in, for I've seen 'em off'en.' This is the tone of jesting contempt with which Dickens always treats such aspects of Regency life.

The only reference in Dickens's correspondence to Tom and Jerry, which I have already quoted, comes, interestingly enough, in connection with *Nicholas Nickleby*. But it was *The Life of an Actor*, in my view, not the Tom and Jerry books, to which Dickens was in some manner indebted in *Nicholas Nickleby*. Certainly in Mulberry Hawk and Lord Verisopht he drew unflattering pictures of the kind of aristocrat who won Egan's regard for their patronage of sport. Hawk, indeed, is explicitly linked with pugilism. When Ralph Nickleby goes to visit the injured nobleman—

'A raw, slight stripling against a man whose very weight might crush him; to say nothing of his skill in—— I am right, I think,' said Ralph, raising his eyes; 'you were a patron of the ring once, were you not ?'

The sick man made an impatient gesture, which Ralph chose to consider as one of acquiescence.

In another part of the novel (Chapter XV) Dickens also expresses his distaste for the kind of amusement with which his contemporaries too readily identified Tom and Jerry. Miss Petowker is discussing Nicholas:

'Why—dear me, how stupid I am,' replied Miss Petowker, hesitating. 'What do you call it, when lords break off door-knockers and beat policemen, and play at coaches with other people's money, and all that sort of thing ?'

'Aristocratic ?' suggested the collector.

'Ah! aristocratic,' replied Miss Petowker; 'something very aristocratic about him, isn't there ?'

Ralph Nickleby himself, in the main a character straight from a thousand melodramatic plays and novels about wicked uncles and oppressive money-lenders, has, nevertheless, many affinities with Old Screw, the knavish money-lender whom Splinter approaches and against whom Bob Logic warns him. The lengthy document which Logic gives Splinter setting out the tricks and deceits of money-lenders could be a blue-print of Ralph Nickleby's financial activities; one of the practices, for instance, of Screw's, which is also one of Ralph's, is giving elaborate entertainments and dinners for his clients and potential gulls.

It is, however, in the Crummles episodes of *Nicholas Nickleby* that Egan seems to have been most in Dickens's mind. True, Dickens had his independent knowledge of theatrical life, although it was clearly less intimate than Egan's, especially where the back-stage *milieu* was concerned. But not only is the general atmosphere of the seedy professional companies in which Peregrine Proteus finds himself very like that associated with the Crummles troupe and his situation, that of a reasonably well-educated and genteel young man among shabby pros, analogous to that of Nicholas, but there are suggestive resemblances in detail between these scenes and *The Life of an Actor*. Peregrine's disappointment at finding that the theatre to which he goes in the provinces is a mere barn is much the same as that of Nicholas and Smike emerging on to the stage of the Portsmouth theatre. Crummles himself shares some of the characteristics of Mr Plausible Screw, the actor-manager who first engages Peregrine, and of Richardson, whom he joins at Bartholomew Fair. The description by Screw of his company and by Richardson of his struggles resembles Mr Crummles's discourses to Nicholas. Crummles and Richardson are seen by their individual presenters as equally absurd and likeable.

In *The Life of an Actor* the female players quarrel over a part; in *Nicholas Nickleby* Nicholas and Lenville have their own quarrel. Peregrine plays Romeo, is a hit and captivates both audience and company; Nicholas does the same. Like Peregrine, both Nicholas and Miss Snevellicci have their 'bespeaks'; there is the same bewildering rapidity in 'getting up a new piece' and in producing a script for it in both novels; the scenes of rehearsals and back-stage titivating have a family likeness also in both. The plays presented, apart from those by Shakespeare, are described by Egan in a lightly affectionate, tongue-in-the-cheek manner; Dickens is much more outrageously funny about them; his sympathy with the players is at least equal to that of Egan, but he has less tolerance for the wretched pieces they presented. His parodies of the high-flown theatrical language and his descriptions of Mr Crummles's histrionics, of the stage appearances of 'The Infant Phenomenon' and of the affectations of the female members of the company far outdo anything in Egan's book. Yet not only did Pierce anticipate Dickens in his introducing into fiction the fourth-rate provincial travelling company and the characters that comprised it, its making do, its financial struggles and its poor pay for the actors, the deplorable state of the theatres and other places where the plays were staged, and the general mixture of good humour, seediness and illusion in such groups, but he treated these things with a generosity of outlook and a sympathy that must have appealed to Dickens. In any case, in no two novels of this age other than *Nicholas Nickleby* and *The Life of an Actor* is there so much common material about travelling theatricals or such a similarity in the way the theatre and its people are shown. That Dickens surpasses Egan in every respect should not lead us to overlook the contribution the latter made towards the final effect.

From *The Old Curiosity Shop* fewer and fewer traces of Egan can be seen in Dickens's work, as his material expands and he finds himself more fully and richly. Yet Egan's world—the Regency world—keeps cropping up in several of the later novels; there is, for instance, the odious Mr Turveydrop, that monstrous relic of the Regency period, in *Bleak House,* and there is the inspector in Chapter II of *Hard Times,* who takes us right back to *Boxiana*:

... in his way, a professed pugilist; always in training, always with a system to force down the general throat like a boulus, always to be heard of at the bar of his little Public-house, ready to fight all England. To continue in fistic phraseology, he had a genius for coming up to the scratch, wherever and whatever it was, and proving himself an ugly customer. He would go in and damage any subject whatever with his right, follow up with his left, stop, exchange, counter, bore his opponent (he always fought All England) to the ropes, and fall upon him neatly. He was certain to knock the wind out of common sense, and render that unlucky adversary deaf to the call of time.

In the same novel the kindly Mr Sleary, of Sleary's Circus Troupe, reminds us again of 'Muster' Richardson. There are, too, the battered ex-pug., Mr Rouncewell's brother, in *Bleak House* and 'The Game Chicken' in *Dombey and Son* (the nickname, incidentally of an actual fighter, 'Hen' Pearce, of Egan's day), to recall to us the days when pugilism was a national pastime and Egan was its chronicler.

But to go hunting for traces of Egan in Dickens's work after 1838 would be to chase quincunxes. To try to make anything out of the fact that Egan describes the convicts at Chatham awaiting transportation to New South Wales and that Dickens does the same in *Great Expectations*, that Mary Rosebud in the *Life in London* books has an echo in Rosa Budd in *Edwin Drood*, that Egan's nickname was 'Pip', and so on would be absurd. Sufficient, I hope, has been said to show not only that Dickens's early books belong to the same world as those of Pierce Egan, but that, in several particulars, Dickens was directly indebted to the 'slang writer' and was conscious of being in competition with such successful popular fiction as *Life in London*. At the same time, while finding material and occasional inspiration in Egan, Dickens, by temperament and class, found himself opposed to almost everything that Egan seemed to him to stand for: Regency looseness, irresponsible Corinthianism, sporting mania, physical brutality, coarseness of outlook and language, lack of refinement in manners, social divisions, monarchical decadence, and vulgarity. He never anywhere in his books shows the least sympathy with the Regency period and is quick to parody its manners and caricature its people. Yet in many ways he is closer in the happy vulgarity of his tone, in his delight in eccentrics, humble folk and Cockney crowds enjoying themselves, and in his attempts to reproduce the speech of the people to Egan and his contemporaries than he is to the great novelists of his own age.

Egan's influence did not end with Dickens. Ainsworth in novels like *Rookwood* and Lytton in *Eugene Aram* drew upon his books and pamphlets for details of low life and upon his edition of Grose as well as upon Vaux and other slang-compilers for the bits of slang and cant that spatter their novels. According to Louis James,[6] Eugene Sue's *The Mysteries of Paris* was inspired by *Life in London*. When G. W. M. Reynolds issued his *Mysteries of London* in 1845–6 he plundered both Sue's work and Egan's original. R. S. Surtees, who is, after Egan, the nineteenth-century writer who most exploited sport in his books, had his own detailed knowledge of hunting and other sports, and could deal with them freed from the spice of gambling or physical brutality. Now and again in his novels some of the episodes suggest that he has been dipping into Egan's sporting anthologies. His early novels, almost contemporaneous with *Finish to Life in London*, share Egan's realism, but most of all they resemble the work of 'Fancy's Child' in what Raymond Chapman calls 'the good-humoured tolerance that the Regency had extended to eccentricity and the Victorians were to lose'.[7]

Quite late in the nineteenth century Egan still retained his power to attract and influence. The young George Bernard Shaw, then vainly trying to break into the field of novel-writing, wrote on 31 May 1883 to Richard Bentley & Son to acknowledge the return, at long last, of the manuscript of *Cashel Byron's Profession*: 'Should you ever contemplate a reprint of the works of the late Pierce Egan, I will be happy, in the capacity of editor, to place at your disposal the historical research I have wasted on "Cashel Byron".'[8] When the novel was eventually published, Shaw prefaced it with a magnificent discussion of prize-fighting in the old bare-knuckle days, its relation to the English spirit, its brutality and the lack of understanding with which English writers had handled it. He quite rightly castigates Dickens for his portrayal of the 'Game Chicken' in *Dombey and Son*.

> It is true [Shaw writes] that *Dombey and Son* contains a pious attempt to caricature a prize-fighter; but no qualified authority will pretend that Dickens caught the Chicken's point of view, or did justice to the social accomplishments of the ring. . . . If Dickens had really known the ring, he would have made the Chicken either a Sayers in professional ability or a Sam Weller in sociability. A successful combination of personal repulsiveness with professional incompetence is as impossible there as at the bar or in the faculty.

His own novel, he claims, was an attempt to 'present the prize-fighter and his pursuits without any romantic glamour', and the main source of his information came from *Boxiana*. He had soaked himself in Egan's volumes, as the novel itself, with all its rich detail straight from *Boxiana*, bears witness and as such a passage from the Preface as this indicates:

> Few living men remember the palmy days when Tom and
> Jerry went to Jackson's rooms (where Byron—not Cashel, but
> the poet—studied 'the noble art') to complete their education as
> Corinthians; when Cribb fought Molyneux and was to Tom
> Spring what Skene was to Cashel Byron; when Kemble engaged
> Dutch Sam to carry on the war with the O.P. rioters; when
> Sharples' portraits of leading bruisers were engraved on steel;
> when *Bell's Life* was a fashionable paper and Pierce Egan's
> *Boxiana* a more expensive publishing enterprise then any modern
> Badminton volume.[9]

Nor has Egan been quite forgotten even in our own day. In A. J. Liebling's splendid book about modern boxers, *The Sweet Science* (1956), he acknowledges Egan as his master and his inspirer. For Liebling Egan is, at different times, the 'Froissart of the London prize-ring', 'the Sire de Joinville of the London prize-ring', and 'the Edward Gibbon and Sir Thomas Malory of the old prize-ring'. And Liebling puts his finger on the matter when he writes: 'Egan's round-by-round stories, with ringside highlights and betting fluctuations, are masterpieces of technical reportage, but he also saw the ring as a juicy hunk of English life, in no way separable from the rest.'[10]

In a sense, every modern sports writer, gifted with the ability to report an event accurately, to capture the feel and colour of the occasion, to transmit something of its excitement and the reactions of the spectators, is Pierce Egan's heir. He took sports reporting away from the stuffy, stilted, impersonal style which had been the norm and made it personal, picturesque, detailed, racy and fun to read; he also saw sport as a social phenomenon of no mean importance and related it to the life of his times. For these achievements, as much as for his value as a literary innovator, a forerunner of greater writers, a well of social history, and for his independent, ebullient, resilient and likeable personality, he deserves a good deal more than the occasional patronizing glancing reference or grudging and usually inaccurate footnote which he is accorded in whichever literary histories happen to notice him.

❧ Notes ❧

Chapter I

1 At my request, the Chief Herald, Irish Genealogical Office, Dublin Castle, initiated an extensive search of all available Irish documents and printed sources without finding any record of Pierce Egan or his father; my own searches of London parish registers have had a similar negative result. However, John O'Hart in his *Irish Pedigrees* shows James Egan as one of Carbery's sons and Pierce as James's son, adding: 'This James's family settled in England.' Unfortunately, O'Hart does not give the sources of his information. The Rev. R. N. Talbot, Rector of Ballyhay Parish, Charleville, County Cork, has examined his various parish records, and finds that the several children of Carbery, as listed by O'Hart, with the exception of James, appear therein. At the same time, O'Hart's claim that James was the name of Pierce's father is substantiated by the apprenticeship details shown in the Stationers' Hall registers and described in this chapter. It seems safe, therefore, to take on trust O'Hart's account of Pierce Egan's origin. It remains unclear, however, whether James Egan came to England before or after Pierce was born.

2 For example, John S. Crone, *A Concise Dictionary of Irish Biography*, Dublin: Talbot Press, 1937, p. 62; Rev. Stephen S. Brown, *Ireland in Fiction*, Dublin: Maunsell, 1919, p. 99.

3 H. D. Miles, *Pugilistica: The History of British Boxing*, 3 vols., Edinburgh: John Grant, 1906 (originally published, 1863) Vol. i, p. 49.

4 I am indebted to Mr Stanley J. Osborne, Beadle and Assistant to the

Clerk, Worshipful Company of Stationers and Newspaper Makers, Stationers' Hall, London, for a copy of this document.

5 Pierce Egan, *Matthews's Comic Annual or The Snuff-Box and the Leetel Bird*, Alfred Miller, 1831, p. xx.

6 Charles Hindley, *The Life and Times of James Catnach*, Reeves & Turner, 1878, p. 382.

7 These details are taken from the registers at Stationers' Hall, London.

8 C. H. Temperley, *A Dictionary of Printers and Printing*, H. Johnson, 1839. Entry under the date 26 May 1809.

9 The Entry of Marriage on this occasion omits details of residence, name and profession of the father of both parties, showing simply 'Pierce Egan, full age, bachelor' and 'Catherine Povey, full age, spinster'. The celebrant was Benjamin Laurence, Curate; the witnesses, Thomas Egan and Sarah Castleton.

10 Pierce Egan, *Epsom Races: The Derby Day, A (Crambo) Sporting Poem:* printed for the author, 1835, p. 49.

Chapter II

1 Hon. Grantley F. Berkeley, *My Life and Recollections*, 4 vols., Hurst & Blackett, 1865, Vol. i, p. 105. This self-satisfied work by an arrogant, blimpish personality gives a remarkable insight into the prejudices of his type and class at the time. Berkeley loathes the Irish and is fanatically anti-Catholic, hating Jesuits to the point of apoplexy and High Churchmen hardly less; all Catholic converts are to him 'perverts'. He more than once took a horse-whip, literally, to editors who offended his susceptibilities and he fought a duel with Maginn. He regarded riding to hounds as the supreme manifestation of English culture. It would be difficult for a caricaturist of early Victorian squires to create a more ludicrous character than Berkeley unwittingly reveals in his complacent autobiography.

2 David Thomson, *England in the 19th Century*, Pelican History of England, 8, p. 19.

3 Badcock, with characteristic inconsistency, spelt his pseudonym both as 'Jon Bee' and 'John Bee'.

4 'John Bee, Esq.', *Slang, A Dictionary of the Turf &c.*, T. Hughes, 1823, pp. 202, 210.

5 'The scratch', whence 'coming up to the scratch', or 'up to scratch'.

6 *Blackwood's Magazine*, August 1819, p. 516.

Notes

Chapter III

1 Stanley Morison, *The English Newspaper*, Cambridge University Press, 1932, p. 242.
2 J. W. Ebsworth, 'Pierce Egan', *Dictionary of National Biography* (successive editions): 'By 1812, his reputation was established as a "reporter of sporting events" in the newspapers, and his *impromptu* epigrams, songs and witticisms enjoyed a wide circulation. In that year, having secured a permanent engagement, which he held until the end of 1823, as the accredited purveyor of sporting news on a paper printed by E. Young, he married and settled.' The other inaccuracies in these sentences will also be noted.
3 See Stanley Morison, *John Bell 1745–1831*, printed for the author at the University Press Cambridge, 1930. Much of the information about the various Bells in this chapter has been taken from Morison's careful account.
4 *Pierce Egan's Life in London and Sporting Guide*, 30 July 1825, p. 629.
5 Blanchard Jerrold, *Life of George Cruikshank*, Chatto & Windus, 1894, p. 87.
6 Pierce Egan, *Sporting Anecdotes, Original and Selected*, Sherwood, Jones & Co., 1825, second edition, p. 351.
7 Bernard Blackmantle, *The English Spy*, Methuen & Co., 1907, pp. 335–9.
8　'Though Pierce Egan's no Poet, yet he honours the shrine
　　Dedicated to Poesy, Wit, Women, and Wine.'
From verses by Egan in reply to Tom Moore's squib, 'Tom Cribb's Memorial to Congress', *Boxiana: New Series*, George Virtue, 1828, Vol. I, p. 112.

Chapter IV

1 Blanchard Jerrold, *Cruikshank, op. cit.*, pp. 82–3.
2 Dorothy George, *Hogarth to Cruikshank, Social Change in Graphic Satire*, Allen Lane, The Penguin Press, 1967, p. 169.
3 William Bates, *George Cruikshank, the Artist, the Humourist and the Man*, Birmingham: Houghton & Hammond, 1878, pp. 23–4; repeated in W. Bates, *The Maclise Portrait-Gallery of Illustrious Literary Characters*, Chatto & Windus, 1883, p. 189.
4 *Life in London* is noted by the O.E.D. as containing the first recorded use of 'slavey'. But see Note 12, below.
5 Egan defines 'covess' as 'Thieves that, just as day begins to break, *sneak* into the passages of houses, if the servant maid had left the door open by accident, and take anything within their reach'.

223

6 Kid-wy—young one (Egan).

7 Scamp—footpad (E.).

8 Bunter—a low, loose woman (E.).

9 Tramp—walking (E.).

10 Lushy—drunk (E.).

11 Scran—victuals (E.).

12 Back-slums. The *O.E.D.* shows 'Blackmantle's' *The English Spy* as containing the earliest use of this term; but Egan had already made it familiar in *Life in London* five years before. Likewise, the *O.E.D.* cites 'Blackmantle' as first using 'mill' for 'a fight', which Egan employed as far back as 1812. 'Fancy-man' is, however, properly assigned to Egan.

13 W. T. Deacon, *Warreniana*, Longmans, Hurst, Rees, Orme, Brown and Green, 1824.

Chapter V

1 This explains the footnote to this passage in the 'Invocation' to *Life in London*: 'ACCUM, be thou kind enough to furnish me with a gentle hint, that I may not only enjoy all thy *nicety* of palate and taste, but reject every poisonous ingredient to the mind', which is headed 'Second Edition, Jan. 8, 1821', and runs: 'Recent circumstances, disclosed to the Subscribers of Life in London, imperatively compel me to state, that the MIND of this *Chemist* will not bear *analysing*, as I had previously anticipated. "Out, damned spot!"'

2 Advertisement in *Pierce Egan's Life in London and Sporting Guide*, 29 January 1826.

3 J. R. Abbey, *Life in England in Aquatint and Lithography, 1770–1860*, privately printed at the Curwen Press, 1953, p. 248.

4 For example, R. V. Tooley, *English Books with Coloured Plates, 1790–1860*, Batsford, 1954, and Catalogue of the British Museum Library.

5 For instance, see *The Fancy or True Sportsman's Guide*, Macgowan & Son, 1826, Vol. i, No. IV, p. 99.

6 Edward Stirling, *Old Drury Lane*, Chatto & Windus, 1861, Vol. i, p. 8.

7 James Robinson Planché, *Recollections and Reflections*, Sampson, Low, Marston & Co., 1901, pp. 29–30.

8 Thomas Dibdin, *Reminiscences*, Colburn, 1827, Vol. ii, p. 213.

9 William Clarke, *Every Night Book or Life After Dark*, T. Richardson, 1827, p. 801.

10 Harriet Arbuthnot, *Journal 1820–1832*, edited by Francis Bamford and the Duke of Wellington, Macmillan, 1950, p. 144.

11 R. M. Levey and J. O'Rorke, *The Annals of the Theatre Royal, Dublin*, Dublin: Joseph Dollard, 1880, p. 10.

12 Anon., *Life in London, A Play in 3 Acts*, Hodgson's Juvenile Drama
Series, Hodgson & Co., n.d. This version reveals a curious idea of
what kind of entertainment and values are suitable for children.
While one song goes:

> What is gaming? 'tis the devil
> That destroys the tranquil mind;
> 'Tis the very root of evil;
> Those who follow it are blind

another contains the lines:

> This bladder's the pride of our table;
> 'Tis filled with right glorious Max!

13 Clement Scott and Cecil Howard, *The Life and Remains of E. L.
Blanchard*, 2 vols., Hutchinson & Co., 1891, entry of 5 March 1870,
Vol. ii, p. 380.
14 *Life in London*, edited by John Camden Hotten, J. C. Hotten, 1869.
From Hotten's Introduction, p. 21.
15 Rev. John Richardson, *Recollections*, 2 vols., Savill & Edwards, 1855,
pp. 242–52.
16 *Boxiana, New Series*, George Virtue, 1829, Vol. ii, p. 281.
17 Charles Knight, *Passages of a Working Life*, 3 vols., Knight & Co.,
1873, Vol. i, pp. 177–8.

Chapter VI

1 Pierce Egan, *The Show Folks, with a Biographical Sketch of Mr
Theodore Lane*, Arnold and Simpkin & Marshall, 1831, pp. 35–8.
2 For example, Ebsworth in his *D.N.B.* article (*op. cit.*): 'In 1821, he
had issued "The Life and Extraordinary Adventures of S. D. Hayward,
denominated the Modern Macheath", a highwayman condemned to
death and executed, 25 Nov. 1821'.
3 Captain Francis Grose, *A Classical Dictionary of the Vulgar Tongue*,
3rd edition, reprinted and edited by Eric Partridge, Routledge &
Kegan Paul, 1963, p. 391.
4 Pierce Egan, *Grose's Classical Dictionary of the Vulgar Tongue,
Revised and Corrected, With the addition of numerous Slang Phrases*,
printed for the editor, 1823: 'In the present edition, for myself, I have
strongly to re-echo the sentiment of the former editors, namely, that
I have neglected no opportunity of excluding indelicate phrases,
which might have been adopted by my predecessors, nor of softening
down others, where propriety pointed out such a source as not only
necessary, but perhaps essential, to render palatable the Classical
Dictionary of the Vulgar Tongue', p. xix.

5 Egan prints a full report of the case at the beginning of Vol. 1 of the *New Series of Boxiana*, 1828.
6 For example, in the British Museum Catalogue.
7 This aspect of the Thurtell trial, as well as many other interesting sidelights, is discussed fully in Eric Watson's *The Trial of Thurtell and Hunt*, Australia: Butterworth & Co., 1920, Notable Trials Series.
8 V. A. R. G. Lytton, *The Life of Edward Bulwer, First Lord Lytton*, 2 vols., Macmillan, 1913, Vol. i, p. 389.

Chapter VII

1 John Camden Hotten, edition of *Life in London, op. cit.*, p. 19.
2 Egan, *Boxiana, New Series*, Vol. i, p. 585; see also Miles, *Pugilistica*, Vol. ii, pp. 354–5.
3 'Blackmantle', *The English Spy*, pp. 208–9.
4 For example, the *Dublin Morning Post* reported that a benefit at the Racquets Court for Neale and Larking was patronized by an 'immense number of swells and tip-top Corinthians of this city'. Quoted by Miles, *Pugilistica*, Vol. ii, p. 301.
5 Among others, J. C. Hotten, edition of *Life in London*, pp. 19–21; Ebsworth in *D.N.B.*; Grantley Berkeley, *Life*, p. 108; Crone, *Irish Biography*; Henry Curwen, *A History of Booksellers—The Old and the New*, Chatto & Windus, n.d., p. 373; F. W. Chandler, *The Literature of Roguery*, New York: Burt Franklin, 1958, 2 vols., Vol. II, p. 383.

Chapter VIII

1 Egan prints the entire outline of the play as submitted to Harris in Chapter I of *Finish to Life in London*.
2 Byron's screen. There is a decided mystery about this statement. Bohun Lynch in *The Prize Ring* (Country Life, 1925) gives a detailed description and photographs of this curiosity, which was adorned with drawings and sketches of boxers, several of them cut from copies of *Boxiana*. According to Lynch, the screen was bought by Murray, the poet's publisher, at the auction of Byron's property in 1816, and installed in the firm's rooms in Albemarle Street, where it was still in 1925. How, then, did Egan come to be, even temporarily, in possession of it? Was it, in fact, the authentic Byron screen he had? It is very unlikely that Byron would have owned two exactly similar screens, and equally unlikely that Egan was in the fake-antique business. Is a puzzlement, as the King of Siam remarked. Incidentally, the theatrical chairs to which Egan refers in the letter are almost

certainly the eight mahogany chairs with the names of characters from *Life in London* in ivory on them which Pierce Egan the Younger left to his own son in his will (see Chapter X).

3 British Museum Manuscript Room. Add. MSS. 2334, f.22.
4 George Raymond, *The Life and Enterprises of Robert William Elliston, Comedian*, G. Routledge & Co., 1857, p. 401.
5 *Pierce Egan's Book of Sports and Mirror of Life*, London: T. T. and J. Tegg, and Glasgow; R. Griffin & Co., 1832, No. 2, p. 32.

Chapter IX

1 Alfred Bunn, *The Stage, Both Before and Behind the Curtain*, 3 vols., Richard Bentley, 1840, Vol. i, pp. 218–20.
2 *Liverpool Mercury*, 1 February 1833.
3 See e.g., *Dublin Weekly Register*, 13 April 1822.
4 John W. Calcraft, *A Defence of the Stage*, Dublin: Mileeken & Son, 1839.
5 J. W. Cole (Calcraft), *The Life and Theatrical Times of Charles Kean, F.S.A.*, Richard Bentley, 1859, 2 vols.
6 *The Diaries of William Charles Macready*, edited by William Toynbee, Chapman & Hall, 1912, Vol. i, p. 110.
7 The Bodleian Library, Oxford.
8 The Birmingham University Library.
9 The Carl H. Pforzheimer Library, New York.
10 *The Journal of William Charles Macready*, edited by J. C. Trewin, Longmans, 1967.

Chapter X

1 Louis James, *Fiction for the Working Man 1830–1850*, Oxford University Press, 1963, p. 59.
2 British Museum Manuscript Room. Add. MSS. 40520, f.92.
3 *Ibid.*, Add. MSS. 42575, f.245.
4 George Augustus Sala, *The Life and Adventures of George Augustus Sala*, Cassell & Co., 1898, pp. 200–202.
5 F. T. Cansick, *A Collection of Curious and Interesting Epitaphs, from the Cemeteries and Churches of St. Pancras, Middlesex*, J. Russell Smith, 1872. Cansick transcribed the final figure as '1840', which may indicate that the tombstone had already weathered considerably.
6 *Bell's Life in London*, 8 August 1849, 'Death of Pierce Egan'.

Chapter XI

1 Charles Knight, *The Old Printer and the Modern Press*, John Murray, 1854, p. 283.
2 Charles Dickens, *Letters*, the Pilgrim Edition, edited by Madeline House and Graham Storey, Oxford: Clarendon Press, 1965, Vol. i, p. 463. The editorial comment on this statement runs: 'The comparison was presumably made on the playbills. The advertisement in *Figaro in London* read "The most perfect picture of living manners since 'Tom and Jerry'". Egan's coarseness of language and glorification of "fast" Regency life would understandably have made Dickens dislike such a comparison. Thomas Hood wrote to him that he had first thought *Pickwick* "only a new strain of Tom-and-Jerryism—which is my aversion" (MS., Huntingdon Library), but after further reading he changed his mind.'
3 Julian Franklyn, *The Cockney*, André Deutsch, 1953, pp. 17–18.
4 J. C. Hotten, *Charles Dickens*, J. C. Hotten, 1870, p. 165.
5 *Ibid.*, pp. 341–3.
6 Louis James, *Fiction for the Working Man*, *op. cit.*, p. 140.
7 Raymond Chapman, *The Victorian Debate*, Weidenfeld & Nicolson, 1968, p. 99.
8 G. Bernard Shaw, *Collected Letters*, edited by Don H. Laurence, Max Reinhardt, 1965, pp. 59–60.
9 *Ibid.*, *Cashel Byron's Profession*, Constable & Co., 1924, pp. xi-xv.
10 A. J. Liebling, *The Sweet Science*, Gollancz, 1956, pp. 14–15.

❧ A Note on Sources ❧

The only printed accounts of Egan's life and activities, apart from brief obituaries, are those in J. W. Ebsworth's *D.N.B.* article, J. C. Hotten's introduction to his edition of *Life in London* and, in part, Charles Hindley's *The True History of Tom and Jerry*. Ebsworth, as has already been emphasized several times, is inaccurate in a number of major details and misleading in others; Hotten, if very incomplete and often vague, and Hindley, if confining himself only to the dramatizations of *Life in London*, offer many useful clues and hints, most of which I have found profitable.

Apart from these, the chief sources for this book have been the files of London, Liverpool, Edinburgh, Brighton, Bristol, and Irish newspapers in the British Museum newspaper section at Colindale, which also possesses complete files of *Pierce Egan's Life in London* and *Pierce Egan's Weekly Courier*, although, unfortunately, its holdings of the *Weekly Dispatch* are defective. Much of the information, for instance, about the dates of the publication of Egan's books, the performances of his plays and his various sporting and dramatic activities has come from reviews and advertisements in newspapers, supplemented by remarks in his own works. A hunch that Egan was apprenticed to a printer led to a rewarding search in the records of the Stationers' Company; an examination of the 1851 Census disclosed the fact that Egan had been twice married, and a consequent re-examination of London marriage registers, also with a happy issue, followed; a remark in Miles's *Pugilistica* concerning Egan's association with Smeeton's printing house sent me to London directories of the time and histories of printing for further information about Smeeton's and Egan's places of business, and so on. For the rest, the nature of his personality and such additional facts of his life, so far as they can be ascertained, have been built up from the biographies and memoirs of his contemporaries, and from the very occasional personal references in his books.

Unfortunately, very few of Egan's letters have survived. It is possible that there are some I have not seen in various libraries or in private hands, but a widespread search and advertising over some years has disclosed only those printed in this book—a meagre haul, indeed. Yet each letter has been valuable, not only in itself, but as providing some useful lead or other. I have been unable to trace any will of Egan's in the various London repositories; he died, of course, before the official recording began at Somerset House. A personal letter to every Egan listed in the London telephone directory, while eliciting some friendly replies, brought no information about living descendants or documents surviving.

❧ Bibliography ❧

Pierce Egan's Works

Egan's letter to Robert Peel, printed in Chapter X, lists on the reverse his publications to that date, December 5 1842. It runs as follows:

Walks Through Bath
The Pilgrims of the Thames
The Book of Sports
Boxiana—5 Vols.
Biographical Memoir of
    George III
Sporting Anecdotes
The Life of Hayward
*Life of George Frederick
    Cooke
*Picture of Paris
A Trip to Ascot Races
Trip to Epsom Races
*Julia and Judy—or the Village
    Curate
Recollections of Thurtell
*The Blind Lover

*Live and Learn: A Comedy
Life in London
Finish to Life in London
Life in Dublin
Life in Liverpool
Tom and Jerry
Panorama of the Sporting
    World
*The Forgotten Ring
The Mistress of Royalty
Anecdotes of the Turf
Classical Dictionary of the
    Vulgar Tongue
Trial of Fauntleroy
*Dandiana &c. &c.
Captain Macheath &c. &c. &c.

Life in London Newpaper by Pierce Egan
&c. &c. &c. in 3 volumes

I have also sent numerous Contributions to Magazines &c.

231

I have not been able to trace the works starred; it is more than likely that several of them, as with *Life in Dublin, Life in Liverpool* and *Tom and Jerry*, were never published. *Julia and Judy, The Blind Lover, Live and Learn*, and, perhaps, *The Forgotten Ring* appear to have been plays, and no play of Egan's achieved print. I have identified the *Memoir of George III* as the work of that name published by 'E. Pierce'. The 'Panorama of the Sporting World' is clearly 'Going to a Fight' or 'A Picture of the Fancy', for which he wrote the now vanished Key, as he did for Lane's 'Ascot Races'. It will be noted that he omits from his list *The Show Folks, Matthews's Comic Annual, Account of the Trial of Thurtell and Hunt, Trial of Bishop and Williams, Life of an Actor, The Fancy Togs' Man* (the rare British Musuem copy of this was destroyed during the war) and *Songs and Parodies from Tom and Jerry*. There seems no way of telling how many other works Egan published or how many contributions he made to magazines, but it appears reasonable to assume that they were, for the most part, fugitive pieces.

Boxiana

As already noted in the text, Vols. I to III, and Vols. I and II of the *New Series*, of *Boxiana* were written by Egan and Vol. IV of *Boxiana* by Jonathan Badcock. Sherwood's retained the copyright of the first three volumes and continued to issue them after Egan ceased to be responsible for them in 1824. But, as is stated in the Advertisement to Vol. IV, Badcock revised the earlier books from 1824 onwards. Consequently, Egan's authentic text will be found only in editions before that date, or in editions based upon pre-1824 ones. The *New Series*, of course, owes nothing to Badcock. Despite this, *Boxiana* is most usually found today in two volumes, I and II, and III and IV, all attributed to Egan. This is the case with the British Museum copies. The *New Series*, not in the British Museum, is held by the London Library.

[In the following lists, the place of publication is London, unless otherwise stated.]

Books and Pamphlets by Pierce Egan

Boxiana: Sketches of Antient and Modern Pugilism ('By one of the Fancy'). Afterwards Vol. I of *Boxiana*. G. Smeeton, 1812. (*Note:* The title-page bears the date 1812, but this page was sent to subscribers of the numbers at the beginning of the series. The completed volume, issued bound in 1813 and 1815, retained the 1812 title-page.)

The Mistress of Royalty or The Loves of Florizel and Perdita. Printed by and for Pierce Egan, 29 Great Marlborough Street, 1814.

Boxiana or Sketches of Modern Pugilism, Vol. II, Sherwood, Neely & Jones, 1818.

Boxiana, Vol. I (a reissue), Sherwood, Neely & Jones, 1818.

Walks Through Bath, Bath: Meyler & Son; Bristol: Barry & Son; London: Sherwood, Neely & Jones, 1819.

A Key to a Picture of the Fancy, Sherwood, Neely & Jones, 1819.

Sporting Anecdotes, Original and Selected, Sherwood, Jones & Co., 1820.

A Concise Biographical Memoir of His Late Majesty George the Third (by 'E. Pierce'), Sherwood, Neely & Jones, 1820. (Preface dated 1 March 1820.)

Life in London or The Day and Night Scenes of Jerry Hawthorn, Esq. and his elegant friend, Corinthian Tom in their Rambles and Sprees through the Metropolis, Sherwood, Neely & Jones, 1821.

Boxiana, or Sketches of Modern Pugilism, Vol. III, Sherwood, Neely & Jones, 1821.

The Songs, Parodies &c. introduced in the Operatic Burletta Called Tom and Jerry or Life in London, Sherwood, Neely & Jones, n.d. (1822).

The Life and Adventures of Samuel Denmore Hayward, The Modern Macheath, Sherwood, Neely & Jones, 1822.

The Life and Extraordinary Adventures of Samuel Denmore Hayward (another edition with a frontispiece and a different title-page), Sherwood, Neely & Jones, 1822.

Grose's Classical Dictionary of the Vulgar Tongue, with the Addition of Numerous Slang Phrases (edited by Egan), printed for the Editor, 1823. (This is clearly a reissue. 'Jon Bee' in his *Slang* (p. ix) of 1823 refers to Egan's *Grose* as having been issued in the previous year and to him as 'the careful editor of 1822'—the 'careful' being, of course, ironical.)

Life in London, Sherwood, Jones & Co., 1823.

The Fancy Togs' Man versus Young Sandboy, the Milling Quaker, 1823.

Pierce Egan's Account of the Trial of John Thurtell and Joseph Hunt, Knight & Lacey, 1824.

Recollections of John Thurtell, Knight & Lacey, 1824.

Pierce Egan's Account of the Trial of Mr Fauntleroy for Forging, Knight & Lacey, 1824.

Sporting Anecdotes, Original and Selected, 'a new edition, considerably revised and improved', Sherwood, Jones & Co., 1825.

The Life of an Actor, 'The poetical descriptions by T. Greenwood', C. S. Arnold, 1825.

Pierce Egan's Anecdotes, Original and Selected, of the Turf, the Chase, the Ring and the Stage, Knight & Lacey and Pierce Egan, 1827.

The Finish to the Adventures of Tom, Jerry and Logic in their pursuits through Life In and Out of London, J. S. Virtue & Co., n.d. (1828).

Boxiana: New Series, Vol. I, George Virtue, 1828.

Boxiana: New Series, Vol. II, George Virtue, 1829.

Matthews's Comic Annual or The Snuff-Box and the Leetel Bird, Alfred Miller, 1831.

The Show Folks: With a Biographical Memoir of Mr Theodore Lane, M. Arnold and Simpkin & Marshall, 1831.

Pierce Egan's Account of the Trial of Bishop, Williams and May for Murder, Sherwood & Co., 1831.

Pierce Egan's Book of Sports and Mirror of Life, London: T. T. & J. Tegg; Glasgow: R. Griffith & Co., 1832. (Also reissued by the same publishers in 1836.)

Epsom Races: The Derby Day, A (Crambo) Sporting Poem, printed for the Author, 1835.

The Pilgrims of the Thames in Search of the National, W. Strange, 1838.

Captain Macheath, 1842.

Every Gentleman's Manual. A Lecture on the Art of Self-Defence, Sherwood & Bowyer, 1845.

Life in London, edited by John Camden Hotten, J. C. Hotten, 1869.

Finish to the Adventures of Tom, Jerry and Logic, Reeves & Turner, 1869. (A further edition was issued by the same firm in 1887.)

The Life of an Actor, Pickering & Chatto, 1892.

Manuscripts

'Tom, Jerry and Logic's Hop at Brighton', British Museum. Add. MSS. 42928. L.C. approval 24–10–1834.

'Life in Dublin or Tom, Jerry and Logic on their Travels', British Museum. Add. MSS. 42964. L.C. approval 3–9–1842.

Imitations of and Derivatives from Egan's Works

ANON., *Real Life in London*, Jones & Co., 1821.

—— *Life in London*, a play in 3 acts, Hodgson's Juvenile Drama, Hodgson & Co., n.d.

—— *The Corinthian Parodies by Tom, Jerry and Logic* (with a frontispiece by I. R. Cruikshank), William Cole, n.d.

—— *Real Life in Ireland* ('By a Real Paddy'), Jones & Co. and J. L. Marks, 1821.

—— *Tom's Demonstration to Jerry How the People May Govern Themselves*, Birmingham: W. Cooper, n.d. (1822 ?).

—— *Dialogue Between Tom and Jerry*, Edinburgh: Menzies, n.d. (1834 ?)

CAREY, DAVID, *Life in Paris*, John Fairburn, 1822.

CATNACH, J., *Life in London or the Sprees of Tom and Jerry, attempted in Cuts and Verse*, 5th edition, J. Catnach, n.d.

—— *The Death, Last Will and Testament of Black Billy: Also The Tears of London for the Death of Tom and Jerry*, 10th edition, n.d.

CLARK, CHARLES ('Thomas Hood the Younger'), *Epsom Races*, Great Totham, Essex: C. Clark's private press, 1838.

DIBDIN, CHARLES, *Life in London or The Larks of Logic, Tom and Jerry*, 2nd edition, John Lowndes, 1822.

GREENWOOD, THOMAS, *The Death of Life in London or Tom and Jerry's Funeral*, John Lowndes, 1823.

MACFARRAN, G., *Tom and Jerry in France or Vive La Bagatelle!* (with a song by D. W. Jerrold, 'Jemmy Green's Tour'), J. Lowndes, n.d. (1823 ?).

MONCRIEFF, WILLIAM T., *Tom and Jerry or Life in London* (with 'A Vocabulary of Flash and Cant'), Dublin: Courtney, 1822.

—— *Tom and Jerry or Life in London*, New York: Samuel French, n.d.

—— *Tom and Jerry or Life in London in 1820*, Thomas Hailes Lacey, n.d.

—— *Songs, Parodies, Duets, Choruses, &c. from Tom and Jerry*, John Lowdnes, n.d.

PEAKE, RICHARD BRINSLEY, *The Life of an Actor*, a farcical comedy in 2 acts, Dicks' Standard Plays No. 582, John Dicks, 1884.

S . . ., M., *Diorama Anglais, ou Promenades Pittoresques à Londres*, Paris: Baudouin Frères, 1823.

SOMERSET, C. A., *The Nautical Tom and Jerry or Life of a True British Sailor*, British Museum. Add. MSS. 42966, L.C. approval, 7-1-1843.

General Books

ABBEY, J. R., *Life in England in Aquatint and Lithography 1770–1860,* privately printed at the Curwen Press, 1953.

ALTICK, RICHARD D., *The English Common Reader, 1800–1900,* Chicago: University of Chicago Press, 1957.

'AN AMATEUR SPORTSMAN', *Sporting Anecdotes, Original and Selected,* J. Cundee and J. Harris, 1807.

ANDREWES, GEORGE, *The Stranger's Guide or Frauds of London Detected,* G. Smeeton, 1808.

—— *A Dictionary of the Slang and Cant Language,* G. Smeeton, 1809.

ANON., *The Art of Boxing,* G. Smeeton, n.d. (1821 ?).

—— *The Stranger's Guide or Frauds of London Detected,* J. Bailey, 1808.

—— *Lives and Portraits of Remarkable Characters,* 2 vols., W. Lewis, 1819.

—— *The Flash Dictionary,* G. Smeeton, 1821.

—— *The Biography of the British Stage,* Sherwood, Jones & Co., 1824.

ARBUTHNOT, HARRIET, *The Journal of Mrs Arbuthnot 1820–32,* ed. by Francis Bamford and the Duke of Wellington, Macmillan & Co., 1950.

BADCOCK, JONATHAN, *Slang: A Dictionary of the Turf, the Ring, the Chase, the Pit, of Bon-Ton and the Varieties of Life,* T. Hughes, 1823.

—— *Boxiana,* Vol. IV, Sherwood, Jones & Co., 1824.

—— *The Annals of Sporting and Fancy Gazette 1822–1828,* Sherwood, Neely & Jones, 1822–8.

—— *The Fancy or True Sportsman's Guide,* 2 vols., J. MacGowan & Son, 1826.

—— *A Living Picture of London for 1828 and Stranger's Guide,* W. Clarke, 1828 (written under the name of 'Jon Bee').

BARNETT, MORRIS, *Monsieur Jacques,* T. H. Lacey, 1857.

BATES, WILLIAM, *George Cruikshank, the Artist, the Humourist and the Man,* Birmingham: Houghton & Hammond, 1878.

—— *The Maclise Portrait Gallery of Illustrious Literary Characters,* Chatto & Windus, 1883.

BERKELEY, HON. GRANTLEY, *My Life and Recollections,* 4 vols., Hurst & Blackett, 1865.

'BLACKMANTLE, BERNARD' (CHARLES MOLLOY WESTMACOTT), *The English Spy,* 2 vols, Sherwood, Jones & Co., 1825–6. (Reprinted by Methuen & Co., 1907.)

BLEACKLEY, HORACE, *Trial of Henry Fauntleroy and Other Famous Trials for Forgery,* Edinburgh and London: W. Hodge & Co., 1924.

BOURNE, H. R. FOX, *English Newspapers,* 2 vols., Chatto & Windus, 1887.

BOYNTON, PERCY H., *London in English Literature*, Chicago: University of Chicago Press, 1913.

BROWN, STEPHEN J., *A Guide to Books on Ireland*, Longmans, Green & Co., 1912.

BRYANT, ARTHUR, *The Age of Elegance 1812–1822*, Collins, 1950.

BUNN, ALFRED, *The Stage, Both Before and Behind the Curtain*, 3 vols., Richard Bentley, 1840.

CALCRAFT, JOHN WILLIAM, *An Address to the Public*, Edinburgh: John Anderson, 1822.

—— *A Defence of the Stage*, Dublin: Mileeken & Son, 1839.

—— *The Life and Theatrical Times of Charles Kean, F.S.A.*, Richard Bentley, 1859 (issued under the name of 'John William Cole').

CANSICK, F. J., *A Collection of Curious and Interesting Epitaphs*, J. Russell Smith, 1872.

CHANCELLOR, E. BERESFORD, *Annals of the Strand*, Chapman & Hall, 1912.

CHANDLER, FRANK WADLEIGH, *The Literature of Roguery*, 2 vols., New York: Burt Franklin, 1958.

CHAPMAN, RAYMOND, *The Victorian Debate: English Literature and Society 1832–1901*, Weidenfeld & Nicolson, 1968.

CHESSON, W. H., *George Cruikshank*, Duckworth & Co., 1908.

(CLARKE, H.), *Lexicon Balatronicum: A Dictionary of Buckish Slang, University Wit and Pickpocket Eloquence by a Member of the Whip Club. Originally compiled by Captain Grose*, C. Chappel, 1811.

CLARKE, WILLIAM, *Every Night Book or Life After Dark*, T. Richardson, 1827.

CRONE, JOHN S., *A Concise Dictionary of Irish Biography*, Dublin: The Talbot Press, 1928.

CRUIKSHANK, GEORGE, *George Cruikshank's Omnibus*, Tilt & Bogue, 1862.

CRUSE, AMY, *The Englishman and His Books in the Early XIXth Century*, George G. Harrap & Co., 1930.

CURWEN, HENRY, *A History of Booksellers—The Old and the New*, Chatto & Windus, n.d.

DARWIN, BERNARD, *John Gully and His Times*, Cassell, 1935.

DAY, J. WENTWORTH, *Inns of Sport*, Whitbread & Co., 1949.

DEACON, W. F., *Warreniana*, Longmans, Hurst, Rees, Orme, Brown & Green, 1824.

DIBDIN, THOMAS, *Reminiscences*, 2 vols., Henry Colburn, 1827.

DICKENS, CHARLES: *Sketches by Boz*, John Macrone, 1836.

—— *The Posthumous Papers of the Pickwick Club*, Chapman & Hall, 1837.

—— *Oliver Twist*, Richard Bentley, 1838.

—— *Oliver Twist*, edited by Kathleen Tillotson, Oxford University Press, 1966.

—— *Nicholas Nickleby*, Chapman & Hall, 1839.

—— *Hard Times*, Bradbury & Evans, 1854.

—— *Little Dorrit*, Bradbury & Evans, 1857.

DICKENS, CHARLES *Great Expectations*, Chapman & Hall, 1861.

—— *Letters*, the Pilgrim Edition, ed. by Madeline House and Graham Storey, The Clarendon Press, Oxford, Vol. I (1965), Vol. II (1969.)

DISHER, MAURICE WILLSON, *Blood and Thunder: Mid-Victorian Melodrama and Its Origins*, Frederick Muller, 1949.

DOUGLAS, SIR GEORGE, *The 'Blackwood' Group*. Edinburgh: Oliphant Anderson, 1897.

DOWLING, FRANCIS: *Fights for the Championship*. Bell's Life, 1855.

—— *Fistiana or the Oracle of the Ring*, W. Clement, 1841.

DUNLAP, WILLIAM, *Memoirs of the Life of George Frederick Cooke*, 2 vols, New York: O. Longworth, 1813.

FAHY, F. A., and DONOGHUE, D. J., *Ireland in London*, Dublin, *Evening Telegraph*, 1889.

FRANKLYN, JULIAN, *The Cockney*, André Deutsch, 1953.

GEORGE, DOROTHY, *Hogarth to Cruikshank: Social Change in Graphic Satire*, Allen Lane, the Penguin Press, 1967.

GETTMANN, ROYAL A., *A Victorian Publisher, A Study of the Bentley Papers*, Cambridge University Press, 1960.

GOLESWORTHY, MAURICE, *Encyclopaedia of Boxing*, Robert Hale, 1960.

GROSE, CAPTAIN FRANCIS, *A Classical Dictionary of the Vulgar Tongue*, 3rd edition reprinted and edited by Eric Partridge, Routledge & Kegan Paul, 1963.

HALDANE, ROBERT A., *Giants of the Ring*, War Facts Press, 1948.

HANCHANT, W. L., *The Newgate Garland or Flowers of Hemp*, Desmond Harmsworth, 1932. (This book contains several extracts from Egan's *Captain Macheath*.)

HINDLEY, CHARLES, *The Life and Times of James Catnach*, Reeves & Turner, 1878.

—— *The True History of Tom and Jerry*, C. Hindley, n.d.

HOLLINGSWORTH, KEITH, *The Newgate Novel 1830–47*, Detroit: Wayne State University Press, 1963.

HOTTEN, JOHN CAMDEN, *The Slang Dictionary*, J. C. Hotten, 1864.

—— *Charles Dickens*, J. C. Hotten, 1870.

HUGHES, S. C., *The Pre-Victorian Drama in Dublin*, Dublin: Hodges, Figgis & Co., 1904.

JACKSON, MASON, *The Pictorial Press: Its Origin and Progress*, Hurst & Blackett, 1885.

JAMES, LOUIS, *Fiction for the Working Man 1830–1850*, Oxford University Press, 1963.

JERROLD, BLANCHARD, *The Life and Remains of Douglas Jerrold*, W. Kent & Co., 1859.

—— *Life of George Cruikshank*, Chatto & Windus, 1894.

JERROLD, DOUGLAS, *The Works, with a Memoir by his son, W. Blanchard Jerrold*, 4 vols., Bradbury & Evans, 1863.

JERROLD, WALTER, *Douglas Jerrold and Punch*, Macmillan, 1910.

KAVANAGH, PETER, *The Irish Theatre*, Tralee: Kerryman Ltd, 1946.

KELLY, MICHAEL, *Reminiscences*, 2 vols., Henry Colburn, 1826.

KNIGHT, CHARLES, *The Old Printer and the Modern Press*, John Murray, 1854.

—— *Passages of a Working Life*, 3 vols., Knight & Co., 1873.

KNOWLES, JAMES SHERIDAN, *Dramatic Works*, Calcutta: W. Rushton, 1838.

KNOWLES, RICHARD BRINSLEY, *Life of James Sheridan Knowles*, James McHenry, 1872.

LEVEY, R. M., and O'RORKE, J., *The Annals of the Theatre Royal, Dublin*, Dublin: Joseph Dollard, 1880.

LIEBLING, A. J., *The Sweet Science*, V. Gollancz, 1956.

LYNCH, BOHUN, *The Prize Ring*, County Life Ltd, 1925.

LYTTON, VICTOR A. G. R., *The Life of Edward Bulwer, First Lord Lytton*, 2 vols., Macmillan, 1913.

MACCOBY, S., *English Radicalism 1832–52*, George Allen & Unwin, 1935.

MAGILL, FRANK, *Cyclopedia of World Authors*, New York: Harper & Bros., 1958.

MATHEWS, MRS C., *Memoirs of Charles Mathews, Comedian*, 4 vols., Richard Bentley, 1838.

MAXTED, HARRY, *The Story of the Prize Ring*, Day & Mason, 1949.

MEEKS, L. H., *Sheridan Knowles and the Theatre of His Time*, Bloomington: Principia Press, 1933.

MILES, HENRY DOWNES, *Pugilistica: The History of British Boxing*, 3 vols., Edinburgh: John Grant, 1906. (First published in 1863.)

—— *Tom Sayers, Sometime Champion of England*, S. C. Beeton, 1866.

MORISON, STANLEY, *John Bell 1745–1831*, printed for the Author at the University Press, Cambridge, 1930.

—— *The English Newspaper*, Cambridge University Press, 1932.

—— *Edward Topham 1751–1820*, Cambridge: printed by W. Lewis at the University Press, 1933.

NEVILL, RALPH, *Old English Sporting Books*, ed. by Geoffrey Holme, Studio Ltd, 1924.

NICHOLSON, RENTON, *Rogue's Progress: The Autobiography of 'Lord Chief Baron' Nicholson*, ed. by John L. Bradley, Longmans, 1966.

NICOLL, ALLARDYCE, *A History of English Drama, 1660–1900*, 6 vols., Cambridge University Press, 1952–9.

'NORTH, CHRISTOPHER', *Noctes Ambrosianae*, 4 vols., Edinburgh and London: Wm. Blackwood & Sons, 1876.

O'HART, JOHN, *Irish Pedigrees*, 2 vols., Dublin: James Duffy & Son, 1887.

OXBERRY, WILLIAM, *Oxberry's Dramatic Biography and Green Room Spy*, 2 vols., G. Virtue, 1827.

—— *Oxberry's Dramatic Biography and Histrionic Anecdotes*, 6 vols., G. Virtue, 1825–6.

PENDRED, JOHN, *The Earliest Directory of the Book Trade (1785)*, ed. by Graham Pollard, The Bibliographical Society, 1955.

PLANCHÉ, JAMES ROBINSON, *Recollections and Reflections*, Sampson, Low, Marston & Co., 1901.

RAYMOND, GEORGE, *The Life and Enterprises of Robert William Elliston, Comedian*, G. Routledge & Co., 1857.

REYNOLDS, JOHN HAMILTON ('PETER CORCORAN'), *The Fancy: a Selection from the Poetical Remains of the Late Peter Corcoran, Gray's Inn, Student at Law*, Taylor & Hessey, 1820.

RICHARDSON, REV. JOHN, *Recollections*, 2 vols., Savill & Edwards, 1855.

SALA, GEORGE AUGUSTUS, *The Life and Adventures of George Augustus Sala, written by Himself*, Cassell, 1898.

SCHWERDT, C. F. G. R., *Hunting, Hawking, Shooting*, 4 vols., privately printed by Waterton & Sons Ltd., 1928.

SCOTT, CLEMENT, and HOWARD, CECIL, *The Life and Reminiscences of E. L. Blanchard*, 2 vols., Hutchinson & Co., 1891.

SHAW, GEORGE BERNARD, *Cashel Byron's Profession*, Constable & Co., 1924.

—— *Collected Letters 1874–1897*, ed. by Don H. Laurence, Max Reinhardt, 1965.

SMEETON, GEORGE, *The Unique*, Vols. 1–3, George Smeeton, 1824.

—— *Doings in London*, George Smeeton, 1828.

—— *Doings in London*, 10th Edition, Orlando Hodgson, 1849.

STEVENSON, LIONEL, *The English Novel; a Panorama*, Constable & Co., 1960.

STIRLING, EDWARD, *Old Drury Lane*, 2 vols., Chatto & Windus, 1861.

STOWER, CALEB, *The Compositor's and Pressman's Guide to the Art of Printing*, B. Crosby & Co., 1808.

SWANN, ELSIE, *Christopher North*, Edinburgh: Oliver & Boyd, 1934.

TEMPERLEY, C. H., *A Dictionary of Printers and Printing*, H. Johnson, 1839.

THACKERAY, W. M., *Roundabout Papers*, Smith, Elder & Co., 1914.

THOMSON, DAVID, *England in the Nineteenth Century*, Pelican History of England, 8, Penguin Books, 1950.

TOOLEY, R. V., *English Books with Coloured Plates, 1790 to 1860*, B. T. Batsford, 1954.

TOYNBEE, WILLIAM (ed.), *The Diaries of William Charles Macready*, 2 vols., Chapman & Hall, 1912.

TREWIN, J. C. (ed.), *The Journal of William Charles Macready*, Longmans, 1967.

—— (ed.) *The Pomping Folk in the 19th Century*, J. M. Dent, 1968.

WATSON, ERIC, R., *The Trial of Thurtell and Hunt*, Australia: Butterworth & Co., Notable Trials Series, 1920.

WHITE, R. J., *Life in Regency England*, B. T. Batsford, 1963.

Bibliography

Articles

ANON., 'Life in London', a review of the first three numbers of Life in London, European Magazine, November 1820.

—— 'On George Cruikshank', Blackwood's Edinburgh Magazine, July 1823, pp. 18–26 (probably by 'Christopher North').

—— 'Boxiana, or Sketches of Pugilism', a series of eight articles, Blackwood's Edinburgh Magazine, No. 1, July 1819, pp. 439–43; No. 2, August 1819, pp. 593–7; No. 3, September 1819, pp. 663–5; No. 4, October 1819, pp. 66–9; No. 5, December 1819, pp. 279–84; No. 6, March 1820, pp. 609–15; No. 7, June 1820, pp. 294–306; No. 8, October 1820, pp. 60–67. (Several of these pieces, if not all, were written, at least in part, by 'Christopher North'.)

—— 'Trial of Bishop, Williams and May', Annual Register, 1831, pp. 316–30.

—— 'Obituary—Pierce Egan', Gentleman's Magazine, Vol. 32, November 1849, p. 548.

—— 'George Cruikshank', Scribner's Monthly, June 1878, pp. 161–77.

—— 'Obituary—Pierce Egan, Jnr.', Athenaeum, 10 July 1880, pp. 49–50.

CAMBRAY, PHILIP G., 'Pierce Egan the Elder' (a letter), The Times Literary Supplement, 21 August 1943.

CHILD, HAROLD: 'Caricature and the Literature of Sport', Cambridge History of English Literature. Cambridge University Press, 1932. Vol. XIV. A valuable survey of the field, which devotes considerable space to Egan's works.

DARWIN, BERNARD: 'Sporting Writers of the 19th Century', Essays Mainly on the Nineteenth Century presented to Sir Humphrey Milford, Geoffrey Cumberlege, Oxford University Press, 1948, pp. 117–26.

J.J., 'London Chit-chat', Blackwood's Edinburgh Magazine, March 1822, pp. 332–3.

MARSH, GEORGE L., 'Pierce Egan the Elder' (a letter), The Times Literary Supplement, 17 July 1943.

NOAKES, AUBREY, 'Pierce Egan the Elder' (a letter), The Times Literary Supplement, 21 August 1943.

—— 'Pierce Egan's Life in London', World Review, December 1944, pp. 57–9.

NORMAN, HUBERT, J., 'Pierce Egan the Elder' (a letter), The Times Literary Supplement, 7 August 1943.

NORTH, CHRISTOPHER, 'Letter to Pierce Egan, Esq.', Blackwood's Edinburgh Magazine, March 1821, pp. 671–7.

WEBB, R. K., 'The Victorian Reading Public', *Universities Quarterly*, November 1957, pp. 24–44.

WEIR, W., 'London Newspapers', *London* (ed. Charles Knight), Henry G. Bohun, 1851, Vol. v, pp. 337–52.

❧ Index ❧